GEORGE GRAHAM
The Glory and the Grief

GEORGE GRAHAM

The Glory and the Grief

His own inside story
with Norman Giller

ANDRE DEUTSCH

First published in Great Britain in 1995 by André Deutsch Ltd
106 Great Russell Street, London WC1B 3LJ

Copyright © George Graham 1995

British Library Cataloguing in Publication Data
A catalogue record for this book is available
from the British Library

ISBN 0 233 98994 3

Printed and bound in Great Britain by
WBC, Bridgend

*This book is dedicated to the memory
of Janet Graham, a Mum in a Million*

The place: Baillieston Secondary School.
The year: 1958.
Teacher: 'What do ye intend tae do when ye leave school, Graham?'
Me: 'I want tae become a f'itballer, sir.'
Teacher: 'Thank goodness then, Graham, that ye've got yer brains in yer
feet, 'cos ye havena any in yer heed.'
Me: 'Thank ye, sir.'

Contents

Author's Note

I wish to thank VCI chief executive Steve Ayres for making this book possible, and Tom Rosenthal and his editorial team at André Deutsch for their patience, encouragement and expertise. In particular, I acknowledge the inspirational input of Norman Giller and the constant, invaluable support of John Hazell; also the diligent editing of Zoë Ross, the production skills of John Cleary, the typesetting of Les Hall and David Caldwell, and the watchful eyes of Caroline Kean and Alex Gordon. Thanks, too, to the army of Arsenal supporters who have showered me with their warmth since my departure from Highbury. Their memories of the good times at Arsenal are my memories, and they will never dim. Most of all, thanks to my daughter Nicole, son Daniel, Susan, brother Andy and all my brothers and sisters for your love and support. *Here's tae ye. Wha's like ye?*

Prologue: The First Seeds

COME with me into the study of my home in Hampstead in north west London, which is like a shrine to Arsenal. Look here, a photograph of me holding the League championship trophy as an Arsenal player, and next to it framed pictures of me with two championship trophies as Arsenal manager. Over here on the opposite wall, more pictures showing me with the FA Cup, the League Cup and, one of my favourites, me with the European Cup Winners' Cup on a wonderful night in Copenhagen.

The study is not just dedicated to the six trophies that I won in eight-and-a-half years as manager of Arsenal. The history of Highbury is here. Look at this one, a photograph of Herbert Chapman and his 'Bank of England' Arsenal team of the 1930s; and alongside it, that's Joe Mercer showing off the FA Cup after he had skippered Arsenal to a 2-0 victory over Liverpool in the 1950 Final at Wembley. Dear old Joe, who was my first manager in football.

Just look at the bookshelves. They are heaving with just about every book ever written about the Arsenal. There are biographies of Herbert Chapman, George Allison, Tom Whittaker and Billy Wright, predecessors of mine in the manager's chair; and there are dozens of memoirs of former players ranging from Cliff Bastin to Liam Brady, and from Alex James to Frank McLintock. There is room for just one more book. This one, in which I shall be revealing how Arsenal gave me the best years of my life and then broke my heart.

Now come with me through the Victorian-domed conservatory and out into my garden, the place where I have found sanity away from the pressures of the last year which might have pushed some people towards the whisky bottle or even a suicide bullet. Here in my garden I feel untouchable. This is where I spend hours planting, weeding,

1

pruning, sowing, hoeing, trimming, digging and watering. Gardening, for me, is like managing a football team. If you plan and prepare properly, you can create something beautiful to the eye. But, if you don't lay the right foundations and sow the seeds with care, you can make a mish-mash of a team. Look there at the shallow trenches I have dug for the planting of next year's roses. Note the perfect symmetry which will mean that my roses grow in a disciplined and decorative formation.

It is here in my lovingly manicured garden and out on the golf course that I have spent the first months of my enforced exile from football, learning to come to terms with the pain you get from a brutal knife stab in the back. Most will claim that it was a self-inflicted wound. I shall let you be the judge of that.

Every Tom, Doc and Harry has had his say about George Graham and the Arsenal Affair. Everybody but George Graham. Now it is my turn. So, if you will take a seat there by the rockery, I shall tell you *my* story.

The glory and the grief of my Arsenal reign.

Hampstead, London, November 1995

1 : The Order of the Boot

February, 1995: The weather is surprisingly mild, so it is time to plant my sweet peas. They are especially effective when grown in clumps, supported with cylinders of netting. I am using autumn-sown seedlings which have wintered in boxes. My garden is a joy to the eye, with *hyacinthus hybrida* and *helleborus niger* in full bloom. But I feel there is a blast of winter yet to come.

IT took eight and a half years for me to win six trophies for Arsenal, and two and a half minutes for the club to kick me out.

I can recall the moment, the minute that I was sacked from the club to which I had given fifteen years of my life, like a knifed man can remember the pain of the blade going into his back. Yes, I know, Arsenal will (perhaps with some justification) claim that the wound was self inflicted, but that does not ease the agony.

From being feted as a rival to even the legendary Herbert Chapman as the greatest manager in Arsenal's history, I was suddenly turned into the leper of football. It seemed that George Graham was the one man, the only man to blame for the oil-slick of sleaze in soccer. I felt not so much a scapegoat as a sacrificial lamb offered up to ease football's conscience.

Now, in my enforced exile, I have time to look myself in the mirror. I look hard and honestly, and I find myself guilty of stupidity and fleeting greed. But I feel I deserve more praise than punishment for the way I tried to put things right after the initial human failings.

I am of the strong opinion that I at least deserved the loyalty and support of the Arsenal board of directors, but they left me feeling like a man cut adrift to be eaten by the sharks. For this, I will never forgive them. And neither will I forgive the Premier League inquiry team who cost me my job with what I considered to be leaking evidence that I am convinced would never have stood up in a court of law.

When Tony Adams was jailed for a drink-driving offence the club, at my insistence, quite rightly stood by him. When Paul Merson confessed to being a gambling, drug-taking alcoholic the club, at my insistence, quite rightly stood by him. When I was in trouble for accepting unsolicited gifts, the club abandoned me.

3

All that I had achieved for the club counted for nothing. I had driven myself into the ground for Arsenal with an obsession that cost me my marriage. When I was divorced after twenty years of marriage, the newspapers talked about my wife and another man. But the real co-respondent was Arsenal Football Club. For eight-and-a-half years I ate, drank and slept Arsenal, putting my wife and family a poor second. I sacrificed my personal life for the club, and I was entitled to expect some loyalty from Arsenal in return. What did they do in my moment of need? They turfed me out, and watched my public execution as I was banned from the game I love. Arsenal will claim they were right to boot me out, but I will argue to my grave that I deserved more sympathetic handling by a club for which I had given my all.

I suffered the most humiliating experience of my life on my last day at Arsenal. It was eleven o'clock on the morning of Tuesday, 21 February 1995, and I returned from a three-mile jog around the roads of Hampstead to find a message on my answer machine from managing director Ken Friar. We were scheduled to play Nottingham Forest that evening, and I wondered if he wanted to talk about match arrangements. When I returned his call, he said tersely: 'The chairman wants to see you here at the ground.'

'When?' I asked.

'Straight away,' he said.

As I showered, I wondered what the chairman could want. The newspapers were full of conjecture about my future, and I knew the Premier League Inquiry report was due on the controversial gift cash payments that I had handed on to Arsenal. But I was fairly relaxed as I drove my club-owned black 7-series BMW to the ground because I had come to a secret agreement with Arsenal to leave at the end of the season with a considerable compensation package. So the sack was the furthest thing from my mind as I drove into the Highbury car park at around 12.15pm, and entered by the back door to avoid the photographers camped out at the front. I wondered what they knew.

I found chairman Peter Hill-Wood in Ken Friar's office along with vice-chairman David Dein. These were the three wise men I had met eight-and-a-half years earlier when they first appointed me manager. Then they were full of good will. Now they were more like executioners.

A stern faced Hill-Wood stood up as I went to enter the office, and he signalled me to follow him. He led me down the corridor into the wood-panelled boardroom, holding in his hand a typewritten sheet of Arsenal-headed notepaper. It was my death warrant.

'We've had advance information on the Premier League report,' he said. 'I'm afraid their findings leave us with no alternative but to terminate your contract with immediate effect.'

I was very nearly speechless, but managed to ask: 'Do I get the right of reply?'

He shook his head and thrust the notepaper into my hand. 'This is is the statement we are issuing,' he said. 'I suggest you show it to your lawyers. That's all I want to say apart from the fact that it's a pity it has ended like this after we've had so many happy times together.'

Happy times? Happy! Is that the best adjective his vocabulary would stretch to? It didn't say much for his Eton education. Happy? I had given him and the Arsenal club *fantastic* times. *Incredible* times.

'Do I get compensation?' I asked.

'No,' he said bluntly. 'Now I suggest you get yourself off the premises as quickly as possible before the media circus arrives. We are releasing the statement to the press in half an hour.'

'Can I make a couple of calls and clear my desk?' I asked, feeling like a condemned man making a final request.

'Yes,' he said, 'but make it quick.'

My mind was reeling as I pushed open the door and walked to my office for the last time. I was in and out of the boardroom in just two-and-a-half minutes. I felt like a servant being dismissed by the lord of the manor, but I wanted to point out that I had provided all the silver-ware on his lordship's sideboard.

I made two calls, the first to my schoolteacher daughter Nicole. I told her not to bother to come to the match against Forest as we had arranged because I had been fired. She was concerned about me, and suggested that we meet for lunch. The second call was to my business manager John Hazell, who could not believe what I was telling him. He had spent much of the previous five months negotiating a deal that would have meant a dignified and properly paid exit.

Now I was having to duck out the back door in a furtive manner, and with empty pockets. Just about the only thing missing was a

5

blanket over my head.

Peter Hill-Wood is a decent chap, and sacking me was probably the hardest thing he had had to do in his life. But I promise you, Peter, you got it wrong.

I know that I had been dismissed on the strength of evidence given to the Premier League by three representatives of the Norwegian club IK Start, from whom we had bought Pal Lydersen in September 1991. The three officials had been interviewed in Norway by Premier League chief executive Rick Parry and Robert Reid QC. They had collectively made a signed statement that pointed the finger at me, insinuating that I had negotiated a deal that was of benefit to me rather than Arsenal Football Club.

Now from what little I know about law, signed statements should be taken individually. But the three IK Start officials were interviewed together in the same room, and were able to hear what each was saying. It was these three faceless people that Peter Hill-Wood and the Arsenal directors preferred to believe rather than me. They took the word of strangers against mine.

Five months later at the Football Association hearing only two of the three IK Start representatives turned up. They gave conflicting evidence when interviewed individually by my QC. But the damage had already been done.

Peter Hill-Wood is on record as saying that it was the evidence from the IK Start officials that convinced him that I had to go. I wonder what he thinks now?

Following my hasty departure from Highbury, I treated myself to a final meal on Arsenal. I left home in such a rush for the meeting with Hill-Wood that I left my money behind. So when I took a tearful Nicole for lunch to a quiet Italian restaurant in North London I paid with my silver club credit card. There were no tears from me. Just a deep, burning anger over the way that I had been kicked out.

While I was toying with my *lasagne verde al forno*, Arsenal were issuing the following statement to the media:

Arsenal Football Club have now been informed by the FA
Premier League inquiry of the results of their investigations

into the alleged irregularities concerning certain transfers, and the board have concluded that Mr Graham did not act in the best interests of the club. The board have therefore terminated Mr Graham's contract as manager. The chairman said it was sad that Mr Graham's distinguished career with Arsenal FC should have to end this way, and he paid tribute to Mr Graham for the success he had brought the club over the past eight-and-a-half years. Stewart Houston will assume the responsibilities of manager.

After my fairly indigestible lunch, I drove the club BMW to the London Bridge office of my lawyers, Berwin Leighton, and had a meeting with my legal advisers and my business manager John Hazell. In our prepared statement, we side-stepped the usual legal jargon. 'The allegations by the Premier League Inquiry are nonsense,' my response stated with heart-felt passion. 'I deeply regret that this kangaroo court judgement should have been reached in such a hole-in-the-corner way.'

We agreed on a damage-limitation policy. Then I drove home to Hampstead, the ex-manager of Arsenal.

As I picked my way through the late-evening traffic I could not help having a grim little smile to myself. After I had captured the sixth trophy for Arsenal – the European Cup Winners' Cup in 1994 – it was suggested by a friend that I could be getting the OBE (Order of the British Empire). But now all I had got was the Order of the Boot, and it was delivered by Peter 'Bites-Yer-Legs' Hill-Wood in just two-and-a-half minutes.

It's a sad old game.

Later that week I flew off to Barbados with my son, Daniel. I needed a break to try to get my head together. While I was away Arsenal started fumigating Highbury of any traces of George Graham. My recorded voice-over words of welcome to the Arsenal museum were substituted by the voice of my old 1970s Arsenal and Scotland team-mate Bob Wilson.

But they will not be able to expunge my name from the record books:

1986-87:
Littlewoods Cup winners: Arsenal. Manager: G. Graham.
1988-89:
League championship winners: Arsenal. Manager: G. Graham.
1990-91:
League championship winners: Arsenal. Manager: G. Graham.
1992-93:
Coca-Cola Cup and FA Cup winners: Arsenal. Manager:
G. Graham.
1993-94:
European Cup Winners' Cup: Arsenal. Manager: G. Graham.

During my holiday I had time to think straight for the first time in months, and I started to put together in my mind the jigsaw of the recent events that had brought me to the lowest point of my life.

As I lay under the Caribbean sun, I could not shake off the belief that Arsenal had arrived at the dismissal decision for one main reason: in my view, they feared that they would have been put in the dock with me. If they did not get rid of the manager, might they have faced the threat of being included in the charges against me?

Arsenal did not mind George Graham having his finances probed and his integrity torn to shreds, but the club had to be protected at all costs. Once I was a non-employee, they were safe from the prying eyes of an investigative committee.

As I walked the beaches of Barbados I began thinking about what Arsenal might have to hide. Like most major clubs, they struggle to conduct a foreign transfer without, to use the vernacular, 'ducking and diving'. There is invariably at least one agent looking for a cut, the player seeking an extra inducement and the selling club not wanting to divulge the true cost of the transaction for any number of reasons. It is all part-and-parcel of the way foreign transfers are often conducted. Is there anybody out there who truly believes that it is only the manager who knows of the hidden extras? When I used to tell Arsenal managing director Ken Friar the requested fee, he would invariably ask: 'Does this include *everything*?' It just stopped short of a nudge, nudge, wink, wink. Can all football club directors answer honestly that they are are not aware that players often get – and here we are back in slang land – 'a bung' to persuade them to make the move?

I had another thought as I made footprints in the sand. Would Arsenal have sacked me had the team been challenging for a third championship under my management rather than tucked down in thirteenth place in the table? Only the Arsenal directors can answer that one. Publicly I am sure they would say 'yes', but I suspect that at least three of them would admit privately that there is no way I would have been kicked out if there had been the chance of another championship and the millions of pounds that would have generated.

As the sun set on my Barbadian holiday, I could not help feeling that I had been left carrying the can ... and it was a can of worms.

So I was more confused than relaxed when I returned from my brief break. The first thing I did was take back the BMW to Duncan Collins, the North London motor dealer who leased it to Arsenal. He kindly loaned me another BMW in its place so that I could get around. Duncan is a Tottenham supporter.

If I could turn the clock back, there is little that I would do differently in my reign as Arsenal manager. The only definite change would be that I would say 'no, no, no' when Norwegian agent Rune Hauge decided he wanted to thank me for all I'd done to help him open doors for transfer business in England. The fact that he wanted to show his appreciation with two generous gifts put a temptation in my way that I was unable to resist. It is no defence, but I am sure that few people could have resisted accepting the money. I have never claimed to be some sort of shining knight, and I am as weak as the next man when it comes to life's temptations. I concede that greed got the better of me, but only temporarily.

Let me tell you about Rune Hauge because he is such a central character in the story that led to my dismissal and subsequent exile from football. As I recall, I first met him in the summer of 1988 when he was visiting Highbury for a meeting with Arsenal vice-chairman David Dein about some commercial business unconnected with the transfer market. He was a very personable character, in his mid-thirties, and with his small, round glasses and fresh, boyish features he looked more like a young college student than a dynamic agent. Likeable as he was, I now, of course, wish I had never clapped eyes on him.

My next meeting with Hauge was on April 26, 1989, when our chief scout Steve Burtenshaw and I travelled to Wrexham to watch Wales play Sweden in a friendly international at the Racecourse Ground. Rune had tipped us off that Swedish midfield player Jonas Thern might be prepared to move from Benfica. Thern was not quite what I was looking for, but there was a player who caught my eye and I asked Hauge whether he might be available. His name was Anders Limpar.

Limpar, however, got involved in a less than successful transfer to the Italian club Cremonese, and it was fifteen months before we could land him. Hauge set up the deal and did the final negotiating with Ken Friar. I was later told by people in the know at Highbury that Limpar was paid the little matter of £200,000 from the transfer fee, not by Arsenal I hasten to add.

Arsenal's wage policy – set by the Board, not me – meant we were unable to match the salary he was receiving from Cremonese, and his cut from the transfer was the only way he could be persuaded to take a big drop in earnings.

Limpar was a sensation when he first arrived at the club, and I remember turning white when he called me to one side after training and said, 'Mr Graham, I have a problem. I have just received my first wages, and the money is far less than I anticipated. I am very unhappy about this. What is to be done about it?'

He was expecting to be paid a net sum, not gross. I had to send him to Ken Friar for an insight into the British PAYE tax system. This little episode was an education to me. It taught me the lesson that foreign players talked in 'net' terms rather than 'gross'. So when you hear a foreign footballer saying that he is on £200,000 a year, he means after tax deductions. For future reference, I made a mental note to always make it clear when negotiating with foreign players that I was talking in 'gross' terms. Net, to me, was where I wanted them to put the ball.

By the time Limpar joined us I had become quite friendly with Hauge. I saw him as a good contact to have in Europe because he was so well connected, and he saw me as a man who could help him do business in England. We worked together on the understanding that I would tell him which clubs might be interested in his players only after I had been given first choice for Arsenal.

Two of the first deals I helped him with involved Andrei Kanchelskis and Peter Schmeichel. I was given first refusal on each of them. Kanchelskis would not have fitted in with Limpar, and by the time I was offered Schmeichel I already had an even better goalkeeper in David Seaman. In each case, I recommended to Hauge that he should contact Manchester United manager Alex Ferguson because I knew they were the type of players for which he was looking. Hauge was delighted with the success of the deals, and said with that precise way he has of speaking: 'I will not forget what you have done for me.'

The way Hauge works is as a broker, as do most agents. He finds out from a club what fee they are expecting for a player, and then he earns for himself whatever he can get above that fee. It is a perfectly legitimate way of doing business, and he is an expert wheeler and dealer.

Apart from the Limpar transfer, Hauge was the middle man in two other deals. The first was for Pal Lydersen in September 1991. He was a Norwegian international full-back who I saw as a useful squad member, able to fill in for either Lee Dixon or Nigel Winterburn should they get injured. The fee I agreed with Hauge was £500,000. 'Does this include *everything*?' asked Ken Friar. I assured him that it did, and I then flew out to Oslo to finalise the deal.

It is important that I make the point here that I went to Oslo only at the insistence of IK Start. Had they not insisted on my going to Norway the IK Start trio of officials would have been denied their moment of glory, and the Premier League Inquiry team would not have been able to use and abuse me, as they eventually did. IK Start made it clear that they wanted to talk directly to me because there was something of a personality clash between Hauge and one of the three club officials involved in the negotiations. One reason I wanted to get everything sewn up quickly was that I knew that Manchester City were on Lydersen's trail. I had seen their scout Bobby Saxon watching him at the same matches where I had been making an assessment of his ability.

I knew that Hauge had worked out a deal with the player, but I was anxious that the total fee did not go above the half a million that I had agreed with Ken Friar. So I reluctantly got involved in the negotiations

11

only to keep the price down, not to push it up as has since been suggested. I came away from Oslo happy that I had got my man and for the originally agreed all-in total of £500,000. In all conscience, I can say that I negotiated in the best interests of Arsenal Football Club.

Now, as I look back, I wish I had never stepped foot in Oslo. It was a trip that eventually cost me my job. That transfer alone triggered my dismissal, and all because the IK Start officials gave evidence that led the Premier League Inquiry team to the conclusion that I had negotiated the transfer for my own ends. I can look anybody in the face and say that is not true.

The second deal brokered for me by Hauge was for John Jensen, who we signed from the Danish club Brondby in July 1992 after he had made a tremendous impression in the European championships while helping Denmark win the title. Hauge told me the asking fee was £2.2 million, which was a fair market price at the time for a player who was the talk of Europe after scoring a sensational goal in the final against Germany. But the canny Scot in me demanded that I barter, and I told Hauge that my valuation of the player was £1.5 million. Now would I have knocked down the price if I was after a cut?

I later learned, long after Jensen had joined us, that Hauge had agreed with Brondby that he would get them £900,000, and then did what I presume was his usual personal business with the player before his company took its cut. The nuts and bolts of the transfer did not interest me. All I was concerned with was the bottom line, and I was able to reassure Ken Friar that, as far as I knew, the £1.5 million fee 'included *everything*'. How Hauge divided the money was his business. It was up to him to satisfy the selling club and the player.

On the day that Jensen arrived at Highbury to complete the formality of signing, I was witness to the start of a conversation between Hauge and Ken Friar in the managing director's office.

Hauge said to Ken: 'I want £100,000 as my commission for setting up the deal.'

As Ken shifted uncomfortably in his chair I made my excuses and left. Hauge later told me that he had settled for £70,000, and that is why the odd fee of £1.57 million has gone into the record books. I must point out here that Ken has always denied this. I am just reporting what I heard, and what Hauge told me.

For Hauge it was just another deal. Another day, another dollar. This is the way agents work, and love them or loathe them they are now an integral part of the modern football world.

Now we need to go back to Christmas 1991 for the story of the first of my two controversial gift payments ... and I stress here and now that as far as I am aware neither of them was connected with the Lydersen and Jensen transfers.

Hauge telephoned me on 22 December to say that he was coming to London the next day, and that he would like to meet up with me. 'I have a Christmas present for you,' he said with a laugh.

I arranged to meet him in the lounge bar at the Park Lane Hotel. This is a regular base for people with Arsenal connections because it is part owned by Highbury directors Richard and Clive Carr.

Hauge came into the bar carrying a hold-all. We ordered a drink each, and then he said, 'I have something in here for you, George.'

He opened up the hold-all, dipped inside and brought out several plastic envelopes. 'Please put this into your briefcase,' he said. 'It is my appreciation for all that you have done to help me open up doors here in England.'

It was obvious that the envelopes contained a lot of money, and it was with a mixture of embarrassment and curiosity that I pushed them into my briefcase.

Please bear in mind that this was all carried out at a table in the lounge bar of the Park Lane Hotel. If I had been arranging some sort of kick-back, does anybody honestly think I would have selected such a public place – a place frequented by Arsenal directors – to carry out the transaction?

When I got home, I opened the envelopes to find they were filled with £50 notes. I decided to take the money straight to the bank, where it was counted. There was £140,500 in all. Happy Christmas, George!

I went hot and cold when I was told the amount. I had not asked for it, but I was neither strong enough nor, I suppose some might say, stupid enough to refuse it. It was eventually alleged that the money had been my share of the 'take' from the Lydersen transfer. That was ridiculous, as anybody who can do their sums will recognise. I understand that Hauge was left with £285,000 from the deal, of which £110,000 went as a 'moving' fee to the player. It makes no sense that Hauge would have paid me £140,500, leaving himself and his company with just £34,500 for all his negotiating work.

I deposited the money in an account that I had at the Allied Irish Bank in London's Berkeley Square. When that became public knowledge, all my detractors pointed to the fact that it must have been a 'bung' because it was suggested that I was tucking it out of sight in Ireland. The truth of the matter is that this was good old-fashioned Scottish housekeeping. It just so happened that the Allied Irish Bank was then paying a much better rate of interest on special deposit accounts. Later, on the expert advice of my bank manager, I transferred the money to the Allied Irish branch in Jersey to set up a Trust for my children, Nicole and Daniel.

To this day I have no idea why my gift was the odd figure of £140,500. Perhaps it was a conversion from a round figure of Norwegian Krone, or maybe it was all the English currency that Hauge could raise at the time. In my lighter moments, I fancied saying: 'Here, Rune, were you £9,500 short?' Well, you have to laugh or go mad.

My second payment came in a much more conventional way in August 1992. Hauge told me he again wanted to express his thanks for the advice and help I had been giving him.

Again, I did not request it. And again I did not refuse it. This time Hauge sent the money by post in the form of a banker's draft. It was for £285,000, and I gratefully had it credited to my Jersey account. It no doubt sounds like a bung, and looks like a bung, but it was a gift. And I did not ask for it.

I did not feel that I was cheating anybody. Hauge was picking my brains, and so I convinced myself that it was reasonable to accept a gift in return for my time and knowledge. He was making big inroads into the English transfer market, and my guidance had helped him to find suitable clubs for his players. His reputation in Europe as an agent who could get things done was soaring. That was due in no small measure to all the advice I was giving him in our numerous conversations. Now, without any prompting from me, he was saying a big thank you. You scratch my back, I'll scratch yours. How many business deals are carried out on this basis in Peter Hill-Wood's beloved City of London? Hundreds, I would guess. Every day.

A question repeatedly asked is, 'Why so much?' Robert Reid QC said to me during the Premier League Inquiry hearing that 'a few bottles of Scotch' might have been acceptable, but not such a substantial amount of money. But how do you measure what I had done for Hauge? Only he knew how much my advice had boosted his business, and he alone decided that £425,000 represented the value of my help that no doubt enabled him to earn millions for his company.

Robert Reid tested my temptation threshold by asking: 'How would you react if you opened the door to find a naked blonde standing there?'

I pondered this before replying, 'Well, it depends on how attractive she is ...'

Deep down I had the gut feeling when I accepted the gifts from Hauge that they could lead to all sorts of complications. But little did I know that the tremors would register on the Richter scale.

Before we move to the earthquaking events of my dismissal and my subsequent exile from football you need to know where I have come from. It has been a long, eventful journey and I invite you to join me back at the start.

Prepare to meet the Boy from Bargeddie.

2 : The Boy From Bargeddie

November 30, 1944: There can only be one plant for a baby boy born in Scotland on St Andrew's Day: the thistle, the national flower of Scotland. The thistle is any of various prickly plants of the composite genus *Cirsium*. The thistle is the ideal plant to represent anybody with a prickly personality. There are some people at Highbury who would find me very prickly.

AS the crow flies, Bargeddie is about 380 miles from the Marble Halls of Highbury but it is so far removed from the high-powered world of football that it could be on another planet. Bargeddie is little more than a village, eight miles from Glasgow and a mile or two from the Strathclyde iron town of Coatbridge. It is in a small, cramped house in Dykehead Road, Bargeddie, Lanarkshire, that my story starts.

It was St Andrew's Day, 30 November 1944, and Winston Churchill was celebrating his sixty-ninth birthday and looking forward to victory over Hitler and the Nazis when I first popped my head into the world. While I was getting my first breath of life my father, Robert, was losing a fight for his. He died on Christmas Day, 1944. I was barely three weeks old. Dad was the victim of tuberculosis, the lung-destroying disease that also robbed my family of my eldest sister, Mary, when she was just nineteen. I was the seventh child and an extra mouth for my suddenly widowed mum, Janet, to feed. I know this reads like the start of a Charles Dickens novel, but that's the way it was. A few decades later I would be lucky enough to collect a couple of Manager of the Year awards, but I was not in the same league as our mum. She was the Manager of the Century.

Just think of what she faced. She was thirty-six years old and left with seven bairns to bring up in a world that was still at war. The only income she had was a pittance of a widow's pension. Yet there was not one day in my young life when I ever went hungry. Mum literally dug with her bare hands to make ends meet. In those pre-motorway days you could take the north road out of Bargeddie and come to lush farm land, and it was on the local farms that mum worked like a slave to feed us. I would be dropped off at a local nursery centre run by a couple of villagers, and mum would disappear off into the fields for eight-hour back-breaking shifts of 'tattie howking' – that's potato picking for non-Scots. She was paid something like two bob for each wire basket that she filled. When things got really desperate she would fill a basket at double speed and then toss the tatties over a hedge into the adjoining field. Later in the evening she would take us all for a walk, me in my pram. She and my brothers and sisters would go to the field to pick up the pilfered potatoes, and then return home with the spoils hidden beneath me inside the pram. For the next few days we would have piping hot potato soup for our main meal.

It is the only dishonest thing she did in her entire life, and with all the right motives. Mum cared about only one thing: feeding and clothing her children, and teaching us right from wrong and to be respectful and well mannered. I would put her up against anybody in the world as a person of great character and principle, and I like to think her managerial skills rubbed off on me. She was a wonderful, God-fearing lady who had been classically pretty in her youth. My dad was a steel worker in Coatbridge until his death at the age of forty-four. I have only got blurred photographs to show me what sort of man he was, but as all the children he produced were tall he must have been a near six footer. Mum was only an inch or two over five foot, but a giant of a person in my eyes.

Dad played a few games for Albion Rovers before the war and his brother, Alex, had a spell with West Ham, so football was in the blood. He grew up in the pit-village region that produced the likes of Matt Busby and Bill Shankly. My three elder brothers, Andy, Tom and Robert, were all good-class players, and even my sisters, Maureen and Janette, could control a ball and give it a fair whack. Our eldest sister, Mary, died when I was six years old, giving Mum another emotional mountain to climb, but she buried her grief and got on with doing her best for the rest of us. Along with mum, Andy was the hero of our family. When dad died, he – as the eldest son – took on the mantle of father figure and quickly got an old head on young shoulders. Andy was the brightest of us all, but gave up the chance of a good education (and a goalkeeping career with Airdrie) to help feed the family. He left school at fifteen and went to work on a farm in Ayrshire, sending all but a few shillings of his wages home to mum every week. To this day

Andy is the man I will listen to before all others. He has great wisdom, and can always penetrate a problem with good common sense. There's a lot of my mum in Andy. Between them, they saw to it that young George had a terrific childhood despite the empty purse and bare larder. I owe them everything.

I want to briefly bounce forward twenty-odd years to when I was established as a player at Chelsea. It was the era of the swinging sixties and I was the 'Beau Brummell of Bargeddie', a walking advertisement for the best tailors in London and always with a mini-skirted beauty on my arm. Oh yes, those were the days, my friends. We reached the FA Cup semi-final and, as a reward, club chairman Joe Mears said he would take all the players to Cannes for a five-day break. We could each take a partner. The boys were having bets as to which of my parade of model girls I would bring on the trip, and I wound them up by telling them that I would be bringing Mrs Graham. The rumour shot round that I had secretly got married, so you can imagine the looks on their faces when I turned up at Heathrow Airport with my favourite girl on my arm: my mum. It was her first trip abroad and she had a fabulous time. We stayed in a five-star hotel and on the first morning I called at her room to take her down to breakfast. She was sitting in her armchair looking out at the panoramic view of the sea, and I did a double take when I saw that the bed had not been slept in.

'Where did you sleep, Mum?' I asked.

'In the bed, of course,' she said.

'Surely the maid's not been already,' I said.

'What maid?' she asked.

'The chambermaid, of course.'

Mum bristled. 'Nobody makes my bed but me,' she said.

That somehow summed up her life. She always made her own bed, and what a great job she did of it.

Now back to Bargeddie.

When I was about four we moved to posh-sounding 95 Abercrombie Crescent. It was situated on a new council estate in Bargeddie. There were no high-rise tower blocks: they were the curse of the sixties. This was the start of the fifties, when the country was just coming out of the gloom of the war. Rationing was soon to end, and the age of austerity was about to give way to what Prime Minister Harold Macmillan (who had great buckets of Scottish blood) labelled the 'never had it so good' times. Never had it so good? We didn't have much, so anything was a bonus. The move to the estate was one of the most exciting things that had happened in my short life. Suddenly, from an old, overcrowded house we were moving into what was, by comparison, something of a palace. The estate was sensibly laid out with neat rows of large two-storey, brick-built buildings. In each block there were four houses, two upstairs and two downstairs. Each house had its own separate entrance, and a back and side garden. We moved into an upstairs house and were able to spread ourselves out to just two to each of the four bedrooms, instead of the four-to-a-room at our previous house.

Mum was so proud of our new home, and kept it spotless with the help of my 'wee sisters' Maureen and Janette. There was a high standard of cleanliness throughout the estate; these were the days when you could happily leave your door unlocked without fear of a burglary. We had basic furniture, with the wireless being the only luxury plus a wind-up gramophone (later a record player) on which my elder brothers and sisters used to play the 78-revs-per-minute sounds of singers like Frankie Laine and Bing Crosby. We used to make our own entertainment by holding sing-along parties at our house and in neighbours' homes, and we followed the Scottish tradition of everybody having to sing a song. My party piece was the first song I ever learned by heart: Al Martino's 1955 version of the western film theme song *The Man from Laramie*. We had nothing, yet we had everything because we knew how to enjoy ourselves and how to get the most out of life through our own efforts.

I used to get free meals at school along with all the other boys who had no fathers in these immediate post-war years, and I was thirteen before I felt a new coat on my back. Mum was incredibly thrifty, and through clever needlework could keep clothes going long beyond normal wear-and-tear time. Most of my clothes used to be hand-me-downs, and it was nothing unusual for me to wear a patched-up jacket that had made the same school journey in earlier years on the backs of Andy, Tom and then Robert. I suppose any psychiatrist will tell you that this is why in later years I became so particular about my clothes. The one vice I have had from my first wage-earning day (I don't count ladies as a vice) is a weakness for buying the smartest possible clothes.

One principle that Mum passed on to me was that you should never, ever get into debt to buy anything. Many families on our estate bought things on tick, but Mum would not entertain the thought of hire purchase. 'If you want something bad enough then it's worth waiting for and saving for,' she used to say. It turned me into a fan of Mr Micawber from Dickens: 'Annual income twenty pounds, annual expenditure nineteen pounds nineteen and six, result happiness. Annual income, twenty pounds, annual expenditure twenty pounds ought and six, result misery.' Rather than get into debt, Mum used to work that much harder in the potato fields and one by one she introduced each of the family to the back-breaking job so that they could all help to bring in the pennies. As the youngest bairn I was spared the work, but many was the time I was pushed home from the fields in a pram sitting on a hidden bag of tatties.

When there was no potato picking, mum used to get a daily tram to Glasgow where she cleaned for a wealthy lady who lived in a mansion. She occasionally took me along with her, and that was when I first got a glimpse of the good things of life. There were striking oil paintings on the walls, carpets you sank into and beautiful furniture. I never once saw or heard Mum give any indication of envy. As far as she was concerned, the new house on the estate was everything she wanted. There was not an envious bone in her body.

Our diet improved enormously when Mum started growing vegetables in the garden, and it was from her that I got the love for gardening that helped keep me sane when the football pressures were at their peak. Mum would chop and season the garden produce, and then stir it all in a giant pot of boiling stock-flavoured water and the end result would be the finest vegetable soups you could ever hope to taste. Even to this day soup remains my favourite part of a meal, but I've yet to come across a restaurant where they can match Mum's cooking.

The best time for the Graham family each year apart from

Christmas (when Mum the Magician somehow managed to get each of her bairns a present), was Harvest Festival. Mum regularly attended the Bargeddie Protestant Parish Church, and demanded that we go every week to Sunday School. After each harvest festival the church would distribute the produce brought to the thanksgiving service to the widows on the estate. Much of it was donated by the local farmers, and we would have huge baskets of fresh fruit, vegetables and tinned food delivered, and we would eat like royalty for a couple of weeks.

I did not miss a father's discipline because Mum, for all her good points, knew how to dish out punishment. If any of us boys dropped below her high standards of behaviour she was quick to produce a leather belt, and she could also deliver a mean back hander to the ears. But from as early as I can remember I was too busy playing football to get into any serious trouble. In fact the only real walloping I got from her was for defying her orders not to play head tennis in the house with Robert, and when I broke a lamp with a misdirected header she chased me up and down the stairs and finally got me by aiming a hand broom that caught me a clattering blow on the back of the head.

The entire estate was 'fitba' crazy. There were few cars to worry anybody and we used to put down coats as goalposts and play in the road, with the pavements as the touchlines. It was our Hampden Park, and we played for hours on end and even had 'floodlit' football from the light of the lamp-posts. This was where I learned the basics of ball skills. I was a real 'tanner ball player', mastering the ball with either foot and spending hours hitting it against a wall and bringing the rebound under control. All the boys on the estate could control the ball thanks to the deadly serious roadway matches, often played with a battered leather ball with a lace that left a weal on your forehead if you headed it. If the boy who owned the ball was called in for supper, we would continue with a tennis ball or an old bladder stuffed with paper. We did not have the distraction of television, and football was the be all and end all of our lives. I have no doubt that it was when these street kickabouts started to die out that we began to see a definite falling off of individual skills in Britain.

Christmas 1953 was very special to this nine-year-old. Mum, in her

Father Christmas role, had, with the help of Andy, somehow scraped together enough pennies to get me my first pair of football boots. Like your first love, you never forget your first pair of boots. Just the memory of them brings back their unique smell. They were Mansfield Hotspurs and made of a blackened leather that was so tough that I had to soak them in warm, soapy water for hours on end to make them supple enough to wear. They had huge toecaps like those on the boots of miners, and God help anybody if I clattered them in the shin. Georgie Bites Yer Legs! There were no studs in the soles, but four rubber bars that ran the width of each boot. For shinpads, mum used to stuff copies of my favourite comics, *The Eagle, The Wizard* or *Tiger*, into old socks and stitch them up and then iron them flat.

It was at school – wearing my Mansfield Hotspurs – that I began to develop my game on proper pitches, first at Bargeddie primary school and then at Baillieston Secondary. I used to swank and tell people that I went to Baillieston High, and if anybody ever queried it I would say, 'Well, it's on top of a hill.' It was a very good secondary modern school, the equivalent to a comprehensive today. There were some first-rate teachers, but I'm afraid their efforts were wasted on me. The only subject I really enjoyed was geography. It must be something to do with being a Sagittarian and enjoying the spirit of freedom. I loved learning about other countries and where places were located, little knowing that one day, thanks to football, I would visit many of them. My worst subject was maths, and if you had told me that one day I would be conducting transfer negotiations with millions of pounds involved I would have wondered who would have counted the money for me (no jokes, please, about Norwegian agents!).

My maths teacher was a strict but caring gentleman called John Stirling. He also took me for football along with our P.E. teacher Mr Black, and while he encouraged my playing he despaired of me as a scholar. I was always looking for the opportunity to dodge maths lessons, and often had a genuine excuse because of representative matches and trials. Once, when I informed Mr Stirling that I would be missing his lesson because of a trial he looked at me and slowly and sadly shook his head. 'Thank goodness, Graham,' he said, 'that ye've got yer brains in yer feet 'cos ye havena any in yer heed.'

When I was eleven I started to contribute to the family income. I got a job delivering groceries, but because we could not afford a bicycle I used to push the delivery items around in an old barrow. I was paid seven bob a week (thirty-five pence), and gave it all to mum but I kept my copper tips. It gave me an appreciation and value of money that has remained with me ever since. I spend heavily on clothes, but am sensible and often cautious when deciding how to invest what's left. We are all of us shaped by our experiences and environment. You cannot come from my sort of background without having caution and a certain thriftiness embedded in you.

Many of my mates at school (my best pal was a very capable footballer called David Robertson) were thinking of a future in the steel industry at nearby Coatbridge. But from as early as thirteen I had my mind set only on becoming a professional footballer. My older brother, Tom, was a full back with Dundee United, and he later moved to Poole Town where he is now happily settled. Robert played good-standard football in Birmingham, and Andy helped run the Swinton amateur team in which I played with my brothers on Saturday afternoons after school matches in the morning. It was Andy who had the greatest influence on me with quiet coaching and words of advice. He used to take me to Broomfield Park to watch Aidrieonians play on a regular basis, and I fell in love with their stylish passing game of football. They had an inside-forward called Ian Macmillan, and I almost purred watching him in action. He was a real thinking man's player, with superb control of the ball and the ability to drift into space and then dismantle the defence with a beautifully weighted pass. That was how I wanted to play the game, and the chance to try to play his way came out of the blue when I joined Arsenal. But more of that later.

I occasionally used to go to watch Rangers play at Ibrox, but even more often I would go to Parkhead to see Celtic in the days of that great entertainer Charlie Tully and the brilliant Bertie Peacock. There was still the unhealthy Catholic-Protestant divide in those days, but I never used to give it a seconds' thought. Our downstairs neighbours, the Gilroys, were a Catholic family, and I used to happily accompany their son, John, to watch Celtic play.

An interlude here for a memory of a match that became a furnace to my ambition to become a full-time footballer. I was lucky to be one of the 128,000 spectators who packed into Hampden to see the unforgettable 1959-60 European Cup final in which Real Madrid swamped Eintracht Frankfurt 7-3. The date was 18 May 1960, and I was fifteen and just preparing to step on to the first rung of the professional football ladder. Now I was about to witness the game played at Everestpeak level.

It was like watching football from another planet. I have since played in hundreds of other games and watched thousands more, but I have never seen one to match it. The skill level was just unbelieveable, and I am proud to say 'I was there'. The footballing aristocrats of Real were untouchable that night, with di Stefano and Puskas performing in tandem. Puskas scored four goals, and di Stefano netted the other three. It was Real's seventh goal that has stayed etched in my memory. Di Stefano moved imperiously from a deep-lying position, exchanging passes with colleagues and always demanding the return of the ball until he ended his advance with a deadly accurate shot that beat the goalkeeper all ends up. It was a goal that deserved to be captured in oils.

The breathless crowd, me included, gave both teams an ovation that lasted a full fifteen minutes after a magnificent match that has been preserved on film as evidence of how the game of football can be played at the highest level. It set a new standard for football and for footballers, but it is only once in a blue moon that you get the coming together of two geniuses of the game like di Stefano and Puskas, both playing at the peak of their power. It was a joy to watch, and it convinced this Boy from Bargeddie that he wanted a future in football.

Professional scouts had been beginning to take notice of me as I sailed through the district and county teams and into the Scottish international under-15 side. For the Airdrie and Coatbridge combined schools side I played at inside-forward alongside the phenomenal Willie Henderson, who was destined for great things at Rangers. I recall one schools final in which we beat Edinburgh 17-3 on aggregate. My most memorable schoolboys match was the international against England at Wembley, even though we lost 5-3. I managed to get on the score sheet on that great soccer stage while playing with prospects of the quality of Jim Forrest, his cousin Alex Willoughby and future Sunderland and Newcastle hero Bobby Moncur. The England team included Len Badger, David Pleat, Barry Fry and a kid from Hackney called Ron Harris. They had not yet hung the 'Chopper' label on him, although the way he tackled even then suggested that he would literally make his mark on the game. Amazingly, we were watched by a crowd of more than 70,000 in the days when schools football was producing a conveyor belt of talent. It was the first time I had heard the real roar of a crowd while on the pitch, and it gave me a taste for the big occasion.

Football was an obsession, and I had little time for other hobbies. I had not even discovered girls but all the music I listened to had romance as the theme. Rock 'n' Roll was taking off in a big way, but I preferred the smoother sounds of Nat 'King' Cole, Billy Eckstine, Vic Damone and the guv'nor, Frank Sinatra. All of them had that indefinable quality called style. And that was what I wanted. Style.

My aim was to play the game the smooth Ian Macmillan way, but because I was a big lad for my age I was encouraged to be more robust than I really wanted to be. Here's an admission that I will only make because I want this to be a true picture of my footballing life: I was a little too faint hearted in those early days for the hurly burly physical challenges of the penalty area. I wanted to be an artist rather than an artisan. The professional scouts were making their reports on me as a target man, something of a grafter, while deep down I wanted to be more of play-maker. When you have seen The Master, Alfredo di Stefano, coming forward from a deep midfield position exchanging wall passes and then, after a forty-yard run, steering the ball into the net it can only make you want to try to imitate and emulate it.

As any of my contemporaries will tell you, speed was never my strong point. I was not nicknamed Stroller without earning the label. Yet it will come as a shock to all those who have ridiculed my slow coach gait to learn that on one day in the Baillieston school athletics championships I won the Under-15 100 yards, 110 yards hurdles, 440 yards and the high jump (I can hear Tommy Doc growling, 'The boys you were running against must have had lead in their shoes'). I was the school record holder in the high jump at both junior and senior level, which explains all those high-flying headed goals I used to collect early in my professional career. (The Doc again: 'Aye, and it also explains how you were able to jump when the tackles were coming at you.').

It was after I had played five times for the Scottish schoolboys team that I had to decide where I wanted to start my career. There were more than a dozen clubs showing an interest, but the first to come for me in a big way was the one for which half the schoolboys in Scotland dreamed of playing: Rangers. It was not a dream that I shared. The Sagittarian in me was demanding that I travel. I was looking o'er the border to that far-off foreign land, England.

Believe me, for a boy from Bargeddie it was a million miles away.

3 : Uncle Joe and Mohair Suits

August, 1960: Beds of the floribunda variety of roses are bringing a riot of colour to our small garden in Bargeddie, which was lovingly kept by my mum. It was from my mother that I first learned the art of gardening, and she was a great believer in the saying, 'As ye shall sow, so shall ye reap.'

RENOWNED Rangers manager Scot Symon stood alongside me in the middle of the pitch at a deserted Ibrox. 'This, laddie,' he said with a sweep of his hand, 'is the greatest place on earth. Once ye pull on a blue Rangers shirt and run out here on tae this pitch ye will know no feeling like it. We want ye tae come here, bring yer heart and soul and ye'll never regret it. There is nae other club like it in the whole wide world.'

It was the sales pitch that I knew he had given dozens of times before, but usually to young hopefuls ready to bite off his hand for the chance to play for Rangers. I was different. My heart was set on going south, and I had the choice of three clubs: Newcastle United, Chelsea and Aston Villa. Mr Symon could not disguise the look of disbelief on his face when I told him: 'Thank ye fer showing me around, sir. I wouldnae want to make a decision right now. I want tae think about it.'

This was not me being mature beyond my years. The game plan had been worked out by my brother Andy. I was fifteen and preparing to leave school to start a career in football, and the first lesson he taught me was not to dive in and make a commitment with anybody.

'Always buy yersel' time tae think,' he advised. 'Ye're in the driving seat because ye have something that they want, which is yer outstanding fitba' talent. Remember, never accept the first offer that is made. Go away, think things through and then make a decision in the cold light of morning.' It was advice that I have heeded throughout my career. The only time I did not hesitate was when Arsenal asked me to become their manager, as I will reveal in a later chapter.

The fact that Rangers wanted me caused a minor family feud. My brother Tom, a full-back with Dundee United, was a 'Gers fanatic who would have given his right leg to pull on the famous blue jersey. He said that I would be mad to turn them down, and that if I refused to sign for them he would not speak to me again. But Andy put the case that I would have a much better chance learning everything about the professional game by moving to an English club. He pointed out that Rangers did not have an apprenticeship scheme and that I would be farmed out to a junior club (the equivalent in England to a senior amateur side), and that I would have to prove myself in a competitive league where they took no prisoners. As a Rangers prospect, I would be the target for the heavy brigade. In England, Andy explained, I would get a proper grounding by daily attendance at the club and that I would learn by mixing and training with the established professionals.

So I said 'nae' to Rangers (Tom and I remain good pals), and took what was described as 'a holiday' with Chelsea and Newcastle. I spent a month with each club, being shown around and playing in trial matches. Ted Drake was the manager at Chelsea, and as a keen student of football history I knew all about his deeds on the pitch with Arsenal and England that included seven goals from eight shots against Aston Villa in the 1930s. He had put together a multi-talented young side known as 'Drake's Ducklings'. When I went down to Stamford Bridge, crop-haired Jimmy Greaves was in the early stages of negotiations for his transfer to AC Milan, and the team included such teenage talents as Bobby Tambling, Barry Bridges, Peter Bonetti, Ken Shellito and a swaggering, streetwise seventeen-year-old Cockney kid called Terry Venables.

Ted Drake, between miming golf shots, told me in that distinctive Hampshire burr of his: 'London is the place you need to be, son, and Chelsea is the heart of London. As you can see from my team, I believe in giving youngsters a fair crack. There will be no hanging around in the reserves here. Show me you can do the business and you will be playing in the First Division before you know it.'

A quick break here for a true Ted Drake story from that larger-than-life character John Sillett. One evening Ted was giving Chelsea skipper John a lift from the ground when he pulled up at traffic lights. They were engrossed in talking tactics, and the traffic lights turned from red to green and then back to red without Ted driving on. When the lights changed to green again and Ted still did not move, an irate driver behind started to sound his horn.

'I think you'd better go now, boss,' said John. 'The lights are green.'

Ted looked at John in amazement and then at the steering wheel. 'Good God,' he said, 'I thought you were driving.'

That's what management does to you.

To be honest, I could not get away from Chelsea quick enough. It was too sprawling a place, the training ground pitch was water-logged after a rain storm and London was just too fast and too big for this boy from Bargeddie. What a difference four years would make.

I was equally overwhelmed by Newcastle; not the place but the club. It was as if I had walked into a home for footballers. Everywhere I looked when I was being shown around St James Park there were players; players kicking footballs; players lapping the pitch; players doing exercises; players sweeping the terraces; players standing around doing sweet Fanny Adams. I was invited to sit in for the pre-season club photograph, and there must have been sixty people lined up with me. Just to make sure I was not dreaming this, I looked up the 1960 record book to see how many players Newcastle had on their staff. There were forty-four in the squad, not counting at least a dozen apprentices. Ironically, one of the players who was in the photograph with me was all set to change the face of football. George Eastham was about to launch his High Court case against 'slave labour' soccer which would coincide with the Jimmy Hill-led campaign to kick out the maximum £20 a week wage. A little over a year later, the Newcastle squad had been chopped by twenty players as clubs started to adapt to having to pay fair wages.

I had been invited for a week's trial at Newcastle by their manager Charlie Mitten, who goes down as one of the more engaging characters to have crossed my path. He visited my home in Bargeddie to try to coax me to sign for Newcastle, but Mum told me to take my time even though Charlie painted a wonderful picture of what life would be like on Tyneside. 'There's nae harm in going ter have a look,' said Mum. 'But listen tae what Andy has got tae say before ye commit yersel'.' Good old Scottish caution; you canna beat it.

Another quick break, this time for a true Charlie Mitten story that was told to me years ago by the late Cockney comedian Tommy Trinder, who was then chairman of Fulham and the man who made Johnny Haynes Britain's first £100-a-week footballer in my first full season in the English game. Tommy told how he once walked into the dressing-room at Craven Cottage during the 1950s to find trainer Frank Penn massaging a greyhound. 'What's that?' asked Tommy. 'Our new centre-forward?'

'It's a greyhound,' said the trainer.

'I can see that,' said Tommy. 'But what's it doing here?'

'It belongs to Charlie Mitten,' (then Fulham's outside left) explained Frank. 'We're getting it in the mood for tonight's big race.'

Charlie came in at that point. 'There you are, guv'nor,' said Charlie. 'Been looking for you to tell you about the dog.'

'Oh, that's most co-operative of you to tell me that we've given a bloody greyhound the run of Craven Cottage,' said Tommy, who was accustomed to Charlie's ducking and diving.

'Do yourself a favour, guv'nor, and get your pound notes on it,' said cheeky Charlie. 'It's running at Slough tonight and it's a racing certainty to finish first.'

'But you can't train greyhounds here,' protested Tommy. 'This is a football club. Well, that's what I like to believe.'

'I think you'll have to turn a blind eye just this once,' said Charlie, famous for his persuasive tongue. 'All the players have got their money on it, and it will upset them if we upset the dog.'

Tommy knew when he was beaten. He shrugged and handed Charlie a white fiver. 'Here,' he said, 'put this on for me when you go to the track.'

The dog trailed in last.

I quickly made up my mind after discussions with Andy that Newcastle was not for me. I would have been just another face in the crowd. The next club to make an approach was Huddersfield Town, and their manager made a big impression. 'If ye join me, sonny,' he said in a voice as Scottish as bagpipes, 'ah'll personally take ye under ma wing. Ye'll learn not only how tae become a fitballer but how tae become a mon.' It was, of course, the inimitable Bill Shankly. Just before the end of the year he moved to Liverpool, and again invited me to join him. But both Huddersfield and Liverpool were in the Second Division, and Andy thought I should set my sights on a First Division club.

My future was decided by the visit of yet another manager to our Bargeddie home, and Mum was bowled over by the natural charm, gentlemanly manners and obvious sincerity of the visitor, Joe Mercer, of Aston Villa; he of the banana-shaped smile and famous bow legs on which he had done proud service for Everton, Arsenal and England. Joe – 'Uncle Joe' to so many people in the game who loved his warm personality – left Mum and Andy in no doubt that he had my best interests at heart, and that I would be looked after at Villa with proper due care and attention.

So it was that I found myself on Glasgow Central station holding a battered brown suitcase and bound for Birmingham on the old steam-driven *Flying Scotsman* (well, I like to think it was, but I am not a hundred per cent sure because I was too nervous to take everything in). There had been a slight delay in my plans because of an operation following appendicitis, but now I was ready for the big challenge of the 'million miles' journey from Bargeddie to England. For the first time in my life I had complete independence. There was no Andy to hold my hand, or Mum to nag me into eating and sleeping at set times; and no safety net if I made a mess of things. 'Make sure ye write regularly,' said Mum, worried out of her wits about her baby boy. 'And eat three square meals a day.' Yes, Mum.

Birmingham was a shock to the system. I was not used to the Brummie accent and many people I met could not tune in to my broad Lanarkshire tones. So for the first few weeks as an Aston Villa apprentice I was involved in some strange and frustrating conversations *('Dear Mum, I hate it here ...')*.

I was not the first footballer from Lanarkshire who struggled to make himself understood. Matt Busby was living in Liverpool during his playing days in the 1930s when a census researcher called at his door. She asked Matt what he did for a living. The young man from the Lanarkshire pit village of Bellshill told her: 'I'm a footballer.' When the papers arrived from the census office, Matt found himself listed as 'a fruit boiler'.

31

Once I settled in and came to terms with the language barrier I found Brummie people the friendliest you could hope to meet. First of all I was put up in digs at Warmley Village with six other groundstaff boys, but I struggled to overcome the homesickness hurdle in the first couple of months. I would go home for long weekends, and Mum had to use really powerful persuasion to get me on to the train back to Birmingham. It was when I palled up with a young professional, Mick Tindall, and moved in with him and his parents that I really began to feel as if I belonged at Villa. Mick and I became great buddies, and it was he who set the smart dress-sense standards that I followed. A family of Birmingham-based Scots, the Samsons, also made life much more bearable by inviting me and two other Scottish apprentices, Jimmy McMorran and Ian Cairns, to their home for lunch every Sunday. While husband Jim sat talking football to us, his wife, Jenny, would cook the sort of meals that you would kill for *('Dear Mum, I love it here ...').* Jenny remains one of my dearest friends to this day and I look on her like a second mum.

I had started at Villa on a wage of five pounds a week, but this was soon increased to a tenner. I used to send a fiver home to Mum and would squirrel away as much as possible of the rest until I had enough to buy decent clothes. No more hand-me-downs.

My first duties on the Villa groundstaff included sweeping the dressing-rooms, cutting the grass and cleaning the boots of the first-team players. I had special responsibility for the size nines of the one and only Derek Dougan when he arrived on a sea of publicity from Blackburn Rovers, having posted a transfer request on the day that he played against Wolves in the 1960 FA Cup final. Doog saw in me a kindred spirit, having made the 'million miles' journey from Belfast to Portsmouth to kick off his football career. He understood my homesickness because he had been through it himself. Doog took me under his wing and I could not have had a better tutor in how to enjoy life. These were his crazy entertainer days when he shaved off most of his hair and became known to the Villa fans who idolized him as 'Cheyenne'. He played hard, on and off the pitch, and quickly picked up a playboy image as he zoomed around the Birmingham nightspots in the original version of the sort of Jaguar car John Thaw drives in the Inspector Morse series. His constant companion was local heavyweight boxing hero Johnny Prescott. What a win double they made, particularly when Johnny often appeared with the notorious Mandy Rice-Davies as a beautiful appendage.

I admired the way Doog lifted himself above a tragedy that would have knocked the heart out of lesser men. He was a passenger in a car on the way home in the early hours after Villa had won the first ever League Cup final at Villa Park on 5 September 1961. The car went out of control on the outskirts of Wolverhampton, and rear-seat passenger Malcolm Williams, a 26-year-old football reporter on the local *Express and Star*, was hurled against the windscreen and killed. Doog broke an arm and had head wounds that required over fifty stitches. The club was numbed by the tragedy and it threw a cloud over the League Cup triumph. There were all sorts of wild rumours that it was a drink-driving crash in what were pre-breathalyser days. Derek and Villa team-mate Bobby Thomson, who was driving the car, assured me that nobody in the car had been drunk, and indeed an autopsy revealed that Malcolm had drunk barely two pints of beer.

Doog had the strength of character to put the tragedy behind him and was back in full swing on and off the pitch within three months. I watched from the sidelines, and occasionally as a companion, as the Dougan whirlwind swept through Villa. He came and went in the space of two years, but he made an impact on the club and on the city that gave him legendary status. These days he says, with a twinkle in those Irish eyes of his, that I was not fit to clean his boots. He was larger than life and, while he rubbed some people up the wrong way with his brash behaviour, there was no doubting that Villa was a more exciting and vibrant place when he was around.

As you can imagine, with characters like Doog and Uncle Joe Mercer around, there was a lot of behind-the-scenes laughter even when the results were not so good. I remember Doog once turning up for training with a Yul Brynner haircut. His head was shaved completely bald. Dear old Joe gave a double take, and said: 'We'll have to get some billiard chalk in the dressing-room on match days. I don't want you miscueing when you're heading for goal.'

Doog later, of course, became a respected and eloquent spokesman for the players as chairman of the Professional Footballers' Association. Cheyenne had become Chairman Mao.

While Doog used to go to the nightspots in his Jag, I would arrive by bus. All my money was going on looking the part, and Mick Tindall and I were trend setters with our shiny Italian-tailored mohair suits with bum-freezer, three button single-breasted jackets, gleaming winkle-picker shoes and fashionably cut hair. Mick went all the way with a Beatles haircut, but I liked my parting too much to go that far. I had discovered a rapport with the lassies of Birmingham and was scoring in the romantic sense as frequently as possible. I was a regular on the last, late-night number 11 bus that took me from the Locarno dance-hall to my digs, and the scent on my mohair suit was not aftershave.

Oh yes, and there was football too. I signed as an Aston Villa professional on my seventeenth birthday, 30 November 1961, and was given an eight pound rise. Now I was sending a tenner home to Mum in Bargeddie and keeping eight for myself *('Dear Mum, No more tattie howking ...')*. My wardrobe was beginning to bulge.

I thought I knew it all about the game until I arrived at Villa, but suddenly I was surrounded by players who were every bit as good, and often better, than me. Coaches Ray Shaw and Bill Baxter gave me a new insight into tactics and I was given the role of target man, playing in the reserves as understudy to the extrovert Doog. The high jumping ability that I had shown at school now became an important part of my armoury as I perfected the sort of 'hanging' headers that were a speciality of one of my favourite players, Denis Law.

I was not forgotten by the Scots, and played in the 'Little World Cup', the tournament for under-18 international teams. My eyes water at the memory. We were drawn against Greece and I scored a hat-trick on the way to a decisive 4-0 victory on the Tooting and Mitcham ground in Surrey. There was a crowd of about 4,000, and at least half of them were Greek. As we came off at the end a mob attacked the Scottish players. I was fighting my way towards the dressing-room when a man wearing an official Greek blazer ran at me and landed with an Eric Cantona-style kung-fu kick right between the posts, so to speak *('It don't half hurt, Mum ...')*. It transpired that he was a team official, and he and the Greek side were banned from the following tournament.

My breakthrough to the Villa first-team came in dramatic fashion just a few days after the Greek riot. It was Villa's last home match of the snow-delayed 1962-63 season, and the opposition were mighty Liverpool including Kop heroes Ian St John, Roger Hunt and Ron Yeats (*'It ain't half hot, Mum ...'*). It could not have gone better for me. I scored the first goal in the seventy-eighth minute with a low left-foot drive and set up the second for Bobby Thomson six minutes later for a 2-0 victory. 'Graham, eighteen-year-old wonderboy!' screamed one over-the-top headline.

This, I thought, meant that I had arrived. But it was a false dawn. It looked as if I was going to be more of a one-match wonder. I played only seven more first-team games over the next year as Villa buckled under a crisis of confidence. In despair I asked coach Bill Baxter what the problem was. He said that they wanted to try a system that did not suit my style. Tony Hateley had been bought from Notts County to replace the Doog, and his aerial power was preferred to mine. Bill sounded an alarm bell during our conversation about my off-the-pitch behaviour, dropping hints that socialising was too often coming before my soccer. This was underlined when I read in a local newspaper that I had collected a reputation as 'a good-time boy'. It was true that I was enjoying myself in my own time, but never at the expense of my football. I was not a big boozer; never have been. But I admit that I could not resist the lassies.

I tried to find out from 'Uncle Joe' Mercer where I stood, but he was under such strain that he made little sense when I talked to him about my future. It was only years later that this marvellous man, sadly no longer with us, admitted to me that he had been on the verge of a nervous breakdown in what was to prove his final season at Villa. 'I kept it quiet but I suffered a mild stroke,' he told me. 'It was brought on by the pressure of work. The job took up every ounce of my energy and thinking time, and I sweated blood for the club for more than five years. I battled back to full health but my reward for all the effort I had put in was the sack.'

Joe had the last laugh on Villa by forming up with Malcolm Allison to make Manchester City one of the teams of the sixties. I should have taken note of how directors can pull the rug from under managers, but management was the farthest thing from my mind. It was playing the game that was my only concern. I wanted first-team football, but Villa had decided I was not right for them. They alerted clubs that I was for sale at a fee of £6,000.

Southampton were the first club to make a serious approach, and their long-serving manager Ted Bates took me on a tour of the club, the town and the beautiful surrounding countryside. An out-and-out gentleman, he was selling me Hampshire as well the Saints. I was impressed, particularly as he had offered me £25 a week, a fiver more than I was earning at Villa. But I remembered brother Andy's advice: Think things over. I went to my brother Tom's home in nearby Poole and slept on my decision. I was all set to accept the Southampton offer when I got a call from Chelsea manager Tommy Docherty, who had watched me score the hat-trick and get a good kicking in the youth match against Greece.

'What have Southampton offered ye?' he asked.

'Twenty-five pounds a week,' I said truthfully.

'Ah'll pay ye thirty,' said the Doc.

I was silently calculating how I could spend the money.

'Hello, George. Are ye still there?'

'Uh, let me think about it,' I said, falling back on to my set script. 'Ah'm going tae Spain fer a holiday tonight and ah promise to get in touch when ah get back.'

I was booked on one of those early-hours package holidays, and was checking in at Gatwick at two o'clock in the morning when I looked up to see the Doc bustling towards me with a sheaf of papers in his hand.

'Ah, George, just the mon I want tae see,' he said, as if it was an accident that we had bumped into each other and that he just happened to be carrying a contract. I signed just before going into the departure lounge. Fasten your safety belts. This could be a bumpy flight.

The boy from Bargeddie was now a Chelsea player. *('Dear Mum, I'm under Doc's orders. Now I'll really have something to write home about ...').*

4 : Bridge of Thighs

July 1964: How fitting that my arrival at Stamford Bridge coincides with the Chelsea Flower Show. There is a splash of Chelsea-blue geraniums, and everything in the garden is lovely as Tommy Docherty sows the seeds of one of the most exciting young teams in the game. But The Doc lacks something that all good gardeners need: patience.

FOR a red-blooded male, stepping foot in the King's Road, Chelsea, at the peak of the Swinging Sixties was like a passport to paradise. There were so many beautiful, long-limbed girls with thigh-high mini-skirts to ogle that I was in danger of my head swivelling off its shoulders. A simple walk from Fulham Broadway station to and from Stamford Bridge was always a delightful distraction. To quote my Cockney tutor Ron 'Chopper' Harris from that era: ''ere, George, clock that Richard.' I quickly picked up the lingo. Richard, as in Richard the Third, bird. Yes, Ron, just look at that bird. I did not just look. I touched and had the time of my life.

Twenty or so years later I would have frowned on any of my Arsenal players being so free and easy, but these were the sixties and times they really were a-changing. Anyway, I could fall back on the old parental theme of, 'don't do what I do; do what I say.' I look back on those Chelsea days as the springtime of my playing career (and you know what they say about a young man's fancy), with the summer to follow at Arsenal.

I will be doing myself and Chelsea a disservice if I paint a picture that gives the impression that I was a non-stop partying playboy. I was never a heavy drinker and I was reasonably discreet and disciplined with the girls in my life. The lady-hunting season came to an end when I met and fell in love with my wife-to-be Marie Zia, who was then a beautiful 20-year-old student actress and a classically-trained dancer. I met Marie while refereeing the Showbiz X1 charity matches, which was my regular Sunday afternoon relaxation. I became good mates with enthusiastic players in the team like Tommy Steele, comedian-actor Dave King, singer Kenny Lynch, boxer Dick Richardson and *Man About the House* star Richard O'Sullivan. I have always considered football a branch of show business. We are there to entertain (I can hear a chorus in the background: 'So what happened with "Boring Boring Arsenal?"'). Marie used to come along to watch an actor boyfriend play, but once she caught the eye of the ref I had her booked! Yes, I enjoyed myself in my spare time, but I also gave football every ounce of effort and concentration. Our pre-season training at Chelsea would have challenged the strength and stamina of commandos, and I have never been fitter in my life than in that Chelsea-blue period of my career.

My early days with Chelsea were spent in a small hotel, The Montana, in Gloucester Road. Then Christine Matthews, a smashing girl who worked in the office at Stamford Bridge (and later became the club Secretary) asked whether I would like to move in with her parents rather than lead a lonely life in an impersonal hotel.

'Where do they live?' I asked.

'Stamford Hill,' she said

That sounded nice and convenient, and so I gratefully accepted the invitation. Stamford Hill, I thought, must be close to Stamford Bridge. Silly me. It was a marathon trek across London from SW6 to N16. But from the moment I met Christine's mum and dad, George and Ada, I could not have felt more at home, even though George was an Arsenal fanatic who kept waylaying me with stories of the great Gunners' teams of the past. It is one of my deep regrets that 'Gentleman' George had passed on by the time I joined Arsenal. It would have given him a terrific kick to see me wearing one of his beloved red-and-white shirts. George and Ada were such warm, welcoming people that I decided the long cross-London trip was worth it, particularly as I was able to travel every day with Ron Harris, who lived in nearby Hackney. We used to get a bus to Manor House tube station, a train to Fulham Broadway, and then take the head-turning walk to Stamford Bridge to catch the team coach to Mitcham in Surrey for training. When I think back on it I feel I must have been mad to take on all that travelling, but it speaks volumes for the way the Matthews' made me feel part of their family. I was relieved, though, when I at last passed my driving test and became a really mobile man-about-town. My first car was a Hillman Minx that I got for a bargain price from a Chelsea fan in South London. I must have stalled it twenty times during my first drive back to Stamford Hill and was bathed in perspiration when I at last completed the journey. I used to have a routine chat-up line before I had the car. My regular haunt was the Tottenham Royal dance-hall, which was the nearest decent 'pick up' place to Stamford Hill. Once I had sorted out the girl most likely, I would ask her to dance and then say, 'By the way, what sort of car have you got?' If she did not have a motor, then she had to be something special for me to stay with her for the evening because I did not want to be stuck with having to pay the fares home. You canna beat a canny Scot!

The moment I arrived at Stamford Bridge my game began to click. Tommy Docherty was piecing together a team that played with a swagger and a flair that mirrored his personality. It was also at times brittle and unpredictable. Just like the Doc. In all my time in the game I have never known anybody quite like Tommy Docherty, who was from the tough Gorbals district of Glasgow. Like me, he was brought up in poor circumstances after the early loss of his father and he tackled life with an explosive energy that often made him seem like an earthquake waiting to happen. He could be the most entertaining and the most exasperating of people, all in the space of minutes. The Doc has had me roaring with laughter and rocking with rage; pumped up to play the game of my life and sometimes totally deflated to the point where I could not raise a gallop. One thing, the Doc was never ever dull. He could be enormously generous one moment, and almost vindictive the next. Just as you felt like getting your hands round his throat he would reduce you to helpless laughter with an earthy one-liner joke from a collection with which he could have made a living as a Glasgow music hall comedian. It was the Doc who said of one of his rivals when the Chelsea directors were interviewing him for the manager's job: 'If you appoint him, you won't get a coach – you'll get a hearse.' And it was the Doc who always told reporters: 'I've got nothing to say... what d'you want tae know?' These days I fully appreciate his joke about football club directors: 'The ideal set-up is to have just three on the board – two dead, and one dying.' Another Docism that carries an element of truth: 'Football is a rat race ... and the rats are winning!'

But it was not laughter all the way with Tommy. He seemed to like to puncture people who got above themselves, and when I made a goal-a-game start to my Chelsea career he took wicked delight in telling people that he had rescued me from doom at Villa. He said it so many times that the Chelsea players started to call me, 'Doomed George'. Another nickname I picked up was 'Gorgeous George'. That was the name of a fan club set up by a group of girls who followed me to every game, home and away. You can just imagine the stick I got from my team-mates for that. I used to respond by telling them they were only jealous. I was also known as 'Big Fry', after the guy in the television commercial who was always being chased by a crowd of girls *('Dear Mum, I'm having the time of my life ...')*.

Chelsea's style of football really suited me. The Doc used me as a target man, and my high-jumping aerial strength became an important factor in the team tactics. I was nodding the ball down to the feet of team-mates or managing to head it into the net with such regularity that the *Daily Express* dubbed me 'The Kangaroo Kid'. Dave Sexton was the inspirational Chelsea coach when I first arrived and he gave me an insight into what can be achieved by *thinking* about the game. He had the ability to make players believe in themselves, and this was the first time that I was made aware of the vital importance of coaching. At Villa, I had been allowed to sink into a valley of depression as I contemplated being on the scrap heap at nineteen. But suddenly, after eye-opening coaching sessions with Dave Sexton, I was feeling invigorated and hungry for action. Little did I know it then, but Dave was sowing the seeds for my future role in the game.

Terry Venables was the biggest influence on the Chelsea team. Even at twenty-one he was a natural leader and he patrolled our midfield with a Napoleonic air, feeding the ball through to nippy front runners with superbly delivered passes. I shall give a player-by-player assessment of the Chelsea team later in this chapter, but it is Terry who will get my main concentration at this point because he became such an important figure in my life. It was a mutual love of good music that first laid the foundation to our friendship. I was struggling to get accepted by the tightly knit Chelsea team when I first arrived, and I was cautious and withdrawn. You had to win the right to acceptance because most of them had grown up together from the Chelsea youth team days, and they were so cutting and quick with their repartee that you were in danger of being made to look a fool if you tried to compete. One afternoon we were on a train trip during a pre-season tour of Sweden when the players started taking turns singing favourite songs. There is not a Scot I know who can resist joining in a sing-song, and I had a good grounding from our parties in Bargeddie. Uninvited, I chipped in with my version of Billy Eckstine's beautiful ballad 'Passing Strangers' that he had recorded in a duet with the 'Divine' Sarah Vaughan. I gave it the full bit in an impersonation of Billy's rich bass-baritone voice. The players applauded and cheered when I had finished. I think it was the first time some of them had heard my voice, singing or speaking. Then Terry, who could (and still can) *really* belt out a song, came up with the classic line: 'That was a superb take-off of Sarah Vaughan. Now how about trying to do it like Billy Eckstine.' It was such a witty remark that I could not take offence, and it completely broke the ice. From that moment on Terry and I became inseparable friends and I was accepted into the Chelsea inner-circle.

After training at Mitcham, Terry, John Hollins, Ron Harris and I often used to call in on Chelsea fan Pat Sherlock, who helped run Mills Music in Tin Pan Alley's Denmark Street. As soon as we arrived in his office he would shout out, 'Reg, get the tea.' Reg, a tubby young lad with glasses, would bring four mugs of tea and then start trying to tell us why Watford were a better team than Chelsea. Some years later when I was at Heathrow with the Scotland team an unbelievable vision came towards me wearing silver, high-heeled boots, a purple fur coat and huge, gold-framed spectacles. 'Do you want me to get you a mug of tea, George?' he asked. It was, of course, Elton John, who I had known as Reg Dwight in his office boy days. I was with him in a boardroom when he was Watford chairman ten years later, and kept calling him Reg. He pulled me to one side and said, 'George, do us a favour. Call me Elton. Reg is not quite the right image!'

I remember my first Christmas at Chelsea when we were playing Blackpool on the Boxing Day. The Doc decided he wanted all the players together on the evening of Christmas Day rather than left to the temptations of parties and over-indulging. We were all booked into a posh hotel in Kensington, and the Doc told us to be in bed by ten o'clock. Then he went out for the evening. What Tommy did not realise is that a Christmas dinner and dance had been organised at the hotel, and when we heard music coming from the ballroom we were drawn towards it like moths to a flame. We were made welcome by the party hosts and Terry, who the previous year had recorded with the Joe Loss Orchestra, was invited up on to the stage to sing with the band. We were having a swinging time when the Doc was spotted getting out of a taxi. Within seconds we had all melted out of sight and rushed to our rooms... everybody but Terry. He was happily singing away on stage, and was into a second chorus of 'Chestnuts Roasting on an Open Fire' when he was suddenly aware of somebody staring at him. Terry looked down from behind the mike into the steely blue eyes of the Doc.

About five minutes later Terry came to the room that we were sharing. 'Thanks a lot, mate,' he said. 'Somebody might have warned me. The Boss has just roasted my chestnuts!'

The next day we beat Blackpool 2-0.

An interlude here for some stories that capture the pranks those Chelsea lads got up to; I've never known any to match them for whacky sense of humour and downright cheek, and I have to confess that I was as bad as any of them. Once, while waiting for a delayed flight at Heathrow Airport, I joined Terry, John Hollins and Eddie McCreadie at an empty BOAC check-in desk in the pre-British Airways days. We were wearing our blue Chelsea blazers and really looked the part of BOAC staff. For a good thirty minutes we were sending passengers all over the terminal in search of departure gates that did not exist. We even got one American passenger to open her case while we inspected it for hidden contraband. Silly, I know, but it was very, very funny at the time. Mind you, there were times when some of the lads could go right over the top. I recall one player secretly peeing in a half-full bottle of champagne that was then passed on to an already sozzled Fleet Street football reporter. His only comment as he swigged from the bottle was that it had not been chilled properly. The same player, one of the great Chelsea characters, once filled a condom with water and pinned it to the back of a passenger's coat at Heathrow. Yes, we had a lot of growing up to do.

Then there was the time we visited a vineyard just outside Adelaide during a playing tour of Australia. We all got absolutely legless while taking part in the wine tasting, and two of the players finished up jumping fully clothed into two huge vats of wine. The Australian wine industry was not then established, and the vineyard owners presented us with bottles of wine each as a PR exercise. Tommy Doc punished us for the exhibition we had made of ourselves by confiscating the wine. He and the Chelsea directors had seen off quite a lot of the bottles before the tour was over. Happy days.

I was on reserve squad wages when I first joined Chelsea, which was half the £60 a week that the first-team players were earning. There was only one place that I could prove myself, and that was on the pitch. I got an early chance to show what I could do when Bobby Tambling pulled out with an injury, and I scored in my debut on 29 August, 1964, against Sunderland, who had fifteen-year-old Derek Forster in goal. I was up and running, and within six weeks the Doc had torn up my reserve-team contract and replaced it with first-team wages that, with pounds-for-points bonuses, brought me in an average £100 a week. *('Dear Mum, The streets of London ARE paved with gold ...').*

Now I was really able to indulge my taste for good-quality clothes. I wore only made-to-measure suits, and beautiful hand-made shirts. Don't forget when judging me to remember all those hand-me-downs I had to wear as a kid. Terry Venables was also keen on fashion, and we decided that, rather than keep on, so to speak, lining the pockets of the tailors, we would put our money into a tailoring business. Ron Harris and Ken Jones, one of the finest, and most knowledgeable of all football writers who remains a good friend to this day, joined the venture, and we set up shop in Soho with Tom, a top tailor pal of ours. We did not exactly lose our trousers, but it folded pretty quickly because we found a marked reluctance by our celebrity clients to pay their bills. You could say we were not suited to the business. We did not exactly help ourselves by telling people that we made Norman Wisdom's suits. They thought we meant his ill-fitting stage suit that was his trademark.

We were also doing measured business out on the pitch, winning the League Cup and reaching two successive FA Cup semi-finals. I was a leading Chelsea scorer two seasons in a row, and I was rewarded with two Scottish Under-23 caps. Tommy Doc showed his caring side when I won my first Under-23 cap against Wales at Kilmarnock's Rugby Park. He flew up to Glasgow, picked up a hire car and drove to my home in Bargeddie. First of all he took my mum out to tea, and then he brought her and my brothers and sisters to watch me play. Like I said, one minute you wanted to throttle him and the next kiss him. The family cheered us on to a 3-0 victory, and I was proud to play in a marvellous forward line that included Charlie Cooke, Peter Cormack and Tottenham flier Jimmy Robertson. Prompting us from midfield was that human dynamo Billy Bremner. Some team.

I got a heavy kick in the calf muscle in the first-half against a powerful Welsh side that included Peter Rodrigues, Terry Hennessey, Mike England, and Ron and Wyn Davies. But I did enough to earn a recall against England Under-23s at Aberdeen's Pittodrie Park. What a battle that was! Alan Ball vs Billy Bremner in midfield. It was like a British bantamweight title fight. Those two wee terriers went at each other hammer and tongs for ninety minutes. Chief second to Ballie was the one and only Nobby Stiles, who was kicking anything that moved. Bremner was not without support. He had the cold-eyed Dennis Hollywood to help him in the rough-house exchanges. How the referee allowed everybody to stay on the field I'll never know. It was one of the hardest matches I had played in, and I was pleased to get off at the end of a goalless game with all my limbs intact.

A week later, the Doc took the Chelsea team off to Duisburg to give West Germany's 1966 World Cup team a warm-up match. They included giants of the game like Franz Beckenbauer and Uwe Seeler, and they treated the match with deadly seriousness. There were 3,000 German-based British soldiers in the crowd and we had them roaring as we floored the Germans with a winning Barry Bridges goal ten minutes from the end. The average age of our team was just twenty-one years, three months.

Everything seemed great, and respected football judges were predicting that we would be champions within two to three years. In one month, at our peak, we beat Liverpool and Leeds in the FA Cup and mighty AC Milan in the Fairs Cup. They were three of the outstanding sides in Europe at the time, and there was a mood of great optimism at Stamford Bridge despite losing our coach Dave Sexton to a managerial job at Orient. But one of those Tommy Docherty earthquakes was waiting to happen. The relationship between the players and the Doc was stretched to breaking point by what became known as The Blackpool Affair. He sent eight of us (Barry Bridges, Eddie McCreadie, John Hollins, Joe Fascione, Bert Murray, Marvin Hinton, Terry Venables and me) home from Blackpool after we had broken an eleven o'clock curfew during a week's training break. I wish I could titillate you by describing the wild night that we had enjoyed, but it was as innocent and as juvenile an act as nipping down the hotel fire escape to go to a nearby bowling alley that had a late-night bar adjoining it. There were a couple of local girls keeping us company, but nobody indulged in any hanky-panky. The Doc was sitting up waiting for us when we returned to the hotel in the early hours, and he decided to use the occasion to show that he was the Boss. We were all packed off home later that day, and he played a reserve team three days later at Burnley that got tanked 6-2. We lost confidence in the Doc after that because we felt he had over-reacted. Looking back with my manager's hat on, I still think Tommy could have handled it better. We were in the wrong, no doubt about that. But the Doc used the silly incident to score points against us, when a verbal rocket and a heavy fine would have done the trick and avoided all the over-the-top publicity and the out-of-order innuendo that crept into many of the newspaper reports.

I noticed with Tommy at Chelsea that he liked to stand on the bridge and walk the deck at the same time, a mistake for any manager to make. During my two years at Chelsea we were a have-boots-will-travel globe-trotting team, visiting outposts such as Australia, the West Indies, Hawaii, West Germany, Sweden, France and Italy. It got to the point where the wives of the married players, like Peter Bonetti and Bobby Tambling, complained to the chairman Joe Mears that their husbands were away too often. For us single blokes, though, it was great and I loved the opportunity to see the world as I had dreamed of during my school geography lessons. Tommy was a great believer that travel broadened the mind and that playing against foreign opposition improved our understanding of the game. He would join us when we used to go out on the town during these trips, and then come the big boss at training the next day. Now I look back I realise that he was then still in his mid-thirties and learning the problems and pitfalls of management. By the time I rejoined him some years later at Manchester United he had clearly realised that a captain cannot mix with the crew.

To this day I have never been able to understand why the Doc chose to break up one of the most exciting young sides of the sixties. He made up his mind to turn the Chelsea team inside out after our 2-0 1966 FA Cup semi-final defeat by Sheffield Wednesday at my old hunting ground of Villa Park. It was our second successive tumble at the semi-final hurdle (Liverpool beat us 2-0 the previous year, again at Villa Park), and just to rub it in, the main architect of the Wednesday victory was Jimmy McCalliog who had been an original Chelsea signing by The Doc. Tommy was full of sympathy when he came into the dressing-room immediately after the match, and he told us with sincerity shining out of his face that we still had a great future ahead of us. Then he went out and told the press just five minutes later that he was going to bring in new blood. 'This team is just not up to the standards we want to set at Chelsea,' he said.

It seemed to me he was shooting himself in the foot. Within weeks he decided to sell Terry Venables, the main man around whom the team was built. Terry had been stripped of the captaincy after the Blackpool Affair, and the relationship between him and the Doc soured to the point where they were like quick-on-the-draw gunfighters, growling 'This club ain't big enough for the both of us.' Tommy accused Terry of undermining his authority by interfering with his tactical plans out on the pitch, and of taking the mickey out of him behind his back during training. It is true that Terry just could not resist giving an opinion on tactics; it was after all he who had to make them work out on the pitch in his role as schemer. And, yes, Terry was an incorrigible mickey-taker – in the Docherty class! Some thirty years on I can see how petty it all was and that with a little bit of common sense the problems could easily have been overcome. But the Doc decided that Terry, the man whose precise passes made the team tick, had to go. He went out and bought Charlie Cooke from Dundee as a replacement, and then sold Venables to Tottenham. He had got rid of the conductor and had brought in a virtuoso. Charlie was one of the finest ball players I ever saw, but he was a holder of the ball while Terry was a deliverer.

I saw no place for myself in a team that was obviously going to change its style, and after turning down my two transfer requests the Doc suddenly changed direction as only he could and sold me to Arsenal for £50,000 plus striker Tommy Baldwin. My love affair with Arsenal was about to start, but I would always have a soft spot for the following Chelsea team that was never really allowed to reach its full potential:

Peter Bonetti: Catty was one of the greatest of all catchers of a ball. He could have fielded at first slip for the England cricket team. His amazing cat-like reflexes meant that even when he was caught out of position he could recover with a reaction save.He played more than six hundred League matches for Chelsea from the age of seventeen and he would have won ten times more than his seven England caps but for the presence of two greats in Gordon Banks and then Peter Shilton. Catty, who did not deserve to be made the scapegoat for England's defeat by West Germany in the 1970 World Cup quarter-finals, disappeared from all our lives when he went off to a remote Scottish island to run a hotel and double up as a postman. I was amused when he reappeared as the respected coach to the Chelsea and England goalkeepers to find his trademark black hair had turned completely white (I can hear the Doc saying: 'Aye, but at least he's got it all ...!'). Catty, now based in the Midlands, is a lovely bloke, and a first-class goalkeeper who always handled with care.

Ken Shellito: It was a tragedy for Ken that his career as Chelsea and England right-back was wrecked at its peak by a crippling knee injury. There have been few, if any, better right-backs produced by England. Netted from East London by famous Chelsea scout Jimmy Thompson along with the likes of Greavsie and Terry Venables, Ken was a beautifully balanced player who could tackle with venom and sprint as quick as the fastest winger. But for his injury, he would have been a serious challenger to George Cohen for the number two shirt in England's 1966 World Cup winning team. I have seen few better club full-back pairings than Ken and Eddie McCreadie. Ken finally settled for coaching after the arrival from West Ham of the stylish Joe Kirkup, and he had a bash at management, including a season in charge at Stamford Bridge and a spell as number two to Tommy Doc at Preston. But I think it's true to say that Ken was much too nice a guy to make a real impact at management level.

Eddie McCreadie: Now we're talking real class. He had been a part-time professional with East Stirling when Tommy Doc persuaded him to try his luck with Chelsea. 'Steady Eddie' developed into one of the most outstanding left-backs in the English First Division, and was one of the first to introduce the overlapping full-back play in an era when wingers were just starting to go out of fashion. He had excellent ball control and could beat defenders in one-on-one situations, and his left-foot crosses set up many a goal for Chelsea and Scotland. Eddie had a go at management and was tremendously successful in motivating the Chelsea team that won promotion back to the First Division in 1977. Then Chelsea refused to pay him what he thought he was worth and Eddie, always a man of high principle, walked out and went off to the United States where he settled to a happy and contented life.

John Hollins: I'm sure that John was born with a spare pair of lungs. There were few in the sixties and seventies who could match his prodigious energy. He would run marathon distances at sprinter's speed from his midfield base, and no matter how the game was going you could not knock the bounce and enthusiasm out of him. John collected two England caps in an era when there was an overspill of top-flight midfield players to choose from. He was not the greatest passer of a ball there has ever been, but he knew how to win it and then give it to players like Terry Venables for expert dispatch. He always played with a smile on his face, and looked as if he was enjoying himself even when pressures were at their peak. I used to break out in a sweat just watching him cover every inch of the pitch. John gave equal effort and determination to QPR and Arsenal and later returned to Stamford Bridge for three so-so years as manager before becoming an intelligent adviser to players.

Marvin Hinton: We used to call Marvin 'Lou' after a notorious

London ticket spiv called 'One-Arm Lou'. This was because he was always on the look-out for match tickets for family and friends. Mind you, he wasn't in the same league as 'Fat Stan' Flashman, who was a regular visitor to the Bridge in the sixties and a close friend of both Ron Harris and Tommy Doc. Come to think of it, the place was full of colourful characters and none more so than Marvin. He arrived from Charlton Athletic and brought his streetwise Croydon brain to the centre of the Chelsea defence. He was a footballing centre-half, happiest when cast as 'sweeper', which in those days was something of a foreign role for British defenders. I recall an astonishing incident involving Lou and Tommy Doc, which summed up the personalities of the pair of them. The Doc was delivering one of his frequent 'now-it's-time-to-be-serious-lads' lectures, and Lou was whispering out of the side of his mouth in a mickey-taking send-up of Tommy. Suddenly the Doc turned and leapt on Lou's back, taking a great Dracula-style bite at his neck. 'There's a love bite for you to take home to show your wife,' he said. 'Tell her Tommy Doc gave it to you. And if she'll believe that, she'll believe anything.' There were never any boring moments when the likes of the Doc and Lou were around!

Ron Harris: We had reached the time in the sixties when every team had to have a tough and effective ball winner. There were the likes of Tommy Smith at Liverpool, Nobby Stiles at Manchester United and Norman 'Bites Yer Legs' Hunter at Leeds. But none of them were as fearsome as 'Chopper' Harris. I knew all about Chopper long before I arrived at Stamford Bridge because we had opposed each other in schoolboy and youth internationals. He was a poker-faced assassin. His face was set in concrete as he used to unleash tackles that made me offer a silent prayer of thanks that he was on my side and not against me, and his unsmiling expression would never change as he went about his business of winning the ball for Chelsea. What a job he did for the team, and he could not give a monkey's as opposing players and fans moaned and groaned about his tough tactics. There was the famous time when Prince Philip was sitting in the VIP box at Stamford Bridge alongside then director Brian Mears. 'Tell me,' asked Prince Philip mischievously, with a twinkle in his eye, 'why do they call this man Chopper?' Just then Ron delivered one of his earth-shaking tackles. 'Oh,' said the Prince. 'I see.' Ron and his less-intimidating brother Allan joined Chelsea straight from school in Hackney. They gave Chelsea great service, Ron in particular, before moving into the coaching world. Allan became a successful right hand man to Terry Venables, and shrewd Ron had a spell as general manager of Aldershot before making a million buying and selling a golf course. Chopper Harris. There was never anybody quite like him.

John Boyle: I always felt a bit sorry for John. A Motherwell boy, he – like me a couple of seasons earlier – was invited down for a trial at Stamford Bridge, and accepted a place as an apprentice. He came under Tommy Doc's spell and was encouraged to play a destroying game that was not really his style. The Doc tried to mould him in the Chopper Harris image, and while it worked in a way there were only limited opportunities for John to make a name for himself. He had a lot more ability and creative skill than he was allowed to show in the ball-winning role that was thrust upon him. John played a defensive midfield role in the 1967 FA Cup final, and was at right-back in the team that captured the European Cup Winners' Cup in 1970 under Dave Sexton. John later played briefly for Brighton and Leyton Orient before injury forced his retirement. He was a good-natured boy with a ready smile, and who always gave his all on the pitch.

Peter Houseman: In his early days under The Doc, Peter struggled for first-team acceptance. He was then an orthodox left winger, who could beat full-backs with a mixture of pace and skill. Peter was from just across the water at Battersea, and so was something of a local hero but it was not until Dave Sexton returned as manager that he got the regular First Division football he deserved. Dave cleverly turned him into a utility player, a role he took on with relish while defending or attacking to suit the needs of the team. He was a proud member of the Chelsea side that won the FA Cup and European Cup Winners' Cup, and was quietly winding down his career at Oxford when he was tragically killed in a motor crash at the age of thirty-two. I had played against him just a few hours before the crash in which both he and his wife were killed, and we shared an after-match drink and talked and laughed about the good old bad old days at Stamford Bridge. Peter was a quiet, unassuming man, who never made a boastful remark in his life yet he had plenty to boast about. He was one of the nicer people to cross my path during those springtime playing days.

Bert Murray: A Hoxton boy, Bert had played in the England schools team with Terry Venables and joined the Stamford Bridge ground staff at the same time. His flying speed down the right wing was ideal for the style that Chelsea were playing in those mid-sixties, and he created a bagful of goals with his measured crosses. Bert, a chirpy Cockney character, moved along with Barry Bridges to Birmingham City where he became quite a favourite after switching to right-back. He wound down his career with Brighton and Peterborough. Bert won England caps at schoolboy, youth and under-23 level, but never quite managed to force his way into the full England team at a time when manager Alf Ramsey was having doubts about the validity of wingers.

Barry Bridges: The fastest thing on two feet, Barry was quick enough to catch pigeons. He used to lead the Chelsea attack with a blinding speed that exaggerated my lack of pace. Barry more than anybody never quite knew where he stood with Tommy Doc. One minute Tommy would be praising him to the sky, the next giving him the cold-shoulder treatment because he did not figure in his plans. A pleasant, easy-going man from Norwich, Barry was good enough to win four England caps but he was the one who had to make way when Peter Osgood arrived on the scene. He had been a productive player for Chelsea, but it all ended in bad feeling. We were at Heathrow Airport waiting for a flight to Barcelona for a Fairs Cup semi-final when Tommy Doc arrived with surprise new signing Charlie Cooke in tow. Barry had been dropped for the previous game, and he saw Cooke's arrival as more evidence that he was on the way out. He stormed away from Heathrow and the plane took off without him. From Chelsea Barry travelled the football roundabout with Birmingham City, Queen's Park Rangers, Millwall and Brighton, always returning home to Eastbourne after matches to help run his family hotel business.

Peter Osgood: I had only one full season playing alongside Ossie, but to this day I don't think I have seen a more naturally gifted footballing centre-forward. It was obvious from his earliest days in the Chelsea youth team and reserves that he had prodigious talent, and Tommy Doc promoted him at the expense of Barry Bridges when he was eighteen. Born in Windsor, Ossie was a late developer who was working as a bricklayer when his talent was at last unearthed thanks to an uncle who wrote to Chelsea recommending him. He played his football with a swagger and a smile, and some of the things he did with the ball were just unbelievable. Ossie was a key man in the Chelsea team that won the FA Cup and European Cup Winners' Cup at the start of the seventies, and he collected another FA Cup winners' medal with Southampton in 1976. He played briefly for Norwich and then had a whirl on the United States circuit before taking his final bow back at Chelsea, where he was one of the biggest idols the Bridge had ever known. Ossie won just four England caps. It should have been twenty times as many for a player of his ability, but he never seemed to take the game seriously enough to win the full trust of Alf Ramsey. If I could find a young Peter Osgood today and take him under my wing, I could make him the greatest player British football has ever produced. That's how good Peter was, and when I see this friendly character these days in his role as an event organiser and Chelsea greeter, I smile and shake my head at the thought of what might have been.

Bobby Tambling: Chelsea have had few better finishers than Bobby Tambling, who was almost in the Jimmy Greaves class for turning a half chance into a goal. He was at his best when cutting in at full pace from the left wing to unleash accurate shots with his deadly left foot. Bobby, who became a Jehovah's Witness, played the game the way he lived his life, with a gentlemanly, dedicated and whole-hearted approach. One of Ted Drake's 'Ducklings', he was equally productive whether out on the left wing or attacking down the middle. I always considered Hampshire boy Bobby a credit to Chelsea in particular and football in general. He won three England caps and scored a club record 164 League goals before finishing his career with Crystal Palace. But I think his heart was always with Chelsea.

Terry Venables: Every side must have an orchestrater, and there was nobody better than Terry at composing and arranging a team from his midfield control point. The description 'playmaker' fitted perfectly on his shoulders that always had something of a swagger. He set a record as a player that will never be equalled, winning a full house of England caps at schoolboy, youth, amateur, under-23 and full international level. Terry, out of the Dagenham territory that produced the likes of Alf Ramsey, Jimmy Greaves and the Allen tribe, was completely at home in the Chelsea midfield, but never quite touched the same dominating heights when moving on to Tottenham, Queen's Park Rangers and then Crystal Palace. He played the game with a lot of flair, a lot of style and a little devilment. I remember the night he scored a hat-trick in a rough-house match against Roma in a Fairs Cup tie at Stamford Bridge. His second goal captured his opportunistic character. Chelsea were awarded a free kick ten yards outside the penalty area. Terry placed the ball as if he was going to take it and then made a great fuss of pacing out the stipulated ten yards, holding up his fingers in mime of a count as he approached Roma's defensive wall. The Roma players, duped into thinking that he was going to have to return to the ball, opened up the wall and allowed him through. Suddenly Venables shouted to John Hollins: 'Give it now!' Hollins steered the ball through the hole that Terry had created in the middle of the wall, and he coolly fired a low shot into the net. The Italians never forgave him, and we got a good kicking in the return leg and had the windows of our coach smashed to smithereens by bricks as we drove away from the ground with a 4-1 aggregate victory in the bag. Great days. Terry and I became such good pals that when I married Marie at Marylebone register office on a Saturday morning in 1967 he was alongside me as my best man. Four hours later we played against each other at Highbury, me for Arsenal and Terry for Tottenham. The Gunners gave Spurs a 4-0 hiding, and as the fourth goal went in I strolled over to Terry and said, 'It's me who should be saving myself for tonight, not you!' Our bond became closer when I was privileged to stand as godfather to his daughter, Nancy. Terry always had an aura about him, and it was clear he would make something of himself after his playing days were over. He has as good a tactical brain as there is in the game, and he was the obvious man for the England job after his managing experience with Palace, Barcelona and Tottenham.

Terry helped make those days at Chelsea among my happiest in football. But then I was off to a club that first of all won my heart and then broke it.

Arsenal here I come.

5 : Arsenal, the Playing Days

September 1966: The month when dahlias dominate in the garden. The most fitting dahlia to represent my change of colours is the Blithe Spirit, which is Arsenal red with a white tip to the petals. If the many different varieties of dahlias are suitably sited, they will flower continuously from August until the first frosts. There was no sign of frost on my arrival at Highbury.

IT was Dave Sexton who was the main instigator of my arrival at Arsenal as a player. During our days together at Stamford Bridge he had detected the deep-seated passion for football that was inside me, and he knew better than anybody that my image as the last play-boy of the King's Road was something of an exaggeration. He was rightly convinced that for me, football came first. Dave, who had taken over as first-team coach at Highbury, persuaded new manager Bertie Mee that I would be right for Arsenal.

After the casual, laid-back atmosphere of Chelsea, Arsenal – with their strict discipline and concentration on getting the job done – was a shock to the system. At Aston Villa I was little more than a school kid feeling his way in a foreign land. At Chelsea I had sown my oats and enjoyed myself on and off the pitch. At Arsenal I grew up.

From the first moment I stepped inside the Marble Halls it felt the same as when I first put on a good tailor-made suit. It felt right, and walking around as an Arsenal player I got a new sense of pride. This may sound corny to anybody who does not understand football history and tradition, but you can almost reach out and feel the past at Highbury. Villa Park also had this aura, but at Arsenal I found it at times almost overpowering. Perhaps it was something to do with Herbert Chapman's bust staring out at you inside the Marble Halls as a reminder of the days when Arsenal ruled the roost in the thirties.

Lovely Billy Wright, now sadly departed, used to tell me how he would sometimes shake his fist at Herbert when walking past the bust to his office. The ghosts of Arsenal's great past used to haunt Billy because he was unable to match their exploits, and in the summer of 1966 he was removed in the sort of way that Don Howe and Terry Neill will tell you seemed to become an Arsenal speciality. Billy's surprise successor was a man little known outside the Marble Halls, Bertie Mee.

One of the beauties of an autobiography is that, as well as telling my side of the story, you can put into print a proper assessment of people that you did not appreciate at the time. Step forward Bertie Mee. It was only when I began to study management that I fully understood the minor miracle he had worked when in charge at Arsenal. He came out of the physiotherapist's room and put together an Arsenal team, on and off the pitch, that could look the ghosts of the club's great past fairly and squarely in the eye. We players used to scoff behind Bertie's back that he was getting all the glory while the work was done by his coaches Dave Sexton, Don Howe and Steve Burtenshaw, chief scout Gordon Clark and, of course, we footballers. The subtleties of delegation were lost on us. It was Bertie's selection of staff and his totally professional organisational skill that was the key to Arsenal's success after nearly two decades of comparative failure. When I became Arsenal manager I used to quite often call on Bertie for sound, considered advice and a confidential second opinion, so he knows that I appreciated him. Now I am delighted to make it public.

I arrived at Arsenal at a time when England's 1966 World Cup triumph had put a new spring in our step, yes even that of a Scot. It proved that British was best, even if the flair of the Brazilians and Argentinians was easier on the eye. Alf Ramsey had pulled it off because he had a plan in his mind. Bertie Mee also had a plan, and he needed a first-rate coach alongside him to help him put it in shape on the pitch. In Dave Sexton he had the best.

Dave, the man I always hold up as the guru of British coaches (while he will name Walter Winterbottom as his inspiration), laid the foundations to the Arsenal success of the 1970s, but was not around to take the credit. We were stunned when Arsenal allowed him to cross back over London to Chelsea as manager, in succession to Tommy Docherty in 1967. There was a mood almost of revolt among the players. 'Where is Arsenal's ambition if they are going to allow a coach of Dave's quality to leave the club?' skipper Frank McLintock asked publicly. It was tame to what we were saying privately.

Bertie did not want Sexton to go and Dave was tortured by the choice. But the lure of managing his old Chelsea club was too strong,

I have only blurred photographs of my father, who died when I was three weeks old. He was a good footballer and, according to mum, tall, dark and handsome.

My mum in a million. I was Manager of the Year a couple of times. She was the manager of the century! The blazer is the one I wore with the Scottish youth squad.

The Grahams, circa 1949, left to right: Maureen, Robert, Janette, Mary (standing behind mum), me, Andrew and Tom. Mary tragically died two years later from the same tuberculosis disease that robbed us of our Dad.

Babies on parade. That's me making my debut in front of the camera in my mother's loving arms (left). More than 25 years on (below) she is giving my daughter Nicole the same cuddle treatment; and that's Nicole in her Dad's arms above. It seems like only yesterday.

I was ten years old when this picture was taken of the Boy from Bargeddie. Note the old leather ball that weighed a ton, and the Mansfield Hotspur football boots. I used to have to soak them in soapy water for hours to make them supple enough to wear.

This is the Scottish international schoolboy cap that I won against England at Wembley in 1959. There was a crowd of 70,000, and I was marked, literally, by a young England defender called Ron Harris. He had yet to collect his 'Chopper' nickname. We lost 5-3.

One of my first school team pictures, the 1956-57 Baillieston Secondary Juniors. That's me four from the left in the front row. There on the left of the front row is my maths and sports teacher John Stirling, who once told me: 'Thank goodness ye've got yer brains in yer feet, Graham, 'cos you havena any in yer heed.'

My son Daniel wears one of my twelve Scotland caps alongside a dad who looks as if he belongs in Madame Tussaud's. Daniel grew up showing more interest in golf than football. I encouraged him because golf is a great passion of mine.

My ex-wife Marie and I had a 20-year marriage that was mostly about good times until I started giving more time to Arsenal Football Club than the family.

A degree of success. Nicole thoroughly earned her honours at Cambridge University, and is now a schoolteacher. That is Daniel joining me in congratulating her on her graduation day. My degree was strictly honorary. I liked to think that I passed with honours on the football pitch and as a manager, but it is Nicole who was blessed with the real brains in our family. I am extremely proud of her.

An armful of trophies, my son and daughter and a beautiful bride on my arm. What more can a father ask for? That's Nicole and Daniel (above) helping me celebrate the double of the League Championship and the Barclays' Manager of the Year award in 1989, and a couple of years later I had the job of proudly giving Nicole away to her husband, Carl. I have come through a minefield of problems with the love of Nicole and Daniel intact. That is more important to me than any football trophy.

The five faces of a footballer. That's me in my springtime Aston Villa days (top left) before the switch in 1964 to Chelsea (top centre). Then, the summertime with Arsenal (top right), followed by an unhappy winter experience with Manchester United (right). I closed my playing career with Crystal Palace (above), and then found an even more rewarding life for myself as a coach and then manager. And I've loved every minute of it.

The teenage years. This is my first Scottish schoolboys team picture (above, front row, third left), and I was eighteen when called into the Aston Villa team (left) for my League debut against Liverpool. I managed to score one goal and lay on the other in a 2-0 victory.

Here's a collector's item (above). There are three future Arsenal managers in this picture. Can you spot them? I am the one heading the goal for Chelsea against Arsenal. Terry Neill is the centre-half that I am outjumping, and that's Don Howe on the extreme right. These were the days when I was dubbed the 'Kangaroo Kid' because of the way I could leap above defenders. Future England manager Terry Venables also played in this match.

It don't half hurt, mum! This is me (left) limping off during Chelsea's FA Cup semi-final against Sheffield Wednesday at Villa Park in 1966. I am being propped up by dear old Chelsea physio Harry Medhurst (who was succeeded by his son, Norman) and Ken Dagnall, one of the better referees of that era. What hurt more than the bruises was that we lost 2-0, and manager Tommy Docherty reacted by breaking up one of the finest young teams in Chelsea history.

I play a watching and waiting role as my Chelsea team-mate Terry Venables tangles with Arsenal centre-half Ian Ure. Terry was the general of the Chelsea team, and one of the finest passers of the ball that I have ever played with. He was also, and remains, a good pal.

Alan Ball and I compete for a ball during a League match between Arsenal and Everton. It was not until Ballie joined Arsenal that I appreciated just what an outstanding player he was, always doing the simple things that gave direction and momentum to the attack.

I perfected shooting with either foot in my Bargeddie road matches, and while I favoured the right I could also score with my left (below). I am hammering the ball wide of Everton goalkeeper Gordon West despite the tackle by Howard Kendall back in the days when both Howard and I had all our hair... before we started pulling it out as managers!.

This (above) was the FA Cup Final goal that Jimmy Hill took away from me after studying action replay footage on his ITV Big Match show. I will always remain convinced that I got a touch, but at least I had the consolation of collecting the Man of the Match award after we had come from behind to beat Liverpool 2-1 to clinch the League and Cup double.

The 'old man' can still do it. This is me heading a goal for Crystal Palace in my last season as a player. A broken leg ended my career, and Terry Venables talked me into coaching the youngsters. It was the best career move I ever made.

and he returned to Stamford Bridge to start creating that magnificent Chelsea team of the Osgood-Hudson-Cooke era. We were shell-shocked at Highbury, but Bertie had total faith in one man who had recently switched to coaching after a broken leg had ended his distinguished playing career with England, West Brom and Arsenal. Don Howe was promoted from reserve-team coach, and proved himself a tactician and coach in the Sexton class. There can be no higher praise. And if anything, he was a better motivator than Dave, who did everything with kid gloves while Don could shout and bully with the best of them when it was necessary.

So with a new coach and with the old hangover of not having won anything for years, we set out to bury the past. Joining me as newcomers to the Arsenal squad were Bob McNab, Bobby Gould and Colin Addison. We slogged our way to the League Cup final in 1968 when a late disputed goal from Terry Cooper beat us. Our goalkeepr Jim Furnell had both Jack Charlton and Paul Madeley blocking him like basketball players as Eddie Gray fired in an in-swinging corner. I managed to head the ball off the goal-line, with Furnell clearly obstructed. But the referee did nothing about it, and we were fuming when Cooper volleyed the ball high into the net from the edge of the penalty area.

A year later we were back at Wembley for a second successive League Cup final that was to prove the turning point for the club. We got stuffed 3-1 by Third Division Swindon Town. No excuses at this distance. Swindon thoroughly deserved their victory on a day when their 'wonder winger' Don Rogers could not put a foot wrong. But it is true that eight of our players, me included, had been weakened by a 'flu virus in the week before the final, and it is a fact that Wembley was such a muddy mess that it equalised the skill factor of the two sides. They had unwisely allowed show jumping horses on the pitch, and the hallowed turf was so churned up that it looked like the field where Mum used to pick the tatties.

I had been summoned into the game as a substitute, and even coming on with fresh legs found every step a challenge because of the clawing mud. A typical opportunist goal by the always enthusiastic Bobby Gould took us into extra-time, and our coach Don Howe wasted his breath trying to talk referee Bill Handley into abandoning the game at the end of 90 minutes because of the mud-heap condition of the pitch. Don knew how weakened many of our team were by the 'flu virus, and the last thing he wanted was us having to slog through another thirty minutes during which the fleet-footed Rogers twice ran away from our mud-bound defenders to score two spectacular goals.

It was the most humiliating defeat that any of us at Arsenal had experienced. We sat in the dressing-room afterwards looking like dazed boxers who had been knocked cold by a sucker punch. Our skipper Frank McLintock was in tears. It was his fourth defeat in four finals at Wembley, and he was convinced that he was some sort of jinx. At his feet lay a crunched up telegram from Leeds manager Don Revie that read: 'Sincerely hope you will be first up the steps this time.' It was a nice gesture by Don, but he had forgotten that in the League Cup the losing team go up the Wembley steps first. In that hour after the defeat I don't think any of us had ever felt so desolate. This was football at its cruellest. Yet out of that despair came an almost fanatical resolve and determination to prove to the village world of football, where we knew there was a lot of sniggering going on, that we were a championship quality side. It is significant that of the twelve players humbled by Swindon, eight played a prominent part in the Double triumph two years later: Bob Wilson, Peter Storey, Bob McNab, Frank McLintock, Peter Simpson, John Radford, Geordie Armstrong and myself. By then, Ian Ure had moved on to Manchester United, Jon Sammels to Leicester City, Bobby Gould to Wolves and David Court to Luton Town. I was told about a rare bust-up between Ure and Bertie Mee. It was over Ian's superstitious preference for what he described as his 'lucky' shirt. Bertie was much too realistic a character to have any time or understanding for the sort of superstitions that abound in football dressing-rooms, and he went out of his way to discourage them. He and Ian had a disagreement over the number shirt Ian should wear in a League match against Coventry. It was not long afterwards that Ian, an eye-catching Scottish international centre-half, was on his way to Manchester United.

It was not luck but determination, dedication and desire that helped us turn the defeat by Swindon to our advantage. Don Howe and McLintock were the main motivators of our revival, taking turns in cajoling and demanding greater effort and more concentration. Don

introduced zonal marking at the back rather than the man-to-man system he had inherited from Dave Sexton, and he, Frank and Bertie
began to pick on players who they thought needed a gee-up. I came in
for more nagging than most because I had this in-built laid-back
approach that gave the impression of casualness that was misleading.
I might have been strolling, but there was just as big a desire inside
me for success as those who showed fierce intensity every time they
ran out on to the pitch. It got to the point where I exchanged punches
with McLintock, who was my best mate off the pitch and the most
inspiring captain I had ever played with. We were coming off at half-
time in a First Division game when Frank insinuated that I was not
pulling my weight. I didn't pull my punch either, and team-mates had
to drag us apart as we eyeballed each other down the tunnel leading to
the dressing-room. It was all forgotten as quickly as it had flared up.
This showed how much we cared about getting it right for Arsenal.

There was a major turning point in our playing careers for both
Frank and me during the 1969-70 season. Frank, who had built his
reputation as a marauding right-half, was persuaded against his will to
switch to the middle of the defence. It was the original idea of chief
scout Gordon Clark, a shrewd judge of players, and Howe and Mee
were quick to see the sense of it. Frank's first reaction was that this
was some sort of demotion, but as he settled in to the role he became
an even bigger influence on the team than when motoring through
from midfield. He took over from that loyal Arsenal servant Terry
Neill alongside Peter Simpson, and for three or four seasons there was
not a better central defensive pairing in the League. Frank will give a
lot of credit for his success to the coaching of Don Howe, who helped
him with his positional play so that his lack of power in the air was
never a handicap.

At about the same time Don and Bertie decided to experiment with
me as a midfield playmaker rather than support striker. Don told me
he wanted me to become 'a good old-fashioned attacking left-half.'
Up until my switch I had been too inconsistent for everybody's taste,
including my own. I was either playing a blinder or disappearing without trace. There was no in between. But from the moment I was given
the responsibility of stamping my authority on the middle of the pitch
I got a new lease of life. Suddenly I had a stage on which I could

unveil the skill I had developed all those years ago in the Bargeddie road matches. It had always been the midfield maestros who had taken my eye from way back when I used to watch Ian Macmillan performing for Airdrie, and it was Alfredo di Stefano's work from midfield that had remained etched in my memory from the Real Madrid-Eintracht match. Operating up front as a target man, you are not allowed the time to pick your passes or dictate the pace. It is all explosive, instinctive stuff. But back in midfield I could suddenly see the entire canvas and used my passing as a sort of artistic brush work. Bob McNab, Geordie Armstrong and I formed a little triangle out on the left and between us created a team within the team. We always knew where to be to get the best out of each other, and it was this understanding that helped to give Arsenal a new dimension and a new impetus. Nobody could accuse me of inconsistency over the following three seasons that were among the most successful in Arsenal's history. I missed only twelve games, and collected twenty-six First Division goals coming through from my midfield base. My speciality was the wall pass, giving the ball and then gliding into space to take the return. It was simplistic but very effective.

Off the pitch I had matured beyond recognition. Older players like Terry Neill and Ian Ure and intelligent players such as Bob Wilson and Frank McLintock set the tone, and there was little of the schoolboy prankster jokes that used to be part and parcel of life at Chelsea. Bertie Mee always used to stress that we were ambassadors for Arsenal Football Club, and he expected us to act with dignity at all times. My 1967 marriage had forced me to grow up, and Marie was a good influence on me. She had a deep understanding and love of the arts, and introduced me to the opera and ballet. Watching Nureyev and Fontaine at Covent Garden was an experience as captivating as seeing di Stefano and Puskas performing on the Hampden Park stage. Mind you, I wonder how precise Nureyev and Fontaine would have been had somebody been trying to kick them up in the air?

We bought a comfortable home in Cockfosters, which was conveniently situated for football at Highbury and training at London Colney. I was now up in the £200-a-week bracket at a time when the average wage outside football was a quarter of that, so we enjoyed a good lifestyle. My Hillman Minx had been part-exchanged for a powerful white Rover saloon, and that was later replaced by a flash two-tone black and gold Ford Capri. With the seventies upon us, I was into flares, wide lapels, kipper ties and Cuban-heel shoes. The arrival of my gorgeous daughter, Nicole, in 1969 gave me a new sense of responsibility, and I was happy to hand over the fashion-leader role to Bob McNab, who had an outrageous taste in floral shirts, velvet, flare-bottomed suits and dazzling kipper ties.

This was the era when I was far more likely to be seen digging in the garden or swinging a golf club rather than in a nightclub. I had got my handicap down close to single figures, and used to get the occasional lesson from Arsenal fanatic Dai Rees, the old Welsh golf wizard who was the pro at the South Herts Golf Club where Arsenal used to spend their home match-day mornings. My lifestyle lacked the hectic pace of my Chelsea days, but it was much more pleasant and rewarding.

The breakthrough for which we had been quietly building came in the 1969-70 Fairs Cup competition. We accounted for Johan Cruyff-motivated Ajax in the semi-finals and came from 3-1 down in the first leg of the final to beat Anderlecht 3-0 on an unforgettable night at Highbury. It was the first time that Arsenal had a major trophy to show off since the one and only Joe Mercer captained them to the League championship back in 1953. The victories over Ajax and Anderlecht did wonders for our confidence and gave us the momentum to go for the jackpot the following season which reached a nail-biting climax.

We came from behind to pip Leeds for the League championship on the last day of the League season, and then came from behind in the FA Cup final five days later to beat Liverpool in extra-time

A capacity 51,192 crowd was drawn to a unique derby match between Tottenham and Arsenal at White Hart Lane on the evening of Monday, 5 May 1971. The result would decide the League championship. There were only two clubs in the race: Leeds United and Arsenal. Tottenham were ten points adrift in third place. Don Revie's exceptional team, football's perennial bridesmaids, had completed their fixtures and could only wait and see if their sixty-four points would be enough. We were on sixty-three points and needed only a scoreless draw to win the championship for a record eighth time by

0.013 of a goal. But a defeat, or a goal-scoring draw, would concede the championship to Leeds.

Next to Leeds, Spurs were about the last team we wanted to visit, particularly as our six defeats had all been away from home. The two North London clubs – like most football neighbours – have always had their own private championship. During the sixties it was Tottenham who had proved they were the top club in North London. But at last Arsenal had a chance to eclipse their rivals, and if we could do the job at White Hart Lane we would be one victory away from equalling the elusive 1960-61 double triumph of Danny Blanchflower's 'Super Spurs'.

There was a wide-spread suspicion, particularly in the vicinity of Leeds, that Tottenham would hand the title to Arsenal. No chance! As we boarded the coach for the trip to White Hart Lane, we heard Tottenham skipper Alan Mullery being interviewed on the radio. 'Arsenal have got as much chance of being handed the League title by Spurs as I have of being given the Crown Jewels,' he said. 'They are the last people we want winning the championship. Everybody is on about the great season Arsenal are having. Well, we're not doing too badly. We've won the League Cup, reached the sixth round of the FA Cup and we're third in the League. Now we mean to round off our season by stopping Arsenal from taking the title.'

So the battle lines had been drawn for a game that nearly didn't start. The streets surrounding White Hart Lane were jammed solid with human bodies and worried police were working overtime to control them. When the gates were locked, it was estimated that there were another 100,000 would-be spectators pushing and shoving their way to nowhere outside the ground. Those who failed to get in missed a match that was memorable because of what was at stake rather than the quality of the football. We were nervously stuck at 0-0 when, with just three minutes to go, the acrobatic Pat Jennings pushed out a header from John Radford. Then George Armstrong calmly lofted the ball into the goalmouth and Ray Kennedy stepped forward to head the ball into the net off the bar. There was an explosive roar as Arsenal fans prematurely celebrated winning the title. But there were still three minutes to go, and a Tottenham equaliser would have tugged the title away from us and given it to Leeds. That was the longest three minutes I have ever known.

In the last desperate seconds it looked as if Tottenham might snatch an equaliser when the ball became lost under a flurry of feet just two yards off the Arsenal goal-line. But Bob Wilson, with characteristic courage, dived in among the blur of boots to clear this final, agonising moment of danger.

At last we were relieved by referee Kevin Howley's final whistle of the match and of his League career.

It was the most dramatic end to a League championship season until our last-kick triumph at the close of the 1988-89 title race. Both finals have a very special place in my memory box. What has stuck in my mind from the night we won the title at Tottenham was how we had to abandon our coach and battle our way through the last hundred yards to the ground because the crowds had brought North London to a halt. We had left the South Herts Golf Club an hour and a half earlier for what was usually a 25-minute drive, and finished up just making it for the kick-off. Then, at the final whistle, there was such a jam of celebrating fans on the pitch that it took some of the players twenty minutes before they could force a way through to the dressing-room. Bertie Mee was worried stiff and was just about to send out a police search party for a missing goalkeeper when Bob Wilson came struggling through the door. 'Where did you all disappear to?' said Bob. 'I wanted to throw my arms around somebody and the only person I could find was referee Kevin Howley. So I cuddled him!'

Five days later we completed the double at Wembley with a spectacular winning goal from Charlie George. All the goals came in extra-time. Steve Heighway, having an outstanding first season with Liverpool, scored at Bob Wilson's unguarded near post in the opening seconds of extra-time. It was a rare positioning mistake by Bob that I always bring up if I want to put him off his putt when we are out together on the golf course. Ten minutes later Eddie Kelly and I chased a pass through the middle of the Liverpool defence, and I am convinced that I got a final touch of the ball on its way into the net. But Jimmy Hill almost triumphantly took the goal away from me the next day when he claimed that ITV cameras proved I had not made contact. Well, I know in my heart that, regardless of what Jimmy believes the cameras showed, I did manage to brush the ball, but I did not mind Eddie Kelly getting the credit. He was a smashing lad, and both of us agreed that it didn't matter who had got the touch as long as the ball went into the net.

Charlie George, who had been having a quiet game, lifted himself into the land of Arsenal legend when, with just nine minutes to go, he scored with a scorching twenty-yard right foot shot. He reacted by stretching flat out on his back on the Wembley pitch. The player who had grown up on the terraces of Highbury had clinched the double for Arsenal. It was *Boys' Own* stuff.

The game had given me the platform for one of the games of my life. I loved every second of it, and I was thrilled to receive the Man of the Match award. There was an incident during extra-time that summed up the will-to-win of Liverpool's iron man skipper Tommy Smith. The Liverpool trainer came on to treat an injured player, and I was standing close by as Tommy took a swig of water from the trainer's bottle. 'Can I have a sip, Tom?' I asked. 'No, you effing can't,' came the reply. 'In that case,' I said, 'I won't let you have any of our victory champagne when this is all over.' It was a brave thing for me to say to one of the most feared men in the game, and I don't think I would have risked it if there were not just a few minutes remaining. It was not wise to get on the wrong side of Tommy Smith.

We had achieved our success from a springboard of a disciplined defence superbly marshalled by McLintock, with Peter Simpson an unheralded hero alongside him. Goalkeeper Bob Wilson was in exceptional form all season, and full-backs Pat Rice and Bob McNab were a perfectly balanced pair who would take it in turns to make positive overlapping runs. Peter 'Cold Eyes' Storey was an assassin of a tackler in midfield in stark contrast to my strolling style. Eddie Kelly also produced many valuable performances when called in to the midfield. George Armstrong was the hidden ace, crisscrossing between the two wing positions from where his passing was always damaging to defences. Charlie George gave the team much-needed flair and invention, while twin strikers John Radford and Ray Kennedy accounted for thirty-four of Arsenal's seventy-one League goals with a partnership that was more about raw power than polish.

It was at Highbury that we won the League championship. We went through the season unbeaten at home, winning eighteen matches and drawing three. A 5-0 defeat at Stoke in September threatened to knock the steam out of us, but we showed determination and character by producing a run of fourteen League matches without a defeat, including eleven victories. Leeds had looked runaway League title winners until overhauled in that last breath-taking week of the season.

I picked up about £4,000 in bonus payments for the Double triumph, which was considerably less than other players in the team because of a loyalty-bonus plan that Arsenal had introduced to encourage players to put their roots down with the club. It was a contentious scheme because loyalty seemed to be encouraged above ability and application, and I was happy that the plan had been scrapped by the time I took over as manager at Highbury. Mind you, the ruling by the European Court of Justice for complete freedom of movement for players could bring the loyalty contracts back into fashion.

There was a camaraderie in that Arsenal squad that I had never known at any other club, and I went out of my way to try to reproduce the Double year team spirit when I became the boss. We would have died for each other, and were ready to fight each other's battles on and off the pitch. In fact we literally fought side by side in the back streets of Rome after a Fairs Cup tie against Lazio. We were just leaving the after-match reception at a restaurant when Ray Kennedy was jumped on by two Lazio players. In no time at all there was a free-for-all, with the Lazio players joined by supporters and they were hitting out at anybody with Arsenal connections. The battle spilled out on to the pavement as we fought our way towards the team coach. It was like a scene from a Francis Ford Coppola film, with bodies flying all over the place. We were outnumbered five to one, but were giving as good as we were getting until pistol-waving police came wading in, hitting out right, left and centre. Even Bertie Mee and Don Howe joined in as they tried to open a way for us to get on to the coach. We were the innocent victims and Lazio collected a hefty fine and a ban from playing in Europe. It was an extraordinary incident and further cemented the bond that had developed among the players.

We had our moments at Arsenal when we were almost as crazy as in those Chelsea days. I recall once when I thought our clowning had cost me my life. We were on a trip to Malta and staying at the Sheraton

Hotel which had a private rock-and-pebble beach. I fancy myself as a good all-round sportsman, but the one thing I have never properly conquered is swimming. As I sat on the rocks with Frank McLintock watching the other lads splashing about in the Med I suddenly got the urge to try some high diving. I had once studied trampolining and had reached a high enough standard to have been awarded a coaching certificate, so I was confident I would have no problems putting together some eye-catching dives. Frank got a lifebuoy and promised to throw it to me the minute I hit the water. So I climbed up into the rocks and then dived, giving it the poseur's bit of going into tucks and attempted spins in poor imitation of Olympic divers. Six times I dived and six times the lifebuoy was waiting for me when I came to the surface. By now, Frank was convinced I must have been kidding him when I said I could not swim properly. When I resurfaced after a seventh dive he still had the lifebuoy in his hand. I was going down for the third time before he realised I was in serious trouble, and two of the other players came swimming to my rescue after I had swallowed a gallon of water. It was the end of my diving career.

During a pre-season training trip to Germany, Bertie Mee and Don Howe organised a gentle, relaxing boat trip down the Rhine to give us a break from the intense training. After a lunch in the boat restaurant, Bertie and Don went upstairs on the deck to enjoy the sunshine. Meanwhile, a group of German day trippers had got stuck into the huge jugs of lager and were encouraging us to join in their swinging and swaying sing-alongs. We did not need that much encouragement, particularly when we started to get a taste for the lager. When Bertie and Don came back downstairs a couple of hours later they could not believe their eyes when they saw half a dozen of their star players – me included – drunk as skunks and leading the singing. We were playing Borussia Dortmund the next day in a friendly match, and several of us went into the game carrying heavy hangovers which were made worse by Don's insistence on pushing us through a vigorous training session that morning as punishment for the drinking incident. I got sent off for the first time in my career after twenty minutes when I reacted by lashing out after one of their defenders had threatened my manhood with a thigh-high tackle. My team-mates were not best pleased with me, they having to battle on with ten men, while I sat out the goalless draw on the touchline bench.

We generally managed to keep our drinking bouts under control, but the club made the same mistake as Chelsea had a few years earlier when they arranged for us to visit a vineyard while on a trip to Switzerland. Inevitably, the wine tasting turned into a swigging session and we staggered back to the coach for the return journey to our hotel. We had a young lady travel courier with us, and the king clown Frank McLintock borrowed her bright orange anorak and started posing around in it. He was on the coach microphone leading the players in a sing-along when there was a loud ripping sound and, as he turned round, we saw that the anorak had split right the way down the back. I know it was stupid, childish stuff, but it was all part of knitting together a team spirit that was a vital ingredient in the success of that Arsenal team.

The only time our team spirit was in danger of being dented was when Peter Marinello arrived in a blaze of publicity. Bertie Mee bought him from Hibernian for £100,000 in January 1970, and in his debut Peter scored a spectacular goal at Old Trafford. Suddenly Marinello was being dubbed as the new George Best, a burden too big for any player to carry. He had his own instant national newspaper column in which he talked about his man-about-town life, when he could hardly find his way to the training ground. Bertie was usually a master at protecting players from the wrong kind of publicity, but it was beyond even his powers to control the unwarranted fuss being made about Marinello.

There was understandable resentment among some of the players, particularly when it was Geordie Armstrong who kept having to make way for him. This was a big mistake because there is no question that it was Geordie, with his insatiable appetite for work, who helped make the team tick. I felt a wee bit sorry for Marinello because he was a nice lad who was having the strings pulled for him by advisers. He could play a bit and was as fast as a whippet, but he had no tactical awareness whatsoever. I thought Jimmy Robertson was a much better bet on the right wing for our style of play, but he was allowed to move to Ipswich to make way for Marinello.

I am sure that in hindsight Bertie would have handled the Marinello transfer in a different way. If he had been brought along quietly and had time to settle to the different pace of football in England he might have made an impact, but from day one he was being compared with George Best, the greatest British player of my (and perhaps any) generation. He just could not live up to it, and he faded from the scene as quickly as he had appeared. I caught up with him some years later at Portsmouth when he was on the verge of bankruptcy, and he admitted to me that he got damaged by too much publicity too soon. It was not his fault, but he was the one who suffered.

Tommy Docherty came back into my life in a dramatic and exciting way in 1971. He had taken over as Scotland team manager after a spell in Portugal, and straight away he selected both myself and English-born Bob Wilson for our first caps. The match was a European Nations Cup international tie against Portugal at Hampden, and the Doc's first team talk in the dressing-room before the game captured perfectly why he is one of my most unforgettable characters. You need to know the full team to fully appreciate my story: Bob Wilson, Sandy Jardine, David Hay, Billy Bremner, Eddie Colquhoun, Pat Stanton, Jimmy Johnstone, Alex Cropley, John O'Hare, myself, Archie Gemmill. This is how I remember the Doc's rousing call to arms:

'Right lads, yer're wearing the greatest shirt ye'll ever wear. Just pride alone will make ye six inches taller when ye run out on tae the pitch. Now remember what we've discussed in training. Billy, ye get closer tae Eusebio than a second skin. George, ah want yer playing a bit deeper early doors and make sure ye come back with their number eight when he looks tae make a break. Sandy, don't forget that their left winger likes tae cut inside. Bob, watch out fer the crosses that they drop just short of the near post. John, keep pulling those big defenders away from the middle, so that George or David can nip through intae space. Pat, plenty of yer usual support work, and Archie ah don't want yer hogging the ball. Let's get some nice passing movements going. Keep yersel' nice and controlled, and make them chase around until they're tripping over their tongues.'

Tommy managed to have a word for everybody with the exception of the one and only Jimmy Johnstone. Now J.J. was one of the few British players you could mention in the same breath as George Best, but the Celtic idol was making a comeback to the Scottish team and was a bit more tense and nervous than usual. The Doc appeared to have finished his team talk, and Jimmy shifted nervously on his seat alongside me. Finally he put up his hand. 'Boss,' he said, 'have ye forgotten that ah'm playing. What d' you want me tae do?'

The Doc summoned him to join him in the middle of the dressing-room and put an arm around his shoulder. 'Ye know that left-back they've got?' J.J. nodded. 'He went tae bed on Sunday night saying tae himsel', "My God, only another three days before ah have tae face that wee Johnstone." He couldna sleep on Monday because he kept seeing the wee red-headed devil running rings round him, and last night he was heard moaning in his sleep, "Come back ye little bastard. Stop making me look an idiot." Ah just caught sight of the poor feller walking intae the dressing-room. He's got huge bags under his eyes. So y'see wee mon, ah don't have tae tell ye whit tae dae. Ye've already got him worried out of his life. Now just go out and play yer usual brilliant game.'

It was a real Shankly-style speech and you could see wee Jimmy visibly growing. He went out and played a blinder, and we won 2-1 in what was a memorable first of twelve internationals in which I was proud to play. Tommy did not think twice about selecting Anglos, but once he had given up the job to take over as manager of Manchester United you could sense the old-style curtain dropping on all but the very best Anglo-Scots. There has nearly always been a blinkered tradition in Scotland to pick home-based players ahead of Anglos, who many Scottish selectors used to look on almost as traitors for daring to play south of the border. Tommy Doc had the sense to pick players on merit, not because of their location.

Arsenal went off the boil after their Double triumph, possibly because we lost Don Howe to West Bromwich Albion. We players were as furious as when Dave Sexton was allowed to move to Chelsea. Some years later Don told me that he would have stayed at Highbury if the directors had given the slightest hint that he would succeed Bertie Mee when he eventually stepped down. But they were too short-sighted to give such a guarantee, and so Don went off to manage the club where he had started his illustrious playing career. What really rubbed it in for Arsenal is that Don took physiotherapist George

Wright and youth coach Brian Whitehouse with him. Steve Burtenshaw, yet another very capable coach, was promoted as Bertie's new right hand man, with Fred Street joining us as physiotherapist from Stoke City.

There was also a change to the playing squad, with Jon Sammels moving to Leicester City for £100,000. Jon had my sympathy because he was a gifted schemer with terrific vision, but he had to sit out much of the Double year on the sidelines, and when he did get his opportunities there was a section of the Highbury crowd who were unmerciful with their criticism of him. We were all sorry to see Jon go because he was such a likeable bloke, but it had reached the point when he no longer wanted to face his barrackers. It can be a very cruel game.

There is one memory involving Jon Sammels of which I am not very proud. Players are notorious for gossiping, and I was furious when I found out from team-mates that Jon was earning five pounds a week more than me. Jon by then had lost his regular first-team place to me and my hackles were up when I realised I was being paid less in an era when five pounds represented five per cent of my basic wage of £100 a week. But more than the pay, it was the principle that was at stake. I demanded to see manager Bertie Mee on the morning of a home game when the team had gathered for a pre-match briefing at South Herts Golf Club. I flew at him in a head-strong fashion that I later had to learn to face from players who thought they had been wronged.

'Either you pay me the same wage as Jon Sammels,' I said, 'or I will not kick another ball for Arsenal.'

It was strong, emotional stuff, and I am not in the slightest bit proud of the blackmail tactics I used.

Bertie was brilliant in the way he handled me. 'You're quite right, George, that you should not be earning less,' he said calmly. 'I shall take the matter up on Monday, but meantime I expect you to be the complete professional and play to the best of your ability for Arsenal. I am sure that when you cool down you will realise that not to kick another ball for Arsenal would be something you would regret for the rest of your life. Now just go out there and show that you are worth that extra five pounds a week.'

I tell the story to illustrate just how it can affect a player when he finds out that a team-mate is getting more money for doing the same job. This, remember, was over a matter of five pounds (which I got added to my wage packet from the following week). Just how will players react when the difference can be measured in thousands? There could be some interesting conversations going on now in the Highbury office of managing director Ken Friar.

We started to lose our way in the League during the 1971-72 season, and Bertie Mee reacted with a bold move in the transfer market for Everton and England playmaker Alan Ball. He cost a British record £220,000 and was worth every penny. I had under-rated Ballie, and found that he was twice as good as I thought. He made the difficult things seem easy, and he always looked to give the simple ball that brought progress. I had always admired his competitive spirit, and now as I played alongside him I got to appreciate his great skill and vision. He was the type of totally committed, stylish player I would have loved to have had in my team as a manager.

Alan joined us too late to qualify for our European Cup quarter-final against an Ajax side approaching the peak of its power, and we were beaten 3-1 on aggregate. It was my unfortunate own goal in the home leg that sealed their victory. Ouch! The players were having a moan at me in the dressing-room after my headed goal had cost us the tie. I looked at Bob Wilson and said with a straight face: 'It was your fault, Willow, not mine.'

'What d'you mean?' said Bob, ready tro protest his innocence.

'Well,' I said, 'you know how great I am in the box. You should have been prepared to save it.'

So we laughed off our disappointment, and that little story sums up the team spirit we had in that Arsenal squad. Mind you, deep down I was not laughing. I was mortified by an own goal that was just an unfortunate accident. It was a classic case of being in the wrong place at the wrong time.

We saved our finest performances in that 1971-72 season for the defence of the FA Cup in what was the Centenary year of the competition, and we reached the final where our old rivals Leeds narrowly beat us 1-0 with a headed goal by Allan Clarke. Alan Ball was inconsolable at the final whistle because once again an FA Cup winners' medal had eluded him. In all my time in the game I have never known anybody take defeat as badly as Alan.

It was beyond my comprehension why, in October 1972, Bertie Mee paid £200,000 for Coventry City centre-half Jeff Blockley. It meant that Frank McLintock's days were numbered when he still had much to give the club. He was desperately hurt by the deal, and he took his inspiring leadership and tactical brain to Queen's Park Rangers.

I was becoming unsettled, and I wondered how I could give a lift to my career. Then the Doc came back into my life. But before I recall my challenging and eventful move to Manchester United, here is my player-by-player assessment of the men who did most to bring Double glory to Arsenal ...

Bob Wilson: I have never known anybody work harder at his game than Bob. He was a qualified schoolteacher when he joined Arsenal as an amateur in the Billy Wright days, and most of the old pros then at Highbury felt he should have stayed with the chalk and blackboard. But 'Willow' silenced his critics by developing into a magnificent goalkeeper who played a vital role in our Double success. Some players are born with natural skills, but Bob manufactured himself and made such a study of goalkeeping that when his playing days were over he was one of the finest coaches of goalkeepers in the game. He applied his great intellect and turned goalkeeping into a science, working out every conceivable angle (apart from how to guard his near post in the 1971 FA Cup final; sorry Bob!). As well as skill and agility, he was unbelievably brave and he used to make us wince with the way he would dive at the feet of forwards, often with a banged head as his reward. Watching him dive in, it was difficult to realise that here was one of the most intelligent men in the game. Bob was always a thought ahead of everybody else at the club and knew from early in his career that he would one day like to work in the media. He started broadcasting with the BBC long before his retirement, and had us falling about with helpless laughter when he told us that in his first test transmission in front of a camera he had told the nation, 'Charlie George has just pissed a late fartness test.' Bob has played an important part in the development of David Seaman as one of the finest

British goalkeepers of all time, and his deep understanding of the game always makes him worth listening to in his position as ITV's football presenter. We won our first Scotland caps together, and for all his refined English accent, Bob, I promise you, has tartan blood. He remains a great credit to our game.

Pat Rice: Pat had to wait patiently in the wings for his chance at right-back, and it was when Peter Storey was moved forward to a midfield anchor role that he made the number two shirt his own. He was capped by Northern Ireland long before establishing himself in the Arsenal defence in 1970, and over the following decade became an exceptional player and an inspiring captain. Pat's strength was his resilience and his speed of recovery. He never knew when he was beaten, and could produce a biting tackle when necessary. His passing from defence was neat without being spectacular and he could trouble rival defences with his enthusiastic overlapping runs. Pat was Arsenal through and though, and jumped at the chance to return to Highbury in a coaching capacity after a spell at Watford. His enthusiasm was always infectious as a player, and he continued to light up training sessions in his new role as a maker of future Arsenal stars.

Bob McNab: There have been few more accomplished or more competitive defensive left-backs than Bob, and if his distribution had been better I reckon he would have gone down as one of the all-time greats. He could mark any winger out of the game, and had the sort of firm but fair tackle that made players think twice about trying to go past him a second time. A proud Yorkshireman from Huddersfield, he would have got many more than his four England caps if fewer of his passes had not strayed into the terraces. Sammy Nelson was another excellent left-back who could use the ball better than Bob, but he had to give second best to him as a defensive master. Nabbers could be a lot of fun, and had a strong life-loving personality. We used to be deadly rivals on the golf course and in the fashion stakes, but he got a better wardrobe together than even me when he started supplementing his income with regular appearances on the ITV World Cup panel for whom he made a big impact with his sensible comments. I always smile at the memory of our first trip abroad together. He joined

Arsenal the same day as me, and soon after we went on a club tour to Cyprus. It was Bob's first overseas trip, and Frank McLintock and I plotted how we could make it memorable for him. We decided that a fully-clothed trip into the sea would be a good start. We innocently walked him to the harbour edge and then gave him a push. As he fell back he grabbed hold of me and not only tugged me into the sea with him but also managed to pull off my watch, which was ruined by the sea water. Frank had to haul me out in what was a dress rehearsal for my near-drowning experience in Malta. Liverpool were the first club to move for Bob when he was transfer listed by Huddersfield. He was given a tour of Anfield by the great Bill Shankly, who was confident of signing him despite the fact that he had also arranged to talk to Bertie Mee at Highbury. When Bob telephoned Shanks to tell him that he had decided to take the Arsenal offer, Bill growled into the telephone: 'They're welcome to you, son. You never could play anyway.' Then he threw the receiver down, leaving Bob open-mouthed on the other end of a suddenly dead line. A skilled carpenter, Bob went off to the United States to make a new life for himself after a brief, injury-dogged career with Wolves.

Frank McLintock: He was as important an influence on the Arsenal Double team as fellow-Scot Dave Mackay had been on the Super Spurs side ten years earlier. Like Mackay, he was a tremendously inspirational captain who could make his team-mates willing to run through brick walls. Frank, born in the tough Gorbals district of Glasgow, started his career with Leicester City as an attacking right-half. Billy Wright bought him for Arsenal after he had made two FA Cup Final appearances with Leicester. He quickly emerged as a natural leader at Highbury, and he was just as inspiring off the pitch with his opinions on anything and everything to do with the game. Scotland gave him a miserly nine caps when his talent deserved ten times that amount. Frank had few who could match his power and enthusiasm as a buccaneering right-half, and he was even more effective when switching to the centre of the defence. He was voted Footballer of the Year after leading Arsenal to the double. The Gunners let him go far too early, and he later gave sterling service to Queen's Park Rangers. He was, and remains, a close pal of mine and we are regular rivals on the golf course. We share the same deep love of football, and also of music. He reckons his Sinatra-style rendering of 'Strangers in the Night' is better than my party speciality which has become 'Let's Take It Nice 'n' Easy'. Frank was always talking tactics and helping younger players with fatherly advice, and all his contemporaries at Highbury thought that if anybody was going to one day make an outstanding manager it would be Frank. But his efforts at managing at Leicester and Brentford never met with the luck he deserved. He has been a successful publican, and is one of the wisest of all advisers to footballers. Arsenal have had few, if any, more inspiring players, and I have had few better or more loyal friends.

Peter Simpson: We called Peter 'Stan' because of his deadpan Stan Laurel expression, even when there was mayhem going on around him in the penalty area. He was the ideal foil at the centre of the defence to the more extrovert McLintock, and they were the rock on which our double team was built. He and Frank complemented each other perfectly, and if it had not been for a genius of a player called Bobby Moore the man from Great Yarmouth would have won a cupboardful of England caps. Peter was the unsung hero of dozens of Arsenal performances, rarely getting the credit he deserved but not caring that his skilled work was going unnoticed by the media. He was an exceptional club man who never put his own interests above the needs of the team. Away from the game Peter was quiet and withdrawn, but with a cutting wit. He smoked like a trooper, loved a glass of champagne and was a real mean card player. Peter and Geordie Armstrong were good muckers and favourites with everybody in the club. He was a one-club loyalist and played more than 400 League matches for Arsenal before injuries took their toll.

John Roberts: Nicknamed Garth because of his powerful physique, John made an important contribution to the double triumph with eighteen League appearances at the heart of the defence when Peter Simpson was recovering from a cartilage operation. Born in Swansea, John started his professional career with his local club at Vetch Field before joining Northampton. He moved to Arsenal in 1969, and we were particularly happy to have him on our side during the back-street battle with the Lazio players and fans. We reckoned he scored at least three clean knockouts, and it became part of Arsenal legend that he was bodily picking up opponents and throwing them over the tops of parked cars. He was a solid and reliable defender whose opportunities at Highbury were restricted by the consistent brilliance of McLintock and Simpson. John, who had muscles on his muscles, was not the most skilful of players, and he is the only player I ever saw who could top a ball when taking a deadball kick. Instead of going into the air, the ball would bounce along the ground like a Barnes Wallis bomb. I once made the mistake of telling John that he was going to be the first footballer to manage to plug a ball. He chased me around and around the London Colney training pitch. When he finally caught up with me, he rolled his knuckles over my head until I cried out for mercy. John was a lovely man to be around but I learned not to take the mickey out of him. The winner of twenty-two Welsh internationals caps, he later travelled the football conveyor belt with Birmingham City, Wrexham and Hull City.

Peter Storey: Peter was out of the Ron Harris school of destroyers. We used to call him 'Snouty', and you could understand why if you watched him eyeing up the opposition at kick-off. He would stand there like a hunting dog sniffing out its prey, training his cold eyes on the man he had been assigned to mark. I have seen players beaten by him before a ball was kicked. He used to frighten the life out of me, and I was on his side. Alf Ramsey was a great fan of his, and awarded him 19 caps as one of the successors to Nobby Stiles as England's midfield anchorman. Any player who took the full weight of his tackle felt that he was with them for days afterwards. Peter, from Farnham in Hampshire, came up through the Arsenal youth ranks, and played more than 400 matches for the first-team before winding down his career with Fulham. The only time I ever saw him scared was when we used to fly to matches abroad. Peter was the worst flyer I ever came across, and he would turn several shades of white and green before and during flights. But once he had his feet on terra firma, there was no more reliable, and sure-footed player to have on your side. He got his personal life in a bit of a mess after he had retired, and spent some time in prison. I found Peter a very amiable character, who was quiet and somewhat mysterious away from football. A real hard man.

Jon Sammels: A good-natured, cheerful character from Ipswich, Jon understandably felt left out of things in our Double year after playing a key role in the team in the previous four years. He was an accomplished playmaker, who could hit deadly accurate long passes and he carried a powerful shot in his right foot. Jon was a former England youth international and won nine Under-23 caps. A section of the Arsenal crowd turned on him in a cruel way, and he and Bertie Mee accepted that it would be best all round if he found a new club where his skill would be appreciated. While we were celebrating the Cup and League triumph he was quietly negotiating his transfer terms with Leicester City. Jon lost out more than others because of my switch to midfield, but he was too much of a gentleman and a realist to make any sort of complaint. He was a favourite with the fans at Leicester, and after hanging up his boots opened a successful driving school.

Eddie Kelly: Eddie was a Glaswegian who arrived at Arsenal from Possilpark Y.M.C.A a few days after his seventeenth birthday in February 1968. Like me, he was not the fastest thing on two feet but he had sound skills and was an enterprising link between defence and attack. He gave under-rated service to Arsenal in the Double year with 21 League appearances, quickly growing with the responsibility he had been given so soon after coming out of the juniors and reserves. He was personable with a bubbling personality that made him good to have at your side in the dressing-room and at the training ground. Eddie became a have-boots-will-travel professional after six years with Arsenal, and played for Queen's Park Rangers, Leicester City, Notts County, Bournemouth and then back to Leicester before winding down his career with Torquay United. He gave his best in every shirt he pulled on.

Charlie George: Charlie was the local hero who came off the Highbury terraces to become an idol of the fans he used to stand alongside. He was discovered by Bob Wilson when our goalkeeper was coaching at a local school. A long-haired, cheeky Cockney with prodigious natural skill, Charlie could make a ball rocket away from his right foot with hardly any back lift. His goal from 20 yards that clinched the Double in the FA Cup final guaranteed him a lasting place in the Arsenal hall of fame. Only a succession of injuries stopped him establishing himself as one of the greatest of all strikers of the seventies. Arsenal needed the flair that he brought to the Highbury stage, and many fans took a long time to forgive the club for selling him to Derby where he won his only England cap. Charlie later played with Southampton and for Brian Clough at Nottingham Forest, but he was never able to scale the heights he touched at Arsenal. He reminded me a lot of Peter Osgood who I had left behind at Chelsea. He had the same in-built inventive skills and the ability to turn a game with one touch of the unexpected, but like Ossie he did not seem to treat the game with total seriousness.

Ray Kennedy: Ray had two careers in one. With Arsenal, he was a formidable, sharp-shooting striker whose left foot was stunningly powerful. He then moved to Liverpool where Bill Shankly converted him into one of the most effective left-sided midfield players in the League. Born in Seaton Delaval, Northumberland, this easy-going character had a meteoric rise to fame with Arsenal after being released on a free transfer by Port Vale manager Sir Stanley Matthews. In his first full season in the Arsenal League team, he provided the goal area punch that helped lift us to the Double. He dropped back into midfield after moving to Liverpool in 1974, winning seventeen England caps and helping the Merseysiders win four League championships, two European Cup finals and the League Cup before moving to Swansea City. Then, in 1984, he returned to his native North-East as a player with Hartlepool while concentrating on a new career as a publican. Tragedy struck in the form of Parkinson's Disease, and all of us in the game are lost in admiration at the courage he has shown in fighting the illness and for the inspiration he has given to others with his I-will-not-be-beaten attitude.

John Radford: His plundering partnership in a twin spearhead with Ray Kennedy was vital to Arsenal's push for the Double. John, a powerfully built Yorkshireman from Hemsworth, had good speed, was difficult to knock off the ball and could unleash a right foot shot that was as powerful as any in the League. He and Ray went together like thunder and lightning. John, capped twice by England, was particularly effective when cutting in from his favourite position wide on the right. He could be dangerous in the air, and was an expert at making decoy runs that deceived defences into leaving room for supporting teammates. After a succession of hamstring problems, John continued his career with West Ham United and then Blackburn Rovers. Later, while an Essex publican, he played for Bishop's Stortford in the Isthmian League and helped them win the 1981 FA Trophy at Wembley. You had to earn John's friendship, and those who did not know him well thought he was dour and moody. But this keen angler had a well-developed sense of humour, and was good company for anybody who had won his respect and trust.

George Armstrong: George was one of the most important members of the team. He could operate on either wing, and would travel miles in every match to hustle opponents and to set up attacks with his probing runs and intelligent passes. The wee man always knew where to position himself to receive rehearsed clearances from Bob Wilson, and time and time again he would launch our counter attacks. I have never met a more generous person (always first to the bar regardless of the size of the round), and his unselfish personality was mirrored in the way he played the game. He always put the team first, and his deadly accurate chip passing dished up a bagful of goals for John Radford and Ray Kennedy. Born in the football hotbed of Hebburn in the North East, we nicknamed him Geordie. He was signed by Billy Wright and came up through the Arsenal youth ranks. Geordie played more than five hundred games for Arsenal before winding down his career with Leicester City and then Stockport County. He won five England Under-23 caps, but was never able to persuade Alf Ramsey to promote him to the full team where his contribution from either wing could have given the team a new dimension. Everybody loved Geordie, and it was a delight to welcome him back to the Highbury staff as a reserve-team coach whose early-morning good humour was a tonic. The Arsenal youngsters could not have a better mentor.

I can get quite misty eyed thinking back to my playing days with these

Highbury heroes. But I had a new football stage on which to perform, one of the few even bigger than the one at Arsenal. The Doc was calling from Old Trafford.

6 : The Doc Calls Again

December, 1972: The garden at my Cockfosters home was ablaze with winter iris and *jasminum nudiflorum* when the call came from the Doc to join him at Old Trafford. I found it as hard to leave my garden as I did to leave Highbury. But I could not resist the chance to try out pastures new.

MY old sparring partner Tommy Docherty summoned me to Old Trafford as his first signing after taking over as manager of Manchester United. It was the biggest challenge of my playing career, and it turned out to be my biggest disappointment. I had the chance to play a lead role on one of the world's great football stages, and in my heart of hearts I know that I did not do myself justice.

United were in turmoil when I arrived the day after Boxing Day, 1972. They were pinned to the bottom of the First Division, and The Doc was going through the place like a tornado trying to sort out the problems that he had inherited: Frank O'Farrell had been sacked a week before Christmas, and Sir Matt Busby – Tommy's idol at the time – persuaded him to give up managing Scotland for the job of restoring United.

The first thing the Doc did was to buy me from Arsenal for £120,000, just a little matter of £114,000 more than he had invested when taking me to Chelsea from Aston Villa. Sir Matt Busby came with him to London to talk the deal through with me. That had an enormous impact on me because Sir Matt, a gentleman of the first order, was a legend in the game – particularly for somebody like me with a similar Lanarkshire village background. Everton and West Ham had also shown interest in signing me, but meeting the incomparable Sir Matt helped sway my decision to sign for United.

Tommy Doc paid me the compliment of describing me to the media as 'Britain's Gunter Netzer', who was one of the world's most accomplished midfield playmakers. It made me smile because Tommy had once told me during one of our up-and-downers at Chelsea that he had seen a cart horse that could run faster than me. But that was Tommy. It was either love or hate, no in between. There was no question that

81

he was in love with United. I had never known the Doc so bubbling and buoyant, even though the club had a relegation battle on its hands.

'This is the greatest club in the world,' Tommy told me, 'and the only one for which I would have given up the Scotland job. But as a gardener, George, you'll understand when I say I've got a lot of weeding out to do.'

Funnily enough, it was only gardening that made me think twice about going to United. I had got our garden at our home in Cockfosters just as I wanted it and was looking forward to seeing the result of all my hard work in the spring. Another issue to consider was that Marie was six months pregnant with our son, Daniel, and I did not want to disrupt her life. But Tommy's enthusiasm rubbed off on me to such an extent that I convinced myself and Marie that it was the right move to make. We rented out our North London home and bought a place in Sale while I gave all my energy and concentration to United.

The Doc took my breath away by telling me that he not only wanted me to play for United but also to captain the team. It was a tremendous privilege but also a burden because from the moment I arrived at United I was struggling to find the peak form of my Arsenal days. There was so much back-stage acrimony in those early months at United that even Captain Bligh would have thought twice about skippering a team that was in a painful transition period. There were a lot of raised eyebrows when Tommy announced me as his captain in succession to the one and only Bobby Charlton. Most people thought that the Doc would automatically hand the captaincy to the assured Martin Buchan, but Tommy considered that he was not yet experienced enough in the English First Division following his move a year earlier from Aberdeen.

It was almost as if Tommy still considered himself manager of Scotland. He was no longer in charge of the team, so he seemed to set out to buy it. Within days of bringing me in from Arsenal he signed Alex Forsyth from Partick Thistle, Jim Holton from Shrewsbury and Lou Macari from Celtic for an anglo-Scottish record fee of £200,000. Already in the United squad were Scots Buchan, Denis Law, Willie Morgan, John Fitzpatrick, Ted MacDougall and the recently retired midfield master, Pat Crerand, who was to become Tommy's number two and, later, his sworn enemy. You could not move five yards without hearing a Scottish accent. The Doc also brought in Tommy Cavanagh as coach. He was a witty, full-of-enthusiasm Scouser who was cast in something of a sergeant major's role by Tommy as he attempted to shake up the sleeping giant that was United at that time.

There was too much behind-the-scenes politics going on for my taste. I kept out of it, but some of the old guard were said to be plotting against the Doc because they resented the way he was ruthlessly reorganising things. Every football club goes through cycles, and for a club that just four years before had won the European Cup this was the low point of the turn in fortunes.

In my first match in a United shirt we were beaten 3-1 at Highbury of all places, and I knew from that opening game that there was a tough mountain climb ahead in my career. Two of my great heroes, Denis Law and Bobby Charlton, were tired giants, and George Best – the most gifted British player of my time – was into one of his disappearing moods. The dressing-room spirit can be gauged by the fact that when Ted MacDougall was substituted by Brian Kidd during one of my early games against Everton, he had showered, dressed and had left the ground before the final whistle.

United fans brought up on some of the finest football to be seen on this planet were treated to some horrendous spectacles as we battled to keep the club afloat in the First Division. The Doc kept denying it, but there was no doubt that we were using the physical route to survival. Big Jim Holton in the middle of our defence was launching himself into tackles that frightened the lives out of opponents, and I have to admit that I was getting more physically involved than ever before. It was desperate stuff and not at all pretty to watch. Yet that did not stop the United fans turning out in their thousands to support the club in their moment of need. A total of 1,027,525 fans turned up for the twenty-one home League matches at Old Trafford, an amazing average of nearly 49,000. Now that is what you call support. The sad thing was that there was a small minority of so-called United supporters who were giving the club – and the well-behaved fans – a bad name with hooligan behaviour that was a growing cancer in the game.

It is indicative of the way we were playing, with defence a priority, that the top scorer for United in that season was Bobby Charlton with just six goals, and two of those were from the penalty spot. I lost none of my admiration for Bobby in what was a tremendously difficult time for him. He had been through all the glory years with United, and it must have broken his heart to be playing with a team that had to kick and rush in a battle for survival. He decided to close his outstanding United career at the end of the season, and I was proud to play along-side him in his farewell match at Stamford Bridge when his standing ovation from a 45,000 crowd spoke volumes for the place he had in the hearts of all football followers.

An interlude here for one of the happier and more lasting memories of my spell with United. We went to Rome for a game against my old rivals Lazio, and devout Roman Catholic Sir Matt Busby arranged a private audience with the Pope at the Vatican.

Pope Paul made such an impression on me with his words of wisdom that I made a point of noting them down. They are worth repeating:

> *Never cease to be conscious of the influence for good that you can exercise. Always seek to live up to the finest ideals, both of sport and right living. Always strive to give an example of manliness, honesty and courtesy both on the field of sport and in your daily lives. Be worthy of imitation by those whose eyes are constantly upon you.*

I cannot think of a better script to pass on to all budding (and established) footballers.

We just managed to avoid relegation at the end of my first season at Old Trafford without divine intervention, and Tommy Doc then started planning for the future... and that future did not include the King of Old Trafford, Denis Law. I will always select Denis as having had the fastest penalty area reflexes of any striker, and it was one of the thrills of my international career that I was able to play with him in the Scotland team while I was at Arsenal. We lined up together in four international matches, the last of them a memorable occasion against Brazil in the Maracana stadium in Rio. By the time I arrived at United, Denis was struggling for form and fitness after a run of injuries and we played in the same League side only three times. He and the Doc had got on like old friends when they were together in the

Scotland squad, but at Old Trafford a coldness and a distance developed between them that could be measured in fathoms. Denis has gone on record saying that he will never forgive Tommy for the way in which he let him go on a free transfer at the end of the season.

The Doc had found a crumbling empire when he arrived at Old Trafford, and it was obvious that he was going to have to hurt a lot of people before he could start rebuilding. I wish I could claim that I played a major role in the resurgence of United, but I rarely managed to produce anything like my best at Old Trafford. There was too much tension and anxiety around, and suddenly all the rhythm went out of my game and Stroller became something of a workhorse. I can look myself in the mirror and swear that I never gave less than a hundred per cent to the team, but I would have been much happier if my contribution had included my old Bargeddie-road skills.

My loss of form had cost me my place in the Scotland team, now under the management of Willie Ormond. I had the satisfaction of scoring two goals against Wales, and made my final appearance in a Scottish jersey a month later at Hampden on 30 June 1973 when I went on as a substitute against a crack Brazil side including Rivelino and Jairzinho. So I finished in the best possible company.

It got no better at United the following season. In fact it got worse. We kicked off with a 3-0 defeat at Highbury (thanks chaps!), and started a relegation battle that lasted virtually the entire season. Rubbing it in on that opening day of the season was Denis Law, who scored two goals for our great rivals Manchester City. A few weeks later he was recalled to Scotland's World Cup squad. That was a real two-fingered salute to the Doc. We could certainly have done with the old Law goal power because we had hit a famine, and this was underlined by the fact that for a time goalkeeper Alex Stepney was our leading marksman with two penalties. Stepney was the only member of United's European Cup winning team who started the new season in the League side, which was proof that The Doc had completed his clearing-out operation.

Brian Kidd was called in for twenty-one games before being sold to Arsenal, and George Best, the only other 1968 hero still in the squad, was encouraged to make a comeback. He played for us in a friendly against Shamrock Rovers and showed flashes of his old magic. The fans were so excited that they invaded the pitch to congratulate him on a goal and the match had to be abandoned. It convinced The Doc that he was ready for a recall and his return coincided with a 1-0 victory over Birmingham City. But the fact that our goal was scored from the penalty spot by Stepney was a sign that all was still far from right.

I thought I had seen it all and done it all in football, but I could not believe some of the stories told to me about the wayward genius George Best. Former manager Wilf McGuinnes said that he had caught him in bed in a leg-over situation with a woman just a couple of hours before a League Cup semi-final. That beat the Chelsea player who used to pay a regular morning visit on home match days to a married lady friend who lived just a goalkick's distance from Stamford Bridge. It was while I was at Old Trafford that George, a real charmer with footballing gifts from the gods, bought the *Club del Sol* in Bootle Street, Manchester, and re-opened it as *Slack Alice*. The Doc was not pleased. 'I want him concentrating only on Manchester United Football Club,' he said.

The Best comeback ran into a brick wall after just 12 First Division appearances. We were hammered 3-0 at Queen's Park Rangers on New Year's Day, 1974, and when we reported back for training there was no sign of George. He was last seen going off to a party after the match, and did not show up at the training ground. The Doc and the United board reacted by suspending him for two weeks and putting him on the transfer list. George told the media that he was quitting the game. 'If I am not good enough to get into a struggling team as bad as United, then it's time I retired,' he said. A little over a month later we looked on open mouthed as George was charged with stealing a cheque-book and fur coat belonging to former Miss World, Marjorie Wallace. He was later cleared of all charges, and I was delighted for him because there has never been an ounce of criminal intent in the wee man who lived life at a reckless pace on and off the pitch. I was proud and privileged to have been on the same pitch as him and in the same team, even though he was just a shadow of the player who had, during the 1960s, looked the greatest thing on two feet.

My favourite George Best story started out as a rumour in

Manchester during my last couple of months at Old Trafford, but it has since been confirmed as true by George himself. Manchester is little more than a big village, and it was whispered in September 1974 that George had won £25,000 with a roll of the dice in a Manchester casino. George left the casino with a former Miss World on his arm and the cash stashed into his pockets. It was the wee small hours of the morning when he returned to a swish hotel accompanied by his beautiful girlfriend. 'A little Irish nightporter showed us up to our room,' recalled George. 'I slipped him a tenner tip and asked him to bring up a bottle of bubbly.' By the time the porter was knocking on the door with the champers, the former Miss World had slipped into a negligée and George was sitting alongside her on the bed counting the winnings. The porter put the tray containing the champagne and two glasses on a side table. As he prepared to leave the room, he coughed apologetically and said in a rich Irish accent: 'Excuse me, George, but would you mind if I were to be asking you something?'

'Of course not,' said George, still counting out his thousands of pounds. 'What is it?'

'Well, George,' said the porter, 'just where did it all go wrong?'

Yes, there's only one Georgie Best.

Anyway, Best had gone and the United defence had been strengthened by the arrival from Brentford of yet another Scot, left-back Stewart Houston, and we started a friendship that would later lead to a close association at Arsenal. It was the United attack, though, that needed a spark of life. Lou Macari, like me, was going through one of those spells when little would go right, and there was an almighty bust up when The Doc dropped him into the reserves. Lou, a fiery character, refused to play for them and was fined £400 and, briefly, transfer listed.

My past flashed before my eyes when Derek Dougan scored the winning goal for Wolves against United at Molineux (I could hear The Doog: 'I told you that you weren't fit to clean my boots!'). I relinquished the captaincy and my place in the team when a 1-0 defeat at Birmingham City dumped us to bottom place in the table. My United career was over after just forty-three League games that the press worked out had cost something around £2,790 a game.

I watched sadly and helplessly from the sidelines as United were demoted to the Second Division. Ironically, it was a back-heeled goal from Denis Law in the Manchester derby that finally doomed United to relegation. Hundreds of United fans spilled onto the pitch after the goal, and with eight minutes still to go and City leading 1-0 the referee abandoned the match, but it was decided by the Football League authorities that the result should stand.

Now I found the unacceptable face of the Doc. Our love-hate relationship touched rock-bottom as he gave me the 'leper' treatment I had seen him use on players in the past. He demoted me to the reserves, and tried to humiliate me by forcing me to train with the youth squad. They were the same tactics that he had used on Lou Macari and which had led to their well-publicised row. But I was determined that Tommy would not force me into a transfer demand that would have cost me a lot of money. I had four frustrating months in the wilderness of reserve-team football, with Pat Crerand as my manager. He was appointed number two to the Doc, but they soon fell out and there was an atmosphere whenever they were together.

I had no intention of falling out with Tommy, hard as he tried to needle me. Finally, in November 1974, he called me into his office. 'We both know it's not working out, George,' he said. 'So how d'ye fancy a move tae Portsmouth?'

Portsmouth? From Manchester United to Portsmouth? Oh well, the Boy from Bargeddie was off on another million-mile trip. And do you know something? I had not even had time to plant a single bulb in our garden at Sale. Now I was off to join The Saint.

7 : The Saint and El Tel

November 1974: Time to pick up the fallen leaves of autumn, and to start planning next summer's delights. Use the leaves for rotting down into leaf-mould or, if they are from beech or oak, to protect tender plants against the ravages of a severe winter. I was now past the autumn of my playing career and into the winter months.

PORTSMOUTH were in an even more perilous position than Manchester United had been when I first moved to Old Trafford. They were stuck at the bottom of the Second Division, and their manager, the one and only Ian St John, had not been able to celebrate a single victory since taking the job ten weeks earlier. He was desperate for points, and agreed to trade veteran Welsh international centre-forward Ron Davies to United in exchange for me. I don't know who was more surprised, Ron to be going to Old Trafford or me to be on my way to Pompey. As Saint's future partner, Jimmy Greaves, is so fond of saying, 'It's a funny old game.'

My arrival at Fratton Park coincided with Saint's first victory after thirteen matches in charge. Pompey beat Sheffield Wednesday 1-0, but I could claim little credit for the morale-boosting win because I pulled a hamstring and limped off after thirty-three minutes. Not the best of starts, but things got better and I played in the last seventeen matches of the season as Portsmouth eased away from the relegation zone.

I look back fondly on my two seasons at Pompey, even though the team did not function too well. Marie and I found a house in Old Portsmouth, just a short walk from the sea front, and it was an invigorating place in which to bring up our children, Nicole and Daniel. There were memories of Arsenal at Fratton Park in the shape of Peter Marinello, who played in the same quick-dribble-and-cross style as in his Highbury days. But the likeable lad from Edinburgh still had the bad old habit of not taking more care with his final ball, and – thoroughly disillusioned with English football – he moved on to Motherwell in December 1975. Saint was not the luckiest of managers, and agonised on the touchline as we lost thirteen of our matches by a single goal. I did my best to get things moving from midfield, and played some of my finest football since leaving Arsenal, but despite all the endeavours of an industrious team we were relegated to the Third Division.

The blackest day for me at Portsmouth came with the news of the passing on of my mother. She had been unwell for some time, and when she died at the age of sixty-eight a light went out in my life. There are not words to express what I, along with my brothers and sisters, owed that wonderful lady. One of my regrets is that she did not live long enough to see me managing at Arsenal. I would have loved to have presented her with one of my Manager of the Year awards; not that it would have been nearly enough to show what I thought of her.

I had a contract that was bringing me in more money than Portsmouth could really afford on Third Division attendances, and when my old mate Terry Venables came in for me the Saint was almost relieved to let me go. Ian, against whom I had made my goal-scoring debut for Aston Villa in his peak playing years with Liverpool, never really seemed manager material to me. He had once finished runner-up in a BBC competition to find a football commentator, and I was not surprised when he switched so successfully to a full-time broadcasting career that has made him a household name.

Terry had started out on a managerial career with Crystal Palace, taking over from his mentor Malcolm Allison as the boss at Selhurst Park. He had put together one of the most exciting young teams in the League, and wanted an old head to steady things down in midfield. Terry had generated a buzzing atmosphere and there was an exciting undercurrent that reminded me of my early days at Chelsea when Terry and I were in the springtime of our playing careers. Now the young whipper snappers at Palace were calling me 'Grandad George', and I was loving every second of conducting them from midfield as their tremendous enthusiasm rubbed off on me. Among their exceptional players was a young left-back I rated just about the best I had ever played with or against: Kenny Sansom, who was later to find fame with Arsenal and England.

If anything I was trying too hard to set an example of total commitment, and I was twice sent off while wearing Palace colours. Each time it was for a poorly timed tackle (I can hear The Doc: 'What was it, George – fishing tackle?'). I was hardly famous for my ball-winning qualities, and I was determined to show the young lads around me that even ball players had to give a hundred per cent in effort.

In 1977 I went to the United States for a loan period with California Surf in the North American League, and in an early game turned on my ankle. It was the greatest pain I had ever experienced. I went for emergency hospital treatment on my return to London where an x-ray revealed that I had severed a tendon. I was put on an operating table and the surgeon broke my ankle so that he could repair the tendon and ligament damage before inserting two one-and-a-half-inch long screws that are still there to this day. Ouch!

I had been lucky with injuries throughout my career, but I was making up for it as I reached the twilight of my playing days. And again it was in the United States where I came a cropper. I was playing for Palace during a summer-tour match against a Memphis team managed by my old Chelsea chum Eddie McCreadie. I went into a straightforward block tackle, and there was that snapping sound that every footballer fears. I knew straight away that I had broken my leg. I was carted off to the local hospital, run by nuns, and had the bone re-set. Palace continued their tour down to Miami while I spent the following week on my back. The boredom was broken only by daily visits from 'Steady Eddie', who each day smuggled into the 'dry' hospital two small bottles of vodka that he kept hidden inside his socks.

When we returned to London, Terry gave me a good friend-to-friend talking to. He knew that I was discussing with our mutual pal Frank McLintock the possibility of going into the pub trade, investing the money that I had tucked away in preparation for my retirement. 'Look,' said Terry, 'you know and I know that your greatest love in life is football. You've got so much you can still give the game. I've watched you working with the kids in training, and you probably don't realise it yourself but you are a born coach. Forget about pubs. Keep your money in the bank, and start coaching seriously. I would like you to start by looking after the Palace youth team. Who knows where it will lead to.'

Terry had not just touched a chord with me, he had played an entire symphony. I had been quietly watching him at work as a coach and his imaginative approach to the job had stirred in me a desperate desire to get involved. Now he was opening the door.

I went home and discussed it with Marie, who agreed it sounded a good idea though the money on offer was not even half what I had been earning as a player. The hardest decision of all was having to take Nicole and Daniel away from private schools because I could no longer afford their fees. Yet it proved the best thing that happened to them. They were both accepted at the excellent Dame Alice Owens School in Potters Bar where Nicole became head girl and won a scholarship to Cambridge. She is now happily married to a skilled carpenter called Carl, and following a career as a schoolteacher. Nicole is a walking record book on football and follows the game avidly, while Daniel has shown only surface interest. A strapping, handsome lad of 6ft 4, his first love is golf and he was an assistant professional for three years before deciding to look for a new path in life. As I write, he is between jobs but I am confident he will do well for himself because he has a sensible head on his shoulders. I look on him as a good mate. A father can ask for no more.

I was like a father-figure to the lads at Palace, and threw myself into the new job with the same sort of enthusiasm and energy that I used to see Dave Sexton and Don Howe showing. Now I was understanding why they always had a light shining in their eyes. There is, I was discovering, nothing more satisfying than coaching. Yes, I was even enjoying it as much as playing the game.

After recovering from my broken leg I buried myself totally in my new career as a coach, and jumped at the chance to follow Terry to Queen's Park Rangers when he took over as manager in 1980 from none other than Tommy Docherty. The football roundabout never ceases to surprise.

For Terry, Queen's Park Rangers was the last stop before his move to Barcelona where he became famed as El Tel as he led them to their first Spanish League championship triumph for eleven years. He always was a natural.

For me, coaching at Queen's Park Rangers was a stepping stone to management, and on 6 December 1982 I eagerly accepted the chance to take on the job of managing Millwall. The Boy from Bargeddie was about to step into the Lions' Den.

8 : Life with the Lions

December 1982: Hyacinths provide bold colour and a strong scent from Christmas to Easter when grown in bowls or pots. They can also give fine displays in outdoor beds at springtime if planted in the autumn after the removal of the summer bedding plants. My hyacinthus were already giving a splash of winter colour to my garden when the call came to join Millwall.

MILLWALL were three places off the bottom of the Third Division when I arrived just before Christmas, 1982. We lost our first two games, and dropped to the bottom. Suddenly the threat of relegation was gaping below me like an executioner's trap door. Welcome to management, George.

When I told Queen's Park Rangers reserve-team coach Theo Foley that I was leaving to take the Millwall job, he said: 'You must be mad.' Then, when I told him Terry Venables had given me permission to offer him the post of assistant manager, he said with his great Irish logic: 'It'll be a pleasure, so it would. Let's be mad together.' Theo, who had managed at Charlton and coached at Millwall, was a great source of strength to me in my managerial baptism and I want to go on record as saying that he deserves a lot of credit for my early success. He played the good guy to my bad guy with the players. I would do the necessary tough talking, and then Theo would come along with the fatherly, arm-round-the-shoulder approach, and between us we would get the required response. It meant I was not always top of the popularity stakes with the players, but it is not a manager's job to try to be liked but to win matches. Theo was an ideal foil for me.

Anyway, off we went on the great adventure, and for the next three-and-a-half years it was an exciting non-stop slog trying to put the Lions of Millwall on the map. I could not have asked for a more demanding, more exhilarating, more exasperating, more educational or happier start to my managerial career. And I could not have asked for a more understanding or supportive chairman than Alan Thorne, who first interviewed me for the job on the recommendation of his son, Byron. Queen's Park Rangers had an exceptional youth team development officer called Chris Geiler, and he invited Byron along to watch our squad training sessions. Byron, a young businessman in his twenties, was fascinated by the way we worked, and was keen on setting up a similar youth team policy at Millwall. I had no idea I was making a good impression on him, but I was delighted some months later when he contacted me to ask if I would like to be considered for the vacant job of Millwall manager.

Byron arranged for me to meet his father, Alan, who was the latest in a long line of benevolent and blindly optimistic chairmen who had taken on the job of trying to put the club on the road to the promised land of the First Division. He was a jovial larger-than-life character who had made a success of his property company in succession to his father, a constructor who had built Millwall's ground in the aptly named Cold Blow Lane (this is all, of course, long before the 1990s switch to the New Den). The club had often felt the cold draught of approaching bankruptcy, and was in a crisis situation when Alan, or Mr Chairman as I respectfully called him, invited me to the London Hilton to discuss the manager's job.

'I've got a hunch,' he told me.

'I thought it was just a bad-tailored suit,' I said with a Tommy Docherty-style punchline.

We were off with a laugh, and then Alan got down to the serious stuff.

'I've got a hunch about you,' he said. 'You're on a shortlist of three for the job. I first of all fancied either of the other two, Ian Greaves and John Hollins, but having listened to Byron enthusing about your theories on coaching and your plans for bringing new ideas to the club, I am going to offer you the job. What sort of money are you looking for?'

'I leave that to you,' I said. 'You know your budget.'

'I was thinking of 20k a year,' he said.

'Think again,' said a voice in my head, while I actually replied: 'That's fine by me. I accept it.'

Alan nearly fell off his chair. 'You surprise me,' he said. 'I was expecting you to push me up, or at least take time to think about it.'

I had broken the golden rule set for me by my brother Andy all those years ago: 'Always buy time to think.' But I was not going to let him get away that easily. 'The reasons that I've accepted it straight away,' I said, 'are because one, I consider it a fair offer, two you are giving me the chance to start a managerial career and three, if I do well then when we come to renegotiate the contract I will be asking for a lot, lot more.'

Within three months, this dynamic man who liked to wear Stetson hats and made light of a diabetes problem, tore up our original contract and doubled my money to make me one of the highest paid managers outside the First Division. So I must have been doing something right in my first attempt at managing a club. And what a club. Millwall's history since their formation in 1885 had been more about taking part than winning. They had never been higher than the Second Division, and their greatest claim to footballing fame was that they had been the first Third Division club to reach an FA Cup semi-final back in 1937.

A little geography lesson, particularly for some Fleet Street observers: Millwall is not in the East End. Millwall, the place, is, but not Millwall the football club. I continually read articles that put the club in East London, when in actual fact they are based on the other side of the river in Lewisham, South London – SE14 to be exact, a short jog away from Tower Bridge and a goalkick from the Old Kent Road. With the Thames rolling close by, the district had a long association with the docks before the introduction of giant containers meant an unloading switch to down the river at Tilbury. The sudden decline of the docks brought mass unemployment (and a lot of resentment) to the area, but by the time I arrived the docklands were being revolutionised and there was a lot of work for local people building apartment blocks for a new generation of 'Yuppies'. You could see poverty on one side of the road and prosperity on the other. It looked to me to be a tinderbox for future problems, but I was not there for politics. Football was my only concern, and thinking of it purely selfishly we were delighted to have London Docklands as the club shirt sponsors.

Millwall have a small band of passionate, totally devoted supporters who will follow them regardless of results. On a good day you could attract more than 10,000 fans to the ground, but the average was nearer 4,000 when I arrived and around 6,000 when I left. Your normal Millwall fan is salt-of-the-earth working class, humorous and quick-witted, South-London-and-proud-of it, a warm friend, a dangerous enemy, and often loudly opinionated, particularly on any matter to do with the club. There is also a strong contingent that come up the A2 from Kent, provided they can bypass local rivals Charlton Athletic, and several hundred give West Ham a miss and come from East London through the nearby Rotherhithe and Blackwall Tunnels, or by tube to New Cross and New Cross Gate stations. I got to love the people of the area, apart from a small, lunatic fringe who scarred the name of the club with mindless hooliganism which was a curse that I (and many others) was never able to cure. Several times I confronted the troublemakers face to face and tried to make them see sense. They would nod their agreement ('You're right, George, mate... we were right out of order'), and then within a week or so would be back to causing mayhem with their loutish behaviour. There were times at Millwall when they almost reduced me to tears of sheer frustration, but I always gritted my teeth and told myself that I must not let them beat me or the club. The crazy thing is that many of them really believed they were some sort of ambassadors for the club. Their chant of 'Nobody likes us, we don't care' could be chilling to hear because it was like an anthem to anarchy. I want to stress that the hooligans made up no more than two or three per cent of the Millwall following, and the large majority of their supporters were the best you could hope to find anywhere. It was sad to see them continually having their good name blackened by a handful of idiots. I have always seen hooliganism as a social rather than a soccer problem, and it is up to the government to take the necessary steps to stamp it out. For a start, they must give magistrates more power to punish the guilty so that the innocent do not suffer. A slap on the wrists is no good for the hardened hooligan.

I refused to let the Millwall hooligans spoil what was a demanding but immensely satisfying first stab at management. During the previous twelve months I had been on a PFA-run management course at Lytham St Annes, and I made a study of how to read accounts (and became so fascinated that I was a regular at Companies House poring through balance sheets), how to handle the media and how to conduct myself in television interviews. But my best lessons had come at first hand from the managers under whom I had served.

From my first manager **Joe Mercer**, I learned the importance of patting players on the back when they had done well, and sometimes even when they hadn't but needed a confidence boost. ('Head up, son, and walk tall, because you're doing a great job,' was one of Uncle Joe's favourite spirit-raising compliments). What I learned *not* to do from Joe was to take on too much at a time. It brought him close to a nervous breakdown at Aston Villa.

From **Tommy Docherty**, I learned to be tough with discipline when necessary ('If you let them, players will trample all over you,' was one quote from the Doc that stayed etched in my memory). What I learned *not* to do from Tommy was talk first and think later. He was often in trouble simply because he was too impulsive.

From **Bertie Mee**, I learned the vital importance of organisation and delegation ('You are as good as the team you gather around you,' Bertie used to say). What I learned *not* to do from Bertie was fall into the trap of socialising with the players. He kept his distance, and earned our respect. Bertie, one of the best organised people I have ever known in my life, never gave familiarity the chance to breed contempt. I worked closely with the players in training, but never made the mistake of allowing friendships to develop with any of them. That can lead to all sorts of trouble for a manager when it comes to selecting the team.

From **Ian St John**, I learned how to communicate. I really admired the way he could handle himself in front of a television camera or when a radio microphone was poked into his face. The Saint had appalling luck when in charge at Portsmouth, and must have been relieved to lay down the burden of management so that he could follow a broadcasting career that really suited him. ('There's got to be an easier way of making a living,' I clearly remember him saying after one of our agonising defeats at Fratton Park.) Communication with the media has become a vital part of football management, and I know there will be a procession of pressmen who would say that I was not nearly forthcoming enough. But I recognise that PR was in some areas a weakness of mine, and it will get my full attention in future.

From **Terry Venables**, I learned the necessity to be inventive and imaginative with the coaching sessions ('You will get no response from bored players,' he used to say. 'Football is a thinking as well as a physical game, and you must change the routine to keep your players on their toes and their interest alive.') What I learned *not* to do from Terry was get on the wrong side of a club chairman. Well I thought I had learned that lesson until I let my guard slip during the last rites at Highbury.

I had also learned from working with two of the best coaches in the business, **Dave Sexton** and **Don Howe**, the importance of doing your homework. I would get reports on all our opponents and would always try to check them out myself before planning tactics. Another thing I discovered from watching Dave and Don at work is that with the right coaching approach average players could be made good players and good players could be made better players. To all those people who knock coaching, I say that nothing will move me from the opinion that there is not a single player in the world who cannot benefit from good coaching. It can be a Baggio or a Romario – he can *still* be made better in some aspect of his game. Yes, a bad coach can damage a player. But a good coach is priceless ... and I have sufficient belief in myself to rate myself in that category.

When it was announced in the newspapers that I was to be the new Millwall manager you would have thought from the reaction of some people that I had come back from the dead. Old footballing friends contacted me to say they thought I had disappeared from the face of the earth. I had been out of sight for five years serving the best possible apprenticeship for management. I could not have bought the experience that I got running the Crystal Palace and then the Queen's Park Rangers youth teams. Sometimes it was hard to the point where I would be standing ankle deep in snow on the touchline of a pitch in the middle of nowhere saying to myself: 'What the blankety-blank are you doing here, George?' But those moments were well outweighed by the satisfaction I got from coaching and encouraging kids with the shining light of hope in their eyes.

Terry Venables allowed me the responsibility of meeting the parents, and I used to go out of my way to emphasise the pitfalls as well as the perks that awaited their young sons. I had to drive it home to them that becoming an apprentice professional was only the first step on what could be a treacherous journey. They needed to know that only ten per cent of youngsters made it through to first-team football, and I said to every lad who played for me: 'If you are going to fail, please don't let it be because of a lack of application and attitude. You can have all the ability in the world, but if you don't give full commitment you are letting yourself down.'

It was my learning experience with the youth teams in the South East Counties League that laid the best possible foundation to my managerial career. Those Saturday mornings spent out on near-deserted grounds coaching and cajoling from the sidelines with stray dogs and dedicated parents for company was time well spent. I learned how a well organised youth structure could bring continuity to a club. Teaching the youngsters the right habits and getting them used to the same system that the seniors were playing made it easier for them to move up the football mountain.

It all meant that when I was invited to move up the mountain to the job of Millwall manager, I was well prepared. I had not come back from the dead, like some people seemed to think. I had been out and about learning my trade.

One of the first things I did when taking over at Millwall was to demand a larger office. I told the chairman: 'If I'm ever going to be carried out of here I want to go out in style.' I feel that a large, well-appointed office is important for a manager if he is going to manage properly. Too many allow themselves to be stuck in rabbit hutch offices, and it cramps their style. You need a good office in which to make an impression, particularly on the parents of boys you are hoping to sign. The chairman took my point about a larger office being good for club PR, and he arranged to have two offices knocked into one.

I had hardly been at Millwall five minutes before I got a reputation as a tough disciplinarian. 'Iron George' was one newspaper description after I had ordered six players in for extra training after a poor performance. I did not see it as discipline. I preferred the description 'professionalism'. There was a casual, what-will-be-will-be attitude at the club, and I was determined to stamp it out. In my first team-talk I told the players they had six weeks to prove themselves to me, otherwise I would be on the look out for replacements who could do the job that needed doing. We were so deep in relegation trouble that I had no time for a soft approach. At the end of the six weeks I asked to see the chairman and his son at the ground. 'Mr Chairman,' I said, 'I've now had time to make an assessment of everybody on the staff, and what I have to tell you is that we need nine new players.'

Alan Thorne looked stunned. 'Are you sure?' he said. 'Only nine! What would that cost the club?'

'I've been out scouting, and I've drawn up a list of the players that can do the job for us,' I explained. 'I can get them all for a total of around two hundred thousand pounds.'

To his credit, the chairman backed me all the way. He must have been having some doubts when, at the end of March and after eight defeats in our last ten matches, we were back at the bottom of the table. But by the right application and attitude we got our act together and we went through the last twelve matches of the season unbeaten to claw our way out of trouble. We beat the threat of relegation by just one point. It was the Great Escape, and I have to admit that some of my principles about always trying to play football went out of the window during those desperate last weeks. We had to fight our way out of trouble with uncompromising stuff that was a long way from the skilful, entertaining style of soccer that I like to preach. In a perfect world I would always like to have my team playing artistic, free-flowing football. But during an England season that can include sun-baked, muddy, saturated, frozen and wind-blown pitches, you have to learn to adapt and adjust to the conditions. I love to watch the Brazilians playing, but I promise you they could not produce their poetry week in and week out in our league where willpower and strength are often as important as the skill factor.

My greatest bonus at Millwall was the buzz I got from coaching. We would work hard in training on set-piece situations, and to see what we had planned come off during a match gave me unbelievable satisfaction. The response of the players was just tremendous and we really looked forward to our training sessions on the playing fields of Dartford College, where BBCTV athletics commentator Stuart Storey had kindly arranged facilities for us. There was a marvellous community spirit in the Millwall area, and so many people in the district wanted to help us that we became like a happy family club for thousands of supporters who refused to let the few hooligans spoil it for them.

The first cracks in my marriage could be traced back to these early days at Millwall. I was working seven days a week, and when not at the club or training ground I was driving for miles watching opponents or looking for new players. I had a second-hand BMW, and literally drove it into the ground while travelling thousands of miles on managerial duties. Marie and the kids hardly saw me. I remembered a story that was told to me about former Tottenham boss Bill Nicholson, who wept when he went to the wedding of one of his daughters. 'I suddenly realised,' said one of the all-time great managers, 'that I had not seen her growing up. I had given all my time and attention to football.' That is how it had become for me. I was eaten up by the game and my job. I would go to the theatre with Marie, and would find that the curtain had come down without my knowing what the plot was because I had been lost in thought about an upcoming game.

Even when I was at home in our lovely old Cockfosters house I would have my mind on the next match, and my sleep pattern was ruined because I would be lying in bed thinking of tactics and new training routines. I also lost sleep over the standard of refereeing, and the daft inconsistencies we were continually experiencing. I filled my secretary's notebook with letters to the Football League and the Football Association on the topic, but nobody seemed to take any notice. Yet I would not have swapped the job for the world. I was completely hooked.

Once we had guaranteed another season of Third Division football I went all out to put together a team that could give us a chance of promotion. It meant wheeling-and-dealing because there was little money to spare. I turned the playing staff inside out and within a year there were only three of the players still on the books who had been at The Den when I took over. We finished ninth in my first full season, and the following year gained promotion as runners-up to Bradford City, and for two successive seasons we made deep inroads into the FA Cup, reaching the quarter-final and then the fifth round.

The team had cost around £215,000 in transfer fees, including one of the best buys I ever made – Les Briley, a snip at £20,000 from

Aldershot. I will always remember the day I signed Les for the saddest of reasons. It was just twelve hours after the Heysel Stadium tragedy in Brussels when thirty-eight people were killed before the kick-off to the Liverpool-Juventus European Cup final after a wall had collapsed following an outbreak of hooliganism. It was a black moment and all of us in football wondered if there was any point to what we were doing, but life (and the game) had to go on. I had gone to Aldershot to watch a striker called Dale Banton, but it was the busy Briley who took my eye with his work-rate and leadership qualities. Les became a bright light at The Den, skippering the team and burning up the midfield with his energy and enthusiasm. He set a shining example both on and off the field with his behaviour and his wholehearted commitment.

It was always my aim to watch players three or four times, home and away. It is vital to check whether a player has the same heart and commitment on away grounds as when in front of friendly fans on home territory. I had earmarked Southend team-mates Anton Otulakowski and Dave Cusack as likely lads for Millwall, and went on a secret scouting mission to Roots Hall to watch them. So that I could keep a low profile I put on a cap and scarf and tucked myself away on the terraces while I had a good look at them. At half-time a young lad came up and said, 'Excuse me, Mr Graham, but can I have your autograph?' In no time at all I was surrounded by youngsters queuing for my signature. So much for my cap-and-scarf disguise.

But the trip proved well worthwhile because I made a double signing that helped give my team its foundation. Dave Cusack was a commanding centre-half, and Anton Otulakowski was a revelation as our left-sided midfield creator. I could never understand why he did not make a major impact in the First Division when given his chance by West Ham, and if he had been younger I would have had no hesitation in taking him with me to Arsenal. Anton and Dave Cusack were union-minded boys who were both keen on PFA matters. They were always keeping me on my toes by bringing up contractual points, and while it sometimes gave me a headache it made me study contracts to such an extent that, thanks to Anton and Dave, I became quite an expert on small-print clauses. Cheers, lads.

Steve Lovell, a Welsh boy I had played alongside near the close of my career with Crystal Palace, banged in goals galore for me, and had great support from his countryman Steve Lowndes. Two other of my former Crystal Palace team-mates, Paul Hinshelwood and Nicky Chatterton, did a great job for me, and Kevin Bremner, a young Scot from way up in the west Highlands, epitomised everything I looked for in a footballer not blessed with natural gifts. He made up for his lack of artistry with a work rate that made me sweat just watching him. His father, a lovely ruddy-faced farmer, used to travel hundreds of miles on a round trip from his home in Banff in the far north of Scotland to watch Kevin play, and it used to fill him with pride to see his son so warmly embraced by the big-hearted and much-maligned Millwall fans. Kevin, younger brother of that good-class pro Des Bremner, is now a coach with Gillingham after a twelve-club playing career. If he can pass on his attitude to his players, they are going to be tremendous competitors.

Coming through from our juniors was a young striker called Teddy Sheringham. I noticed that he was always looking to score spectacular goals, chipping from way out and shooting from impossible angles. Once I had convinced him that he would be twice as successful if he got in the box to poach simple tap-in goals to go with his art gallery efforts he began to look the part of a future England international. Even at the age of seventeen you could see that he had outstanding talent, and it was no surprise to me when he developed into one of the finest strikers in the League. Millwall did very nicely out of Teddy, collecting £2million for him from Nottingham Forest manager Brian Clough in 1991. Not bad for a player who had cost the club nothing.

My biggest pay-out was the £55,000 invested in a young striker from Lincoln City called John Fashanu. He had been living in the shadow of his older brother, Justin, who moved from Norwich City to Nottingham Forest for £1million. I saw a raw talent in the former Barnardo's Boy that I knew could be honed, but I could not quite believe my ears when John told me after signing: 'I enjoy playing, but I want to make it clear that I don't like training.'

'Fine, John,' I said. 'I will tell the other players that in future we will not train and just turn up on match days.' I think John got the message, and I got the best out of him on the pitch even though he continued to hate training. He tackled a difficult job at Millwall with great dignity off the pitch. He was one of the few black players the club had ever had, but he took it all in his stride and he was an excellent PR for the club with his community work and in helping us to develop the vital family spirit of which we were all so proud. I was very reluctant to part with him after eighteen months, but I was forced to sell him to Wimbledon for £125,000 after the small hooligan element in our crowd had landed us in financial trouble. They made several pitch invasions during our FA Cup quarter-final tie at Kenilworth Road and terrorised parts of the town on what was one of my saddest days in football. Luton manager David Pleat, an old footballing acquaintance from way back when we played against each other at schoolboy international level, said to me: 'They're going to kill our great game, George.' I feared that he was right. They certainly almost killed off Millwall. A series of crowd disturbances led to the FA forcing us to make home and away games all-ticket affairs. Our attendances dropped alarmingly and the only way we could survive was by selling. So it was goodbye to Fash, who had certainly livened up the place with his colourful and at times peppery personality and his hurly-burly style of attacking play. But we didn't miss him on the training pitch!

Conscious of the troublemaking reputation of a section of our crowd, I went out of my way to make sure our players did not incite them with their behaviour on the pitch. I introduced a system of fines which punished any dissent and reckless play. There were also fines for anybody who was late, went on to the pitch with their shirt out or without shinpads. I encouraged the players to have pride in their appearance and pride in their performance. I was particularly hot on anybody being late because I considered this disrespectful to the other players. I always made the point: 'If office workers can be at their desks by nine o'clock each morning, I don't think it is asking too much of you to be at the training ground by ten.' With bonuses, the Millwall players were as well paid as any outside the First Division and I wanted them to be totally professional on and off the pitch, and to set an example to any young fans who looked on them as role models. There were a lot of more talented squads in the League, but those Millwall boys would have matched any for strength of character and I was very proud of them.

There was one occasion when a couple of players who objected to my hard-line tactics telephoned the chairman behind my back to complain. They were docked money as a punishment. I gave and demanded loyalty. The chairman was there to run the club. I ran the team. I had made up my mind right from day one that I wanted to be a manager who really managed, and I would accept no interference unless there was a good reason. It was, after all, my neck on the block if things went wrong. I met Alan Thorne and his son regularly for talks on club matters, but the chairman knew better than to try to tell me how to run the team, just as I would not have considered trying to tell him how to run the club.

I came out in support of the ban on our fans travelling away after the Luton fiasco, and this brought me some ugly fan mail. But I was just sick to death of the trouble being caused by a minority of thugs and I was in favour of anything that might stop them coming anywhere near a ground where Millwall were playing. It was heartbreaking for the thousands of decent, law-abiding Millwall followers, but if the hooligans could not be beaten they were in danger of putting the proud old club out of business.

Theo Foley and I both felt we had laid the foundation for a team that could take us all the way into the First Division (it was a foundation on which our successors John Docherty and Frank McLintock later built the first Millwall team to reach the top table in these pre-Premiership days). It was soul destroying for us to have to sell a player of Fashanu's goal-snatching ability, and all because of the behaviour of the hooligan minority.

I was less than professional for just one week in my three and a half years with the Lions. It was the spring of 1986 and I was talking to my old pal Terry Venables in one of our long-distance telephone calls between Barcelona and London.

'I really envy you working with all those class players,' I said. 'I'm limited to what I can do with my boys here at Millwall.'

'Why not give yourself a break and come and see how we do things,' said Terry. 'You'll be amazed at the set-up we've got here. You'll find it's like being on another planet compared with Millwall.'

On the spur of the moment I said, 'You're on.' I told Theo Foley to tell anybody who inquired that I had gone to Scotland on a scouting trip. In actual fact I nipped down to Barcelona for a week, and studied coaching under one of the masters, El Tel. The main reason I kept the trip secret is that I did not want people putting two and two together and making five. Sure enough there was a rumour that I had gone to Barcelona as a right-hand man to Terry, but nobody could find me to substantiate the story.

Terry was right about the difference between Barcelona and Millwall. Comparing the Nou Camp stadium with The Den (or most British grounds for that matter) was like contrasting a cathedral with a cattleshed. It is only in recent years that top British clubs have caught up with the standards of the major grounds on the Continent. I trained with Terry and the Barcelona players and made note of the way every player worked out with a ball, and noticed how the defenders were just as comfortable with their control as the midfield players and forwards. Terry rattled out his instructions in Spanish, and was tremendously impressive in the way he had some of the most accomplished players in the world hanging on his every word. They knew an outstanding coach when they heard one.

I returned to Millwall refreshed and brimming with new ideas... and with a sun tan. When I was asked about the tan, I replied: 'That's what we call windburn in Scotland.'

But before I could put ideas picked up in Barcelona into practise with Millwall, I was off on a rollercoaster ride that was to bring me my greatest highs and my most depressing lows.

The Boy from Bargeddie was going home to Highbury.

9 : Home to Highbury

May 1986: The rhododendrons and azaleas are in full flower, and there is a smell of advancing summer in the air. Rhododendrons require little or no pruning, but to avoid damage to the young growth, snap off the dead flowers with your finger and thumb. Secateurs could cause lasting harm to the shoots. I have some serious pruning work to do at Highbury.

IT was Millwall chairman Alan Thorne who first told me that Arsenal were interested in interviewing me for the job of manager at Highbury. I was astonished because I was convinced that my old pal Terry Venables was going to get the post. It was supposed to have been a closely guarded secret that Terry had signed a letter of agreement with them, but to his and Arsenal's great embarrassment the news leaked out before the incumbent manager, Don Howe, had been informed. Don, a man of great principle, resigned on the spot.

I still expected Terry to get the job, although the newspapers were now bringing the names of Alex Ferguson, Howard Kendall, David Pleat and Graham Taylor into the frame. There was only passing mention of me, and so I was genuinely shocked and excited when Alan Thorne rang me on the morning of 12 May 1986, to say: 'I always promised you that if a major club asked to talk to you I would let you know. Well, it's happened as I knew it would. Arsenal chairman Peter Hill-Wood wants to see you.'

Arsenal? That was not just a major club. They were, for me, *the* club. Alan added: 'You are free to talk to them, but let me stress two things. One is that I would rather you stayed here with us and saw out the year remaining on your contract. Two, if you do decide to go to Arsenal we will be wanting substantial compensation. All it remains for me to do is wish you luck.'

Alan had played it straight down the line with me throughout our extremely happy association, and I considered myself lucky to have had such a fine chairman supporting me as I took the first step into the minefield of football management. But both he and I knew that if it was a straight choice between Arsenal and Millwall (or Arsenal and any club, for that matter) I would choose to go 'home' to Highbury where I had spent the best years of my playing career.

A secret rendezvous was arranged with Peter Hill-Wood at his smart town house just off the King's Road, which brought back memories of my happy Chelsea days. I was ushered into his beautifully furnished lounge to find him in the company of Arsenal vice-chairman David Dein and managing director Ken Friar. I knew Ken well from my playing career at Arsenal when he was the club secretary, and he had since developed into one of the finest and most respected administrators in the League. David Dein was a relative newcomer to the board, and the talk in the game was that he was the thrusting power behind the throne. Peter Hill-Wood had taken over as chairman of Arsenal in 1982 following the death of his father, Denis, a distinguished City businessman who had been in the chair when I was a player and who I counted as one of the finest, old-style English gentlemen ever to cross my path. Peter was the third Hill-Wood to take the chair at Highbury, following in the footsteps of his father and grandfather, Samuel Hill-Wood.

He started our meeting by asking me to outline my views on the game, and to propose what steps I would take to make Arsenal once again contenders for the championship. I told them that I had been raised in the best Arsenal traditions, which meant that I believed in a well-organised, totally professional team. I also pointed out that if I were to get the job I would become very much a tracksuit manager because I was of the strong opinion that the main role of a manager was to coach his players. I was not interested in sitting behind a desk. I wanted to be out on the training ground instilling tactics and skills that would, I was convinced, make Arsenal strong challengers for the championship they had last won when I was a player back in the 'Double' year of 1970-71.

They were obviously relieved when I stressed the vital importance of strict discipline, both on and off the pitch – another Arsenal tradition that in recent months had been torpedoed by some well-publicised incidents that damaged the image of the club. I sensed that I was making an impression and decided to go for broke. 'As Arsenal manager, I would not tolerate my players mixing socially with members of the board,' I said. 'I have heard that the players have been socialising with a director and his wife. This is just not on, and if I was Arsenal manager it would be stopped immediately. It can undermine a manager and lead to all sorts of misunderstandings and problems if his players are going out on the town with directors or going over his head to board members.'

There were a lot of rumours flying in the village world of football about one of the directors and his wife going night-clubbing with first-team players and also inviting them into their home. I wanted to make it clear right from the outset – even before I was offered the job – that this is something I would not accept. 'I would expect any player to come through me before approaching a director,' I said, and got nodded approval from all three wise men.'I would also want to handle all press inquiries rather than have you, Mr Chairman, or any director giving quotes that could be at cross purposes with what I want to convey.' We had entered an era in which publicity-seeking chairmen were continually in the headlines. I did not consider it a change for the better, and preferred the old days when few supporters could have named their club chairman.

Hill-Wood had been getting a lot of flak from Arsenal fans following some poor results and the mess of Don Howe's departure. 'What would you want from me?' he asked.

'I would just want you to come to the ground on a Saturday and enjoy the game, Mr Chairman,' I said. 'My aim would be to make life easier for you. I would take full responsibility for running the team, Ken, as managing director, can run the business side and you, sir, can just sit back, relax and have a good time.'

The Chairman laughed, and there was an almost visible relaxing of his face. This Old Etonian executive of Hambros Bank, touching fifty, was not the type who could stomach supporters screaming insults at him.

I went out into the dining room while the three of them had a quiet discussion, and I wondered to myself if I had gone 'over the top' with my demands. But I consoled myself with the thought that if they decided against giving me the job I still had things to do at Millwall where I was perfectly happy. Within ten minutes I was summoned back to be greeted by handshakes from each of them.

'Congratualtions,' said Peter Hill-Wood. 'You are the new Arsenal manager, provided, of course, you are happy with our terms.'

Happy? I was ecstatic. It was a dream come true to be managing the club I rated the best in the world. Mind you, I was not over-impressed by the terms – £60,000 a year over three years. I knew there were First Division managers earning more than twice that, but it was enough for the job of my dreams. Millwall were paid £60,000 compensation, so they had done well out of me considering that I had led them to the Second Division and given them a profit of something around £40,000 on transfer deals.

It later transpired that when the move for Terry Venables broke down because the story of his agreement had been leaked, he told Peter Hill-Wood: 'There's an obvious man for the job. George Graham is Arsenal through and through.'

Thanks, Terry. He was right, of course. I was like a stick of rock with Arsenal stamped all the way through me. There were suggestions that I was only keeping the Arsenal seat warm for Terry, but Peter Hill-Wood knocked that down very firmly and told the press: 'George is the unanimous choice for the job, and if he brings us success he can stay as long as he likes.' He later told me that I had been considered as successor to Terry Neill three years earlier, but it was felt that I then lacked the necessary experience.

My first shock on agreeing to take the job was to find that Arsenal were around £1 million in debt. 'You can spend up to one million pounds in the transfer market,' Hill-Wood told me, 'and we can find more for you if you consider it absolutely necessary. That is a matter entirely for you to decide.'

My second shock was to discover the contractual mess that I had inherited. A dozen of the players were nearly out of contract. I was astonished that a club of Arsenal's stature had allowed this situation to develop, and I was determined to sort it out as quickly as possible.

I celebrated getting the job with a champagne dinner with Marie and some good old friends, including our Double year skipper Frank McLintock. He was now a manager at Brentford, and the whisper went round that I would be taking him to Highbury as my number two. Much as I rated Frank, I had no intention of appointing him to my staff. Our friendship was too valuable for me to risk it by working together. I have seen too many friends falling out over differences of opinion on football matters. The best example I can think of is when bosom buddies Brian Clough and Peter Taylor, inseparable 'Siamese twins' of football, had split with bad blood between them. Frank was honest enough to tell me to my face that he was as jealous as hell of me, but – like a true friend – he backed me all the way. He and I remain good pals to this day.

Theo Foley, my strong right hand at Millwall, was my choice as assistant manager, and it was a role he performed superbly until, in my view, he started to get too close to the players. His laughing-and-joking approach to the job had at first been the perfect balance to my deadly serious attitude, but then it reached the stage where I considered that the players had lost a little discipline. I decided that we could get a vital edge back into our training if Theo swapped jobs with reserve team manager Stewart Houston. Rather than take what he considered a demotion, Theo moved on to become manager of his old club Northampton, and he went with my best wishes and thanks for all that he had done for me. It was a sad day for me when he left because I always thought we would have a long-lasting run together, and I knew we were going to miss his sunshine personality. He is a smashing bloke and we still keep in touch with each other.

Steve Burtenshaw, who had been acting manager following the resignation of Don Howe in March, reverted to chief scout, and good old reliable Pat Rice returned to the club as youth team manager. There would eventually also be room on the coaching staff for Geordie Armstrong because I wanted people around me who had been brought up with the best Arsenal habits and standards.

The first thing I did when inheriting the little downstairs office in which Bertie Mee used to reign was to turn the desk round to face the door rather than the wall. I wanted to be able to look straight into the eyes of whoever came into this squashed room that held unhappy memories for me. I set out to make it feel more like my own office rather than the haunt of a procession of my predecessors. This was the claustrophobic office in which I used to make frequent visits to see Bertie Mee to ask why I was the player being dropped after a defeat. It was Bertie's way of motivating me, and it worked – but I used to moan like hell. I'm not so sure that as a manager I would have fancied handling the player George Graham. He could be a real pain at times.

The timing was not right for me to ask for a bigger office in keeping with one of the top managerial jobs in football, but once I had got a championship under my belt I demanded a move upstairs to a sizeable room that made both me and any visitors feel as if they were in a special place and not in the broom cupboard. If you are not going to think big and act big as manager of a club like Arsenal you might as well crawl under the carpet. The opportunity for a move came when they carried out some major restructuring under the main stand, and I had an executive-style office built that will have delighted the manager ghosts of Arsenal's past. Previously, only Herbert Chapman had what I would call a proper office. In fact it was the best room at Highbury – a large, elegant oak-panelled office in which you could smell the history of the place. Herbert had combined the manager and chief administrator's job, but when he went to the great dressing-room in the sky, Bob Wall took over his office for administration and from then on the managers were relegated downstairs to a cubby hole in which you could not swing a cat (or even a seven iron when I wanted to practise my golf swing). Ken Friar had inherited the office from Bob Wall, and I made the mistake of one day confiding in Terry Venables that it was my ambition to get the office for myself because of its historical significance dating back to the Chapman era of the 1930s. From then on Terry would drop into every conversation the question: 'Got the oak-panelled office yet?' I never did realise my ambition.

As I was settling into the job on my second day back at Highbury there was also managerial musical chairs down the road at our great North London rivals Tottenham. They had appointed my old schooldays footballing foe David Pleat as manager, and we swapped 'good luck' messages. We both faced the biggest challenge of our lives.

Working closely with Ken Friar and Steve Burtenshaw, I went through all the contracts of the players and set about sorting them out. Tony Woodcock, Paul Mariner, David Rocastle, David O'Leary and Paul Davis were among those who had been allowed to virtually drift out of contract. My first job was to rubber-stamp a free transfer for Mariner that had been arranged before my arrival. Tony Woodcock was also allowed to go so that he could build a future for himself as a coach in Germany, where he had played with great success for Cologne. I renegotiated new contracts with the other players, but stressed to each of them – and everybody in the squad – that nobody could count themselves as an automatic choice for the first-team. 'The Arsenal shirt must be worn with pride,' I told them, 'and you have to earn the right to wear it.'

Howard Wilkinson, then in charge at Sheffield Wednesday, telephoned in my first week to casually inquire about David Rocastle. This set the alarm bells ringing in my mind because I knew Howard had been impressed by Rocastle when he was handling the England Under-21 team. David was on holiday in the Caribbean, and I ordered that he had to be met at the airport on his return and brought straight to my office at Highbury. If necessary I was prepared to lock the door so that he could not leave without signing a new contract. As it turned out I found him the easiest person in the world to deal with and he willingly signed himself to Arsenal, and he became one of my favourite people. It would be a lovely world if everybody had David's pleasant manner and natural charisma. And he could really play the game.

I had done my homework before talking to the players, and I knew that I had a lot of weeding out to do. My aim was to quickly break the three cliques that had been allowed to build up. There were the prima donnas who wanted the star treatment without earning it, and there were two pools of former youth team players who had grown up together from their apprenticeship days and were distinctive by their colour, on the one side white players and the other side black. There was no racial tension, but they went their separate ways. I was determined to have them all pulling together in one direction and not against each other. I had a quote from from the late, great American football coach Vince Lombardi printed out and placed on my office desk because it captured my thoughts and feelings about team togetherness:

> You have to start by teaching the fundamentals. A player has got to know the basics of the game and how to play his position. Next you have got to keep him in line, that's discipline. The men have to play as a team, not as a bunch of individuals.

There's no room for prima donnas, but there have been a lot of coaches with good football clubs who know the fundamentals and have plenty of discipline, but still do not win the game. Then you come to the third ingredient: If you are going to play together as a team, you have got to care for one another. Each player has to be thinking of the player next to him, saying to himself, 'If I don't block that man, one of my team-mates is going to get his leg broken. I have to do my job well in order that my team-mate can do his.' The difference between mediocrity and greatness is the feeling these players have for each other. Most people call it team-spirit. When the players are inspired with that special feeling, you know you've got a winning team.

From day one of returning home to Highbury my objective was to get that special team spirit. It was also Lombardi who first came up with the quote: 'Winning is not everything. It's the only thing.' I never met the man, but I felt as if I knew him because he thought the way that I thought, and there was no more successful coach in American Football history. The rules of our game may have been different, but the aims were the same. *Winning*.

In my first team meeting with the players I made a few of them gulp when I forcibly made the point that I would not under any circumstance tolerate lack of discipline on or off the field. I had been told about card games on the team coach in which hundreds of pounds exchanged hands, and I made it a rule that in future only friendly card games could be played. Few things can destroy club spirit quicker than playing alongside a team-mate to whom you have just lost a packet at the card table.

As when I first took over at Millwall, I introduced a strict code of conduct, with fines promised for any player who stepped out of line. A couple of the players had recently been involved in drink-driving incidents, and I made it clear that this was the unacceptable face of professional football. There was an undeniable sense of complacency about the place, and I was determined to leave the players in no doubt whatsoever that I was going to shake them up. Average weekly wages of the first-team players then were around £1,500. It made the top-whack £200 a week I used to earn with Arsenal seem chicken feed. The players were going to have to earn their money.

To give you a taste of my hectic early days in charge at Arsenal, these are diary-style notes on the sort of jobs I had to tackle:

Monday: Called Charlie Nicholas in today and told him I was unhappy with his 'Champagne Charlie' image. 'You're a super player,' I told him, 'but you're letting yourself and the club down with your behaviour. You have not begun to show the marvellous skill that made you a star at Celtic. You'll have no bigger fan than me if you start playing like I know you can, but if you continue to live a faster life off the pitch than on it then I shall come down on you like a ton of bricks. It's Arsenal Football Club not nightclubs that should be getting your full attention. Oh, and by the way, Charlie, get rid of the earring and I want you (and all the players) wearing a tie and club blazer on match days. The casual days are over.' What I want to get home to Charlie and every player is that there is a time for work and a time for play. I had enjoyed myself off the pitch in my playing days, but I always (well, nearly always) got my priorities right and made sure that my football came first.

Tuesday: Gave David O'Leary a new one-year contract. He was starting out as a young apprentice at Highbury when I was in my last year as an Arsenal player, and now he is one of the longest-serving players in the club's history. David could not quite believe his ears when I told him that I wanted him to prove himself to me, along with everybody else. There has been no greater Arsenal loyalist, but this is a new beginning for all of us. Heard today that Terry Butcher has joined Graeme Souness at Rangers. I had been half interested in signing him, but held off because I think that in young Tony Adams we have a potential world-class central defender. Am looking to Adams and O'Leary to give us a strong foundation in defence.

Wednesday: Told Marie I could not make our theatre date because I am nipping down to Plymouth to watch Kerry Dixon play in a friendly for Chelsea. That's the third time I've let her down in as many weeks. She said it's a wonder I don't take my bed to the club. Now why didn't I think of that?

Thursday: Gave Graham Rix and Steve Williams a good talking to today. Told them they should take a long hard look at themselves. Both are talented players, but I've warned them that they are both at the crossroads. It will be very easy for them to start going downhill unless they are prepared to continue giving the club a hundred per cent.

Friday: Young Martin Keown is on his way to Aston Villa. He is making financial demands that I have no intention of meeting. Why should I pay him more than, for instance, Tony Adams, David Rocastle and David O'Leary? He is frustrated after two loan spells at Brighton, but money is the motivation that is taking him away from Highbury (The transfer tribunal forced us to take a cut-price £200,000 and six years later it cost us £2 million to buy him back. He would have earned a lot more money and success if he had stayed with us, but you cannot force a player to sign a contract.)

Saturday: The fixtures for the new season have just been published. Arsenal's first match under my management will be at home against Manchester United. Ouch!

We got off to a winning start against United, Charlie Nicholas snatching a late winner. He nipped into the six yard box to score a tap-in goal, and I was delighted because I had been nagging at him in training that he should be looking to make more of an impact in the penalty area. I was particularly pleased with the performance of nineteen-year-old Tony Adams in the centre of the defence, and I was more convinced than ever that he would develop into an exceptional player. David 'Rocky' Rocastle was another Arsenal-reared player who gave an outstanding performance, and it was his explosive energy that gave us a decided edge over United in midfield. With young talent like Adams and Rocastle, I could afford to feel optimistic about the future.

We were beaten only three times in our first twenty-five League games. It was a dream start, but I knew deep down that this team was not good enough to win the championship – and that was the two-year target I had set myself. There was a growing chorus of criticism that I had not made a move into the transfer market, but I was determined not to buy for the sake of it. The players I brought in had to be right. You cannot go out and buy long-term success. First of all you need a strong foundation, and I was determined to build from the bottom. I know there were a few behind-my-back sniggers when I at last made my first buy, paying a modest £65,000 for Perry Groves from Fourth Division Colchester. But Perry, who I had tracked while at Millwall, gave terrific value for the money and did the job I wanted from him.

Despite my telling everybody that we were not yet ready to challenge for the championship, we went into the New Year as First Division leaders and put together a sequence of seventeen League matches without a defeat. It ended in a horrible, bad-tempered way with a 2-0 loss at Old Trafford. The referee, in my opinion, had a poor game. He quite rightly sent off the inexperienced David Rocastle for retaliating, but his out-of-character 'crime' was nothing to what one of the United players was allowed to get away with as he rushed around making dangerously wild tackles. Seven players were booked, and it raised a barrier of bitterness between the two teams that took a long, long time to go away, as a later match would prove.

I had gone to Old Trafford looking forward to meeting for the first time Alex Ferguson, a manager for whom I had tremendous respect. He had worked wonders at Aberdeen before taking over at United in November, 1986, and it was my intention after the match to sit down with him and try to find out what his secret was. I was a real fan. But the bad temper of the match boiled over onto the touchline benches and my first exchanges with Alex were of the industrial language type as we eyeballed each other down the players' tunnel on the way to the dressing-rooms. We later became good pals and could laugh about it, but at the time we were very close to a physical confrontation which was not quite the example we should have been setting. Football has a way of grabbing hold of your emotions and turning perfectly sane men wide-eyed with anger or ecstasy. Joe Mercer summed it up best when he once said to me: 'Football can make you look more ridiculous than drink.' There was perhaps an even more appropriate quote from that great fount of sports wisdom, Vince Lombardi. After a particularly hard and wild match, he said: 'Has this become a game for madmen? And have I become one of them?'

Well the madness had not got to me (yet), and suddenly in my first season back home at Highbury I had Wembley in my sights. Everything I wanted to see from an Arsenal side was revealed against

Tottenham in our Littlewoods Cup semi-final saga in that footballing hotbed of North London where passions can run just as high as in the Manchester, Liverpool and Glasgow derbies. We lost the first leg at Highbury 1-0 to a Clive Allen goal when injuries to David Rocastle and Viv Anderson robbed us of our usual rhythm as we sank to our first home defeat of the season.

In the second leg we were trailing 1-0 at half-time, again to an Allen goal, when we got motivation from an unexpected source. I was just about to give my half-time tactical talk when over the Tannoy we could hear a Tottenham official giving out details of where Spurs supporters could purchase tickets for the Final. His final mocking taunt, which angered every one of our supporters and wound up our players, was: 'Spurs are on their way to Wembley.' They were publicly counting their chickens, or rather their cockerels. My team talk was rendered redundant.The disembodied voice had done a perfect job in giving the Arsenal players the incentive to go out and battle for their pride. Our magnificent second-half performance produced goals from Niall Quinn and Viv Anderson to set up a replay. I tossed with David Pleat for the right to select the venue. He won and, naturally, picked White Hart Lane.

With less than ten minutes to go in a raw, thundering replay we were again 1-0 down to yet another goal from Clive Allen. David Pleat must have been quietly congratulating himself in marking his first season in charge at Tottenham with a visit to Wembley when we came back from the dead for the second time in four days. Charlie Nicholas had come off with a damaged ankle, and I sent on in his place the unsung Ian Allinson, who responded to his sudden unexpected challenge with a low shot that squeezed past goalkeeper Ray Clemence at the near post. The game was into injury time and a penalty shoot-out was looking inevitable when David Rocastle connected with a half-power left foot shot and the ball threaded under the body of the diving Clemence to put us in the lead for the first time in the tie and into the Final at Wembley. It was a famous victory that inspired a chant from our supporters: 'One nil down, two-one up, we knocked Tottenham out of the Cup.' It also spawned the irreverent but widely read fanzine *One Nil Down, Two-One Up* that provides an alternative voice on Arsenal affairs.

I had not been so excited by a victory since another memorable night at White Hart Lane back in 1971 when I was in the Arsenal team that beat Tottenham to set up the League and FA Cup Double. The character and resilience that shone out of my players in those two titanic games gave me my biggest kick since returning home to Highbury. You could almost warm your hands on the team spirit.

Suddenly, in my first season, there was talk of an Arsenal treble – the League championship, the Littlewoods Cup and the FA Cup. But I refused to get sucked in by the runaway optimism because I knew we lacked the necessary goal power. Young Niall Quinn was doing a brave and workmanlike job leading our attack, but – at 6ft 4in – he was such a towering target player that too many of our advances on goal were telegraphed. There was plenty of money in the bank, particularly as I had sold Stewart Robson to West Ham for £700,000, but I was refusing to be lured into paying an inflated price for any newcomers.

As our goals started to dry up, I made enquiries for Kerry Dixon at Chelsea and John Barnes at Watford, but got no encouragement. It was Barnes who played a prominent part in lifting Watford to a 3-1 FA Cup quarter-final win against us, a defeat that left us fuming because the crucial third goal was scored while a linesman was flagging for an Arsenal penalty that was over-ruled by the referee. I dashed home from a club break in Portugal on the March transfer deadline day to clinch the £750,000 signing of Alan Smith from Leicester City, who had only agreed to let me have their quality striker on the understanding that he would stay with them until the end of the season to help their fight against relegation. Other clubs in relegation trouble complained to the Football Association over the arrangement and this scuppered any future loan-back deals.

Liverpool, the club that had given all of us a lead in how to build on success year in and year out, were our opponents in the Littlewoods Cup final at Wembley. Ian Rush, primed for his transfer to Juventus, gave us that sinking feeling when he put Liverpool into the lead in the twenty-third minute. It was his 202nd goal for the Anfield giants, and, astonishingly, they had never failed to win a game in which he scored over a stretch of 145 matches. But again we had the character to come from behind, and we made nonsense of the Rush factor with two

Charlie Nicholas goals. The first came just six minutes after the Rush strike, and Charlie's winner eight minutes from the final whistle was set up by the under-rated Perry Groves, who came on as substitute for the tiring Niall Quinn. Alan Hansen, Liverpool's world-class central defender, later told David O'Leary: 'Our hearts sank when we saw a fresh Groves coming into the game. We were frightened to death of his pace.' And it was Perry's pace that gave Charlie Nicholas the chance to enjoy the greatest moment in his Arsenal career. He thrived on appearing on the Wembley stage, and rose to the occasion in a manner that underlined how great his input to Arsenal could have been with the right commitment.

Thanks to Charlie's two goals – both scored from inside the six-yard box – I had landed my first major trophy as Arsenal manager, and well ahead of the schedule I had set myself. Vice-chairman David Dein was first into the dressing-room after we had paraded the cup to our ecstatic fans. He brought a crate of champagne with him. David really knew how to celebrate.

I had twice been on the losing side with Arsenal in League Cup finals as a player, so this victory tasted sweeter than most. But I did not get carried away. This, I knew, was just going to be the start. I quickly pushed the Littlewoods Cup success out of my mind and put the blinkers back on. I called myself, 'the Scot with tunnel vision.' The toast I proposed with David Dein's champagne was, 'Here's to greater things.'

We slipped to fourth place in the championship race because of our sudden impotence in front of goal, but at the end of the season during which we had led the First Division for twelve weeks I could look back with great satisfaction on what we had achieved. It was time to sit down and take stock after twelve months in which I had hardly paused for breath. First of all I looked at the pluses: goalkeeper John Lukic had been a sound last line of defence, Viv Anderson and Kenny Samson were an exceptional pair of full backs, and David O'Leary and Tony Adams had looked the most formidable centre-back partners in the League. Our black pearls David Rocastle and Paul Davis were full of promise, and Steve Williams had bossed the midfield with skill and determination. Youngsters Niall Quinn and Martin Hayes per-

One of the sweetest moments of my life. It's the night we captured the first League championship at Anfield, and (above) I acknowledge the cheers of the Arsenal fans who managed to drown out the Kop choir. This is one of my favourite pictures (right) as I bring the trophy up the steps past the famous and forbidding 'This is Anfield' sign. That is my daughter Nicole just a step behind.

Herbert Chapman (left) was the legendary Arsenal manager with whom I was always being compared, and this (right) is how I might have looked had I been managing even before Herbert. His bust stands in the marble halls of Highbury, and he greeted me with stony silence (below) when I showed him the first of the two League championship trophies that I won. We had more than managing in common. Herbert served a year in exile back in 1919 following a financial scandal.

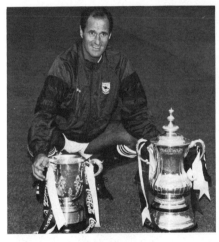

This (top) is when I belonged to Highbury and I felt Highbury belonged to me. It was like a mausoleum when I took over, and during my eight-and-a-half-years the ground was transformed into as fine a stadium as there is in Europe with an all-seater capacity of 39,000. It was the success of the team that helped generate the money to get the refurbishing work done, including the winning of the FA Cup and Coca-Cola Cup (above) and then the European Cup Winner's Cup (right) in successive seasons.

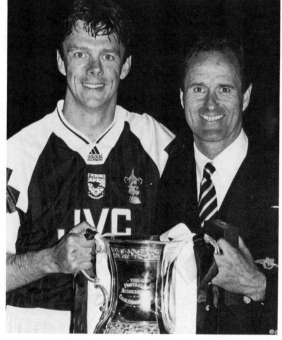

A couple of cups helped to make the 1992-93 season memorable. It was the first time in history that a club had won two domestic cups in the same season. Raising the FA Cup and League Cup with me (above) are, left to right, Tony Adams, Eddie McGoldrick, David Seaman and Ian Wright. Holding the FA Cup with me (right) is Arsenal stalwart David O'Leary, who played a record 558 League games for the club.

Two shots of me at my favourite place of work, on the training ground at London Colney. I am no doubt telling the players (above) that football is as much a thinking game as a physical one. And I am probably working out the tactics for a set-piece situation (right). We prided ourselves on the organisation of our set-pieces, and scored dozens of goals that were plotted at London Colney.

I am flanked here by the best backroom team in the business (above, left to right): Pat Rice, Stewart Houston, Gary Lewin, Theo Foley, Steve Burtenshaw and Terry Murphy. George Armstrong joined the team when that lovely character Theo went off to manage Northampton Town. The players and I got all the plaudits for our success, but we could not have done it without the input of these Highbury loyalists.

Frank McLintock, my best pal in and out of football. He rivalled even Dave Mackay as an inspirational captain. The awards we are holding were presented by Rothmans in 1994 for our achievements in the game.

It was one of my great pleasures while manager at Arsenal to welcome back to Highbury former club skipper Joe Mercer, who had started me off on the football trail when in charge at Aston Villa. Joe was at his old haunt for the opening of the Arsenal museum, and the shield we are holding between us marks the hat-trick of League championship triumphs in the 1930s.

Here I am with the walking, talking legend Bill Shankly, who had twice tried to sign me as a youngster in Bargeddie — first for Huddersfield and then for Liverpool. Shanks and I are pictured at Wembley on the eve of the 1971 FA Cup Final. He was one of the game's great psychologists. 'The pitch looks ver-r-ry slippery,' he said to our goalkeeper Bob Wilson. I wouldnae fancy having to make saves on it.' But Bill's attempt to plant a seed of doubt did not work. We won 2-1 to clinch the double.

Tommy Docherty (above, first left) could have made a living as a comedian. I have never met anybody like him for cracking jokes and getting humour out of any situation. Here he is giving Dickie (now Lord) Attenborough a taste of his humour at Stamford Bridge on the day that Dickie was made vice-President of Chelsea. The players enjoying the Doc's medicine are, left to right, Bobby Tambling, Peter Bonetti, Ken Shellito, Ron Harris and myself. There could not have been a bigger contrast between the Doc and my next manager, Bertie Mee, who is greeting me (right) on my first day at Arsenal. Bertie was a serious-minded, dignified man who was a master at delegation. I will always have enormous respect for him.

The highs and lows of my playing career. It is one of the great days of my life (above) as I check out the Wembley turf with Ray Kennedy (centre) and Charlie George before the FA Cup Final victory over Liverpool in 1970-71. Nine years later it was all over after I had broken a leg in a meaningless tour match in Memphis while with Crystal Palace. 'Steady Eddie' McCreadie (below, left) was manager of the American team, and visited me every day in hospital with a miniature bottle of vodka tucked inside his socks. Cheers, Eddie.

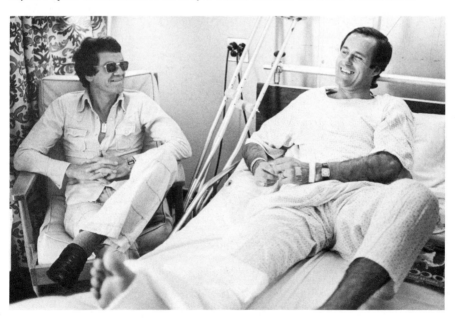

I kiss the hand of His Holiness Pope Paul VI during an audience that he gave to Manchester United's team before a match against Lazio in Rome. Tommy Docherty(centre), a Roman Catholic, described it as the most moving and memorable day of his life. That's the distinctive head of Bobby Charlton in the background. Pope Paul told us: 'Be worthy of imitation by those whose eyes are constantly upon you.'

I am first in line in an all-star line-up being introduced to the Princess of Wales during a charity function in London in 1989. Lined up alongside me are boxer Lloyd Honeyghan, Cliff (now Sir Cliff) Richard, tennis legend Fred Perry and athletics master Sebastian Coe. Tennis has become a new love of mine, and it was a treat to meet the now sadly departed Fred Perry, who told me that Arsenal were the greatest club in the world when he was winning his three successive Wimbledon titles in the 1930s.

On the cheque:

BARCLAYS

3 APRIL 19 91

Pay ARSENAL CHARITABLE TRUST or order

ELEVEN HUNDRED POUNDS £1,100

ISLINGTON FIRE STATION

It is well known that Prime Minister John Major is a Chelsea fan, but he was happy to take part in the presentation of this cheque for the Arsenal Charitable Trust. He told me that he used to regularly watch Chelsea in my playing days at The Bridge. The Duke of Kent (below, centre) makes no secret of the fact that he is an Arsenal supporter, and proudly parades here with the FA Cup and Coca-Cola Cup with skipper Tony Adams and myself.

Two managers I admire above most others. That's my long-time pal Terry Venables (left) after he had won the FA Cup with Tottenham in the same 1990-91 season that I captured a second League championship with Arsenal. Below, I am trying to steal the Premiership trophy from Manchester United boss Alex Ferguson. Our teams had their ups and downs, but I never lost my admiration for Alex and his managerial know-how.

formed better than I had a right to expect taking into account their lack of experience. Hayes, in particular, performed above himself for much of the season and emerged as our top goal scorer. Perry Groves also gave some sparkling performances considering that he had made the giant step up from the Fourth Division. Charlie Nicholas and Graham Rix both had an up and down season, mainly because of injury problems, but they had applied themselves well and Charlie had popped up with some crucial goals. The one big minus was a failure to put the finishing touch to good approach work, and this is where I was looking to Alan Smith to make a major difference.

By the time the following season came around I had bought Nigel Winterburn from Wimbledon for £350,000 and sold Viv Anderson to Manchester United for a tribunal-set fee of £250,000. I give the background to many of the transfers that I negotiated in the 'Exile's Files' chapter. One player who does not feature is centre-forward Kerry Dixon, but it was not for the want of trying. I made four determined bids to buy him from Chelsea, but I was never able to clinch a deal for a player who, at his peak, would have made an ideal partner for Alan Smith. I actually once got Chelsea manager John Hollins, my old Stamford Bridge team-mate, to agree to sell him, but then chairman Ken Bates returned from a summer holiday and called it off.

The Arsenal board were so pleased with my first year in charge that Peter Hill-Wood gave me a new five-year contract at a salary of £80,000, with incentive bonuses for any trophies that I could land. I had an added spur, so to speak, when my old pal Terry Venables moved in down the road at Tottenham for what would become an eventful reign as first the manager and then chief executive. Our friendship was in no way dented, but we became more cautious in our conversations because we were eyeing the same players. I was, for instance, very keen on Terry Fenwick, who both Terry and I knew well as a fine competitive player at Crystal Palace and then Queen's Park Rangers. Terry beat me to his signature just to underscore the fact that while he was my friend he was also a considerable rival.

Charlie Nicholas, who only fleetingly reached the standards that I expected of him, returned to Scotland with Aberdeen, and I strengthened the squad by buying Lee Dixon from Stoke City, Kevin

Richardson from Watford and Brian Marwood from Sheffield Wednesday for a total outlay of less than one and a half million pounds.

It was a strange, and ultimately frustrating second season in charge. We produced an impressive winning run of fourteen League and cup matches, and reached the final of the Littlewoods Cup for a second successive year. Good judges were tipping us for the championship when we led the First Division for three weeks in November, but we lost our momentum and finished a disappointing sixth.

I got a taste of appearing in front of an FA disciplinary committee when I was fined £250 for having a go at the referee during our goal-less draw at Oxford. Referees have never been my favourite people, and I have a low tolerance threshold with them. In a way they have my sympathy because they are being turned into robots by FIFA direc-tives that demand a set course of action regardless of common-sense. All I ask of referees is that they work within the spirit of the game, making decisions with discretion. Too many of them ignore the fact that the rule book allows them an opinion. They continually take the easy way out by flashing a yellow card when a well-chosen word in the ear would quickly bring a situation under control.

I remember referees like Jim Finney, Gordon Hill, Jack Taylor, Ken Dagnall, Kevin Howley, Tommy Dawes and Leo Callaghan in my playing day who would chat to you during a game. 'Do that again, and you're in the book,' they would say. They no longer seem quite so human, and the days of Britain having the best referees are long gone. The finest now are to be found in Europe, and particularly in Holland.

After Philip Don, one of our most respected referees, had sent off Tony Adams for an innocuous so-called professional foul, I wrote a letter of complaint to the Football Association, and made the point that he had treated Tony as if he were a headmaster. In their reply, the FA showed a rare sense of humour by adding a PS: 'Oh by the way, Mr Don *is* a headmaster.'

The edge went off our game in my second season following a last-minute defeat by Luton in a nail-biting thriller of a Littlewoods Cup final. The turning point of the match came when the usually reliable Nigel Winterburn had a second-half penalty saved by reserve goalkeeper Andy Dibble. That would have given us a two-goal lead and a stranglehold on the trophy, but the save gave Luton a tremendous confidence boost and they lifted their game. All credit to Luton – 1-0 leaders at half-time – for the way they battled back and snatched a late winner through Brian Stein. It was the sort of see-sawing match that puts years on managers, but I had the satisfaction of being at Wembley for the second time in my two years in charge at Highbury. We also gave a good account of ourselves in the FA Cup before going down 2-1 to Brian Clough's Nottingham Forest in the quarter-finals.

While I was getting it right at Highbury, my private life was becoming a tangled mess. I was giving so much of my time and concentration to Arsenal that I could not see the approaching storm in my marriage. Marie was unable to raise any enthusiasm for football. She preferred her own pursuits and hobbies to the game that was my life, and more and more we were going our separate ways.

A divorce became inevitable. It was a painful and bitter break-up, and as I look back I would say that Arsenal Football Club was the real co-respondent. I have happy memories of most of the twenty years we spent together before I became too wrapped up in my job to recognise that a wall of indifference was developing between us. Marie did a marvellous job bringing up our great kids, Nicole and Daniel, while I was throwing myself into my new career as first a coach and then a manager. I cannot claim to have always been a dutiful husband and father, but when Marie, Nicole and Daniel read this book I hope they will understand that I loved them and, thank God, out of the wreckage of my marriage I have managed to secure a close relationship with both my daughter and son. That means more to me than anything.

Somehow I managed to stay sane during what was the most difficult period of my life. The strain showed in a worrying loss of weight. I lost a stone during the months leading up to the divorce, and it was my tight band of close friends who helped me through the bad times with their company and their advice. The biggest rock for me was my business manager John Hazell, who has been my guide and comforter through the pain of the divorce and also the despair of my split with Arsenal and the surrounding controversy. With good friends like John and my total concentration on making Arsenal a lasting force in football, I was able to battle through the domestic minefield that was much of my own making. I was also lucky to have in Carmen, my Spanish housekeeper, somebody who was completely loyal and trustworthy. *Muchos gracias, Carmen.*

I have always believed in trying to keep my private life private, and even here in my autobiography I do not feel it right that I should open up about the ladies in my life. I have too much respect for them to name names. What has angered me is the way the press continually pry into any relationship I might have, even though I am now a single man. It is nobody's business but mine and whichever lady I might be with.

Football is my real mistress, and I miss her greatly now that I am in enforced exile. But I shall have her back. We cannot resist each other.

While my marriage was breaking up, I had become a man obsessed ... obsessed with Arsenal Football Club and with trying to win the top domestic prize: the League championship.

10 : The First Championship

Summer 1989: Everything's coming up roses. Now is the time for summer pruning and dead-heading, which means the removal of faded blooms. When cutting blooms from established roses, it is important to make a sloping cut above a leaf to encourage new shoots. One rose fades; another takes its place. One player goes; another takes his place.

IF I live to be a hundred, I know that I will never experience a moment or a match quite like the one in which Arsenal clinched their first championship under my management. Not even a Hollywood screenwriter with an over-active imagination or the Roy of the Rovers creator could have conjured a climax to equal it. The title was not only decided by virtually the last kick of the match but also by the last kick of the season. That was dramatic enough, but the fact that it happened at, of all places, Anfield made it even more unbelievable. This was the work of the great scriptwriter in the sky.

To understand the full impact of winning the title at Anfield you need to know just what Liverpool means to me and to most professionals in the game. Bill Shankly was just turning them into the premier club in the land when I arrived in England to start my career, and over the next thirty years I got a close-up view, first as a player and then as a manager, of the conveyor belt of outstanding teams turned out by Liverpool. Manchester United had more glamour, Leeds were exceptional for a short span and Arsenal, Tottenham, Manchester City, Forest and Everton had their moments, but none of them could match Liverpool for consistency. They were the club I unashamedly set out to copy when I arrived back at Arsenal as manager. I did not want a team of five-minute wonders. I wanted to build a Shankly-style dynasty.

So you can imagine the Everest facing us when we went to Anfield for the last match of the 1988-89 season with the championship within reach of both Liverpool and Arsenal. We needed to win by two clear goals to clinch the title on goal difference. Kenny Dalglish, who had impressively carried on the Liverpool tradition of Shanks and Bob Paisley, had the cushion of knowing that even if his team lost by the odd goal the championship was staying on Merseyside, where Everton had been the defending champions in an earthquaking season. There was heavy emotion written into the tapestry of this match in a million. The city of Liverpool was still weighed down with mourning in the wake of the terrible Hillsborough tragedy on 15 April when ninety-five spectators were killed in a crowd crush during the Liverpool-Forest FA Cup semi-final. The Liverpool team were paying their respects to the memory of their fans in the way they knew best: by winning matches and trophies.

On 20 May, two extra-time goals by Ian Rush had lifted Liverpool to an exciting 3-2 victory over Everton in the FA Cup Final. Now, just six days later, they had the Double in their sights for the second time in three seasons, and the media statisticians were falling over themselves to point out that Arsenal had lost their last seven matches at Anfield, and that we had not scored two goals in one game there in fifteen years. Eighteen years earlier it had been Liverpool standing between Arsenal and the League-and-FA Cup double. We came from behind to win at Wembley in what was the last season that Arsenal had won the championship. In my first year as manager at Highbury we had come from behind to beat Liverpool in the Littlewoods Cup final. It was against Liverpool that I had made a goal-scoring League debut for Aston Villa. I had Liverpool coming out of my ears.

Kenny Dalglish was bringing his team into the showdown at Anfield on the back of an express train 24-match unbeaten run, while we were in danger of coming off the rails after leading the First Division table since a Boxing Day victory at Charlton. We should have sewn up the title before travelling to Anfield, but nerves got the better of what was a relatively young and inexperienced team and we picked up only one point from our final two home games against Derby and Wimbledon. Almost to a man, the media wrote us off as having little or no chance at Liverpool. The bookmakers were offering 16-1 against Arsenal winning 2-0.

This, then, was the backdrop to the most vital team talk I had given in my fairly short managerial career. Everything I said and did in the build-up to the game was designed to take the pressure off my players. Our training was much more relaxed than usual, and I encouraged a light-hearted, jokey climate far removed from the usual seriousness with which I like to tackle training.

The one dampener came twenty-four hours before the match when Paul Merson was banned from driving for eighteen months on a drink-driving charge. I used it as a lesson for all the players that they needed to be sensible with their drinking. Paul had been properly punished, and promised that he would watch his drinking in future. There is only so much a manager or a club can do to control the social lives of their players. They are adults earning an awful lot of money, and you can only try to teach them how to behave responsibly. You cannot be with them twenty-four hours a day, and you have to trust them to try to avoid the temptations that come their way, particularly in a vast city like London. There were going to be a lot more headaches coming my way from Paul, but I could not help liking the boy with his engaging smile and easy-going personality. Only Paul could have got away with having his untidy thatch of fair hair, making him look as if he had been dragged through a hedge backwards. He was a superstitious lad, and every time I told him to get his hair cut he pointed out that Arsenal had not lost since his last cut. I am in no way superstitious, but I thought I had better go along with him just in case!

That explains why Paul had his hair down close to his shoulders when we left by coach from our London Colney training headquarters at breakfast-time on the Friday morning of the match. The atmosphere on board was so laid-back you would have thought we were going off on a short holiday rather than on the most important football trip of our lives. David O'Leary had helped put us in the right frame of mind by telling us that it was the sixth birthday of his son, John. 'I've told him that I shall be bringing him back a championship medal as a present,' he said. 'So don't be letting him down lads.'

David sat at the back of the coach playing a friendly card game of hearts with Tony Adams, Niall Quinn and Brian Marwood, who was out of the match with injury but remained an important member of the squad because of his confident manner. The rest of the lads dozed, listened to their Walkmans or read the newspapers. We would usually have a video of the opposition on board to watch during the journey, but on this occasion I wanted the players to forget about who we were playing. 'Look at this headline,' said David Rocastle, holding up the *Daily Mirror* that shouted: 'ARSENAL DO NOT HAVE A PRAYER'.

I think it was Paul Merson who called out from the back, 'Let us pray...' The lads were also wound up by an article in the *Sun* by Graeme Souness, who was manager at Rangers at the time and was completely dismissive of us. It all worked in our favour and made us more determined to prove everybody wrong.

We were settled into our hotel in the centre of Liverpool by lunchtime, and I sent all the players to their rooms to relax. They were down for a light tea of toast and honey at five o'clock, and then I told the waiters to leave us alone and to shut the doors behind them. There we were, the enemy, right in the heart of Liverpool as I delivered this team talk that came from the top of my head and the bottom of my heart:

'You are just a couple of hours away from the match of your lives, and you are in the perfect position of having nothing to lose and everything to gain. The press and all the know-alls on television and radio have written you off. According to them, you have not got a hope in hell. But I know, and you know, differently. All the pressure tonight is going to be on Liverpool. They will not be able to breathe out there for the weight of expectancy. Their fans, the media and probably even some of their players think the title is in the bag. The television cameras will be bringing the game live to the nation, and all the viewers at home will be sitting there expecting to see a Liverpool victory. If we don't win the title, we can still walk proudly away from Anfield saying what a great season we've had. It's the best season since we all got together, and it's going to get even better. But just think, if we win the title tonight. That will really shove it down the throats of all those people who shout "Boring Boring Arsenal".

'I'm lucky because I've played in an Arsenal team that has won the championship. I promise you there's nothing quite like it, and you can experience that feeling tonight. Liverpool will expect us to go out looking for an early goal, but I am more concerned that we don't *concede* an early goal. So what I want us to do is play it very tight in the first-half. We will have David sweeping up behind Tony and Steve at the back, and I would like you, Lee and Nigel, to be pretty cautious about breaking forward for the first half hour or so. Let's be nice and patient. I will be quite happy to see it at 0-0 at half-time because that will put added pressure on them for the second-half. Paul and Alan, you will find it quite lonely up front but if you could nick a goal just before half-time then that would really turn the screws on them. But I stress again that more important than scoring in the first-half, we must do our best not to let in a goal. We must not get in a position where we are having to score four goals.

'I want you, David, Mickey and Kevin, to close down on any Liverpool player in possession in midfield. Don't give them the time or the space to get their passing movements going. Liverpool like to play with rhythm, so we must make sure they are disjointed by deny-ing them space and the opportunity to start stringing passes together. If it's goalless at half-time and then we can score early in the second-half, I think you will find Liverpool falling apart under the pressure. You will I reckon then have twenty-five minutes or so to get the sec-ond goal, and then Liverpool will be forced to come out and I predict that we will win this one 3-0 (wrong, George!). Just remember, what-ever happens out there tonight I am proud of what you have achieved this season. Go out and play without fear because you've got nothing to lose. But just think of what there is to gain. Good luck lads, and thanks for all you've done to get us this close to the championship.'

It was hardly Churchillian stuff (Winston and I shared the same birthday, not the same vocabulary), but you needed to be there to know that I had touched a chord with the players. There was a light coming from their eyes that radiated confidence and determination (although my 3-0 prediction was greeted with raised eyebrows that suggested they thought the Boss might have gone potty). I would think the only equivalent to the camaraderie we felt at that moment must be when a general sends his troops into battle. There was a spe-cial, unbreakable bond between us, and all the players were ready to fight for each other. We walked tall out of our hotel and reboarded the coach for the twenty minute police-escorted run to 'Fortress Anfield'.

There were still more than seventy minutes to go before the kick-off when we arrived, but Anfield was already jammed with singing, chanting fans. Our outnumbered supporters were managing to com-pete with the famous Kop choir. We immediately went down the steps past the huge board with the legend 'This Is Anfield' and out onto the pitch. 'Boring Boring Arsenal' was the instant welcome from the Kop as we inspected a ground that was firm and in excellent condition considering this was the final match of the season. 'Arsenal, champions' was the premature and hopefully prophetic response from our fans. I am often asked whether vocal support can lift a team. The answer is an emphatic 'yes', just as a crowd getting on the backs of their players can have an adverse effect. When supporters are right behind you, it is all part and parcel of that camaraderie we felt in the hotel. The Anfield crowd are reckoned to be worth a goal start to their team, but that had been cancelled out by the tremendous support from the travelling army of Highbury fans. We were not walking alone. They also serve who only stand and shout (or sit and shout in all-seater stadia!).

In the dressing-room all the jokes and banter of the early part of the day were now buried in the pre-match tension. There is little a manager can do or say at this point because the concentration of the players is focused totally on the game, and by now they know exactly what is expected of them. I just repeated my main message: 'You have nothing to lose. Go out there and do all the right things well. You need not play with any fear. Just keep it nice and tight and be patient. Deny them space and don't let them grab an early goal. Good luck.' I then handed over to skipper Tony Adams to make his usual forthright final demands. 'We've come this far, lads, and we're not letting the title slip now,' he said, smacking a fist into the palm of his hand. 'They've all written us off. Now let's get out there and prove them all wrong. Let's go!' There may have been an expletive or two in there somewhere as our fiercely committed captain brandished his fist, winding up his team-mates with the common industrial language of football. Tony is not a wordsmith, but he has such presence and self-belief that players are instantly inspired by him. He is a real man's captain. Only a team player who has been involved in a major event can understand the sense of togetherness that sends the dressing-room temperature soaring in the moments before going out for the kick-off. It's an indescribable feeling, but you can almost reach out and touch it. It's a combination of harmony, brotherhood and a desire to do well not only for one's self but for each other. In short, it's team spirit and that is what I had worked on introducing into the dressing-room from the first moment I returned home to Highbury.

As the players prepared to leave the dressing-room, I shook each of them by the hand and they were all shaking hands with each other on their way to the door. They looked a little uncomfortable as they were each handed a bouquet of flowers, which were to be presented to the Liverpool fans as a mark of respect following the Hillsborough disaster. We also donated a cheque for £30,000 to the appeal fund. As I walked out into the corridor I caught a brief glimpse of Kenny Dalglish. He was wearing his usual weather-proof Liverpool jacket. I was in my Arsenal blazer and club tie. Sixteen years earlier we had been in the same Tommy Docherty-selected Scotland teams. Now we wanted to see each other beaten into the ground. We briefly waved to each other across the corridor, and quietly wished each other luck (neither of us meaning it). He looked much more strained than I felt. I can rarely recall feeling so confident about a game. Building a team is like putting together a jigsaw puzzle, and I knew that all my pieces were in place.

I made my way up to the centre stand and took my place in the directors' box alongside Peter Hill-Wood and David Dein. The tension was etched much more into their faces than that of the players. 'We're going to be all right,' I said. 'We've got the game plan to cause a major upset.' I like to sit in the stand to watch at least the first-half of a game because you get a better overall picture of the action, and it is easier to take notes and work out tactics. At away games I desperately missed the telephone intercom system that had been fitted for me at Highbury where I could make direct, instant contact with Theo Foley or Stewart Houston on the touchline bench.

Everything went perfectly to plan in the first-half of what was to be one of the most dramatic matches in footballing history, and we just shaded it without having any luck in front of goal. Steve Bould frightened the life out of Liverpool early in the game when his header was cleared off the line by Steve Nicol, but it was goalless at half-time, which suited me down to the ground. You could already see Liverpool getting the jitters. So much was expected from them, and they were struggling to produce anything like their usual flowing form. This was because of a mixture of the pressure on them, and the way we were working like beavers to make sure they did not have time to breathe on the ball let alone bring it under control. They had expected us to come out looking for an early goal and played a strangely, for them, restrictive game. I am sure, in hindsight, Kenny Dalglish will have wished he had ordered his team to go out to win rather than try to avoid a two-goal defeat. It was not the prettiest first-half of football seen at Anfield, but it was beautiful to my eye.

The players were trooping into the dressing-room by the time I got back downstairs at the end of the first-half. There was not a lot I needed to say. 'We can be more positive and adventurous for the opening twenty minutes of the second-half,' I said. 'Lee and Nigel, if the opportunity presents itself push right forward and get your crosses in from the flanks. David and Mickey, come through on support runs whenever you feel it's right. I want us to bring Alan and Paul more into the game now because it's important we try to get an early goal. If we get one, I know the second will follow. This could be the greatest forty-five minutes of your lives. Good luck.'

Our physio Gary Lewin was doing his usual thorough job massaging life back into tired limbs, and Theo Foley was going round to each individual player and whispering words of encouragement. Everybody was playing their part in what was a tremendous team effort.

There was the ritual hand shaking and back-slapping on the way out for the second-half. This time I followed the players down the steps past the 'This Is Anfield' notice that Bill Shankly had put up to try to frighten the life out of the opposition. For many players it had the opposite effect because it gave them a sense of occasion and made them lift their game (not that I would have ever dared say that to Shanks's face). I took my place on the touchline bench alongside Theo. From being in the stand, it's as different down on the line as being at the wheel after sitting on top in a bus. You are nose-to-nose with the action, and it is sometimes difficult to get a proper perspective of what is happening. You also tend to get emotionally involved, which is something you control when you are sitting in the stand. I was soon joining Theo in shouting myself hoarse with instructions which, if truth is known, the players can rarely hear because of the din of the crowd. But the shouting gives you a sense of involvement, and an animated manager and coach on the line can make even the laziest player increase his effort and commitment. Not that any of the Arsenal players needed lifting in this match. I had rarely seen such concentrated effort in all my years in the game.

The early second-half goal that we desperately needed came in controversial circumstances, or at least that's how the Liverpool players and Kenny Dalglish interpreted it. Referee David Hutchinson awarded an indirect free-kick in the 52nd minute after Liverpool skipper Ronnie Whelan had fouled David Rocastle. Nigel Winterburn floated in a free-kick and Alan Smith guided the ball into the net with a delicate glancing header. The referee was surrounded by protesting Liverpool players and a fuming Kenny Dalglish came running from the touchline bench area to join in the argument. They were insisting that the ball had gone straight into the net from an indirect free-kick, but there was no doubt whatsoever in my mind that Smudger had got a touch. He is one of the most honest people I have met, and it was good enough for me when he claimed the goal, which was his twenty-fifth of the season and his twenty-third in the League. All this despite missing two matches with a fractured cheekbone. What a buy he had proved to be. Thanks Smudger.

One more goal and the title was ours, provided we did not allow them to score. It's a simple old game! We were having to play an attacking game, yet somehow remembering to keep things tight at the back. Suddenly I found being perched on the touchline bench was like sitting on a barbed-wire fence.

With just fifteen minutes left and Liverpool beginning to shut up shop, Mickey Thomas was put through by Kevin Richardson. It was a golden opportunity but he snatched at his shot and the ball was comfortably smothered by Bruce Grobbelaar. That was the only time during the game when I felt a sinking moment of despair. Little did we know that for Thomas this was just a dress rehearsal.

I needed to send on a fresh pair of legs, and gave Martin Hayes a brief to attack down the left wing as I sent him on for Paul Merson. Then, with just minutes left and Liverpool within sight of the title, I went for broke and pulled off Steve Bould so that Perry Groves could join our desperate attack.

The game (and the season) was into its final minute when Kevin Richardson went down with cramp. As Gary Lewin ran on to massage him, I noticed the Liverpool bench were congratulating each other as if they had got the title won; and out on the pitch John Barnes and

John Aldridge gave each other the high-fives as if their night's work was done. On the restart it was Barnes who collected the ball, and instead of doing the old pro's time-wasting trick of aiming for the corner flag he decided to try to dribble inside. Richardson, dragging his cramped leg, somehow managed to dispossess him and pushed the ball back to our goalkeeper John Lukic. He threw the ball immediately to Lee Dixon, who transferred it into the path of Alan Smith. There were ninety-two minutes showing on the clock when Smudger passed the ball ahead of the galloping Mickey Thomas in the centre of the pitch and deep inside Liverpool territory. Even though Mickey was going flat out, it was all as if it was in a slow-motion action replay as he moved wide of the oncoming Steve Nicol. The ball came off Nicol's outstretched boot back into Mickey's path and as he zeroed in on Bruce Grobbelaar I think everybody either stopped breathing (if you were for Liverpool) or shouted 's-h-o-o-t' (if you were for Arsenal). Mickey was as calm as if in a five-a-side practice session as he dipped his shoulder to send Grobbelaar one way while shooting the goal of a lifetime. I had been telling everybody that the championship would go right down to the wire, but this was ridiculous!

There was just time for Mickey to perform one of his gymnastic somersaults before he was engulfed by celebrating team-mates. Theo and I were going demented on the touchline trying to make everybody keep their concentration. Anybody who recalls the final three-goal minutes of the 1979 Arsenal-Manchester United FA Cup final will know that a game is not over until it's over. Liverpool kicked off and a dash for goal was halted by, of all people, Mickey Thomas who tested my blood pressure by dribbling it back towards our penalty area. The football purist in me disappeared into the night air as I screamed, 'Whack it away!' But, cool-as-you-like, Mickey played the ball back to goalkeeper John Lukic as the final whistle signalled that the championship once again belonged to Arsenal.

I have a store of photographic images in my memory of the crazy, chaotic scenes that followed. There was David O'Leary, in his fourteenth year as an Arsenal player, unable to hold back the tears, and saying, 'I've got my son his birthday present.' There was Kenny Dalglish, with a face so long and hard that you could have broken a pick axe handle on it, being sporting enough to say, 'Well done,

George.' There were the Liverpool players, some flat on their backs, others on their haunches, shattered by their defeat; and in contrast small chains of Arsenal players hugging and kissing each other like consenting adults. I made a vain attempt to make the players act with some decorum and dignity because I was still deeply aware of the Hillsborough disaster, but this was one night when you could not begrudge them their celebrations. (Dear old Joe Mercer used to preach that you should treat victory and defeat with the same dignity, but I think even Joe would have found it hard to contain himself in an atmosphere that had suddenly made Anfield sound more like Highbury.) There was the moment when proud Tony Adams collected the championship trophy, and held it up with a flourish towards the Press box where the reporters who had written us off were composing 'Arsenal Miracle' stories. Tony must have been hoping that the reporter who had a few weeks earlier so insensitively labelled him a donkey might have been skulking behind his typewriter. There was the wildly untidy team photographs out in the middle of the Anfield pitch, while we all – myself included – joined in the Arsenal songs being poured out by our deliriously happy fans. There was the marvellously sporting response from the Liverpool fans who generously applauded our lap of honour and gave us a special version of 'You'll Never Walk Alone' plus joke-only 'Boring Boring Arsenal' chants. The warm reception from the Liverpool supporters made nonsense of the attempt by Anfield officials to stop the trophy presentation being carried out on the pitch. All credit to Barclays chairman Sir John Quinton, who insisted that Arsenal deserved to have the presentation made in public and not behind closed doors. Best of all of my memories, there was the moment when my daughter, Nicole, and son, Daniel, managed to get on to the pitch from their stand seats for a quiet cuddle that meant more to me than anything. It was proof, if proof was needed, that out of the wreckage of my broken marriage I had managed to retain their love and support.

Brian Moore, who had commentated on the 'live' match for ITV, looked as whacked as any of the players. 'I have never known a finish like it,' he said. 'It has to go down as one of the greatest televised football moments of all time.'

Back in the dressing-room we started a long night of champagne toasts, with David Dein leading us into the party spirit. Liverpool players Peter Beardsley and Bruce Grobbelaar swallowed their bitter disappointment enough to come in to congratulate us. It was a gesture greatly appreciated by all of the Arsenal squad, even though Bruce could only bring himself to say through a fixed grin: 'Sod the lot of you!' I went round and shook the hand of every player, not needing to say anything. They had done exactly what I had asked of them, and every one was a hero. This included Brian Marwood and Paul Davis, both of whom were unlucky to have their season spoiled by injury. It was particularly aggravating for Paul, who picked up a thigh strain just minutes after being told he had been called up for the first time by England. Had he been fit, it is unlikely that Mickey Thomas would have made the starting line-up. Fate's a funny thing.

We saw to it that Paul, Brian and everybody on the Arsenal staff were made to feel part of our celebrations, and the coach trip back to London was one of the most memorable of our lives. We were accompanied the entire way by a convoy of Arsenal fans honking their horns. The players disappeared into the night on our return, and I later learned they had danced and sung the night away at a club called, appropriately, Winners. I went off home alone, made myself a hot drink and then climbed into bed feeling totally drained. As I drifted off to sleep I was warmed by the thought that I was only the eighth person to win the League championship as both a player and manager.

I was in illustrious company. The previous seven had been Ted Drake (Arsenal player, Chelsea manager), Joe Mercer (Everton and Arsenal player, Manchester City manager), Bill Nicholson (Tottenham, player and manager), Bob Paisley (Liverpool, player and manager), Dave Mackay (Tottenham player, Derby manager), Howard Kendall (Everton, player and manager) and Kenny Dalglish (Liverpool, player and manager). To have my name linked with theirs gave me a quiet feeling of pride that money could not buy.

The Boy from Bargeddie slept soundly.

It was with great sadness that I learned the morning after our title triumph that one of the great managers, Don Revie, had died on the very day that we won the championship. Don had succumbed to motor neurone disease at the age of sixty-one, a tragic end for a man who was

untouchable at his peak as a club manager. The Leeds United team
that he built in the 1960s won few friends with the ferociousness of
some of their football. But once they calmed down and concentrated
on making the most of their skill I reckon they were just about the best
English club side I had ever seen. The team featuring the midfield balance and brilliance of Bremner and Giles, the thrust of Clarke and
Jones, the shooting velocity of Lorimer, the skill of Eddie Gray, the
forbidding strength of Charlton and Hunter, the full-back mastery of
Reaney and Cooper and the all-round talent of Madeley was just about
as good a combination as you could get.

It was all pieced together by Revie, who was a grand master of
organisation. He was nowhere near as effective as an England manager when he missed the day-to-day involvement with his players, but
there have been very few in his class at club level. I cannot say it was
a pleasure to play against his team, but it is a privilege now to say that
I was on the same pitch. They were something very special, and Don
Revie must get the credit for masterminding their incredible run of
success and near-misses.

The League championship was won on the playing fields of London
Colney. They are the training headquarters of Arsenal, owned by
University College Hospital and tucked away just off the M25 on the
Greater London/Hertfordshire borders. It was at London Colney that
the plans were laid, the tactics and playing patterns practised and per-
fected and our style and team-spirit created.

As I sit out my enforced exile, the thing I miss most of all are the
training and coaching sessions. I feel as frustrated as a pianist who
finds every piano-lid locked. In my eight years as Arsenal manager,
you could count the training days I missed on the fingers of a one-
armed bandit. The training pitch was like a second home to me, and I
got more job satisfaction there than at the ground on match-days. I
always worked with the first-team players, and would call in the
reserves and youth team players when I wanted opposition against
which to experiment. After the pre-season strength and stamina work,
most of our attention during the playing months would be on tactics
and skills and I would see to it that each player had a ball to work
with. This might sound an odd thing to say to an outsider, but there are

managers – mainly from the old school – who prefer their players to be starved of the ball so that they are hungry for it come match day. That is not a theory that I have ever subscribed to, and that's going right the way back to my Bargeddie days when I used to spend hours working on my ball control.

My main concentration, particularly in my first three seasons in charge, was on getting the back four working as a unit. It's half the battle if you can get your defence right. It is pointless having a team that is great on the eye going forward if you are going to keep leaking goals at the other end. I liked the way Dave Sexton used to put it: 'A boxer always pulls back his fist before throwing a punch and a gun-fighter always pulls back the trigger before firing a shot.' That sums it up nicely. I wanted a team that could pull back and then rifle forward on the counter attack.

So it was vital that I got the back four working in harmony. First of all it was Viv Anderson, Tony Adams, David O'Leary and Kenny Sansom, and they could not believe how hard I worked them to ensure they were covering each other properly and taking the right positions for deadball situations. The back line formation later became Lee Dixon, Tony Adams, Steve Bould and Nigel Winterburn, and I worked them into the ground until they had perfected zonal marking. I would sometimes use a pitch-width rope that the players would hold on to as they tugged and pulled each other while they disciplined themselves to staying in their zone. Then I would release one of the full-backs, and the remaining three players had to stay attached to the rope and take on responsibility for covering a wider zone with lateral movement.

The reward for all the strenuous work came on match days when they proved themselves time and again to be the finest back four in the League. We also worked extremely hard on set-piece attacking and defending situations. While I was at Millwall we were able to use the same ploy several times in a season without being rumbled, but the extensive television coverage of our Arsenal matches meant we needed many more permutations for set-piece play, particularly from free-kicks.

During our first championship season I experimented with a sweeper system that is much more common on the continent than in

British football. I introduced it against Manchester United at Old Trafford with eight matches to go, and at the back of my mind was the crucial contest with Liverpool when I knew I would want to play a spare man at the back. With Brian Marwood out injured, I took the opportunity to bring in David O'Leary and played him in a shuttle role behind Tony Adams and Steve Bould.

I could not fathom the way it was reported by some critics. They described the new formation as 5-3-2, and accused me of being too negative and defence minded. What they failed to realise is that the new system gave those fine exponents of over-lapping play, Lee Dixon and Nigel Winterburn, scope for more positive work in support of the attack. They could move forward safe in the knowledge that David O'Leary was there to cover for them. It also allowed Rocky Rocastle greater freedom to push forward, and to all those critics who claimed we were too defensive during that first championship season just let me remind them that Arsenal were top scorers in the First Division with seventy-three goals. If I had to describe the formation it was 1-2-5-2, with six of the players encouraged to be attack-minded. The sweeper system was an experiment that worked well.

The general style that I developed was a 4-4-2 system not unlike that perfected by Liverpool and Everton, and which was flourished by the outstanding AC Milan team of the last decade. Rinus Michels, mastermind of the exceptional Ajax team of the 1970s, was one of the pioneers of what I call 'the pressing game'. Put simply, it meant that if the opposition had the ball our nearest player would press down on the man in possession while his team-mates pressed any opponent who might be in a position to receive a pass. When we had the ball, our players pressed forward to find the space where they could receive a pass. If we lost the ball, it was imperative that we try to win it back as early as possible and, ideally, in the opponents' half. This is where our midfield players, David Rocastle, Mickey Thomas and Kevin Richardson, came into their own with the pressing game, and one of the major reasons for our success was the speed with which we would win the ball back. There was such a great camaraderie in the team that everybody worked to support each other on and off the ball, and this sharing of the workload meant we developed an unbeatable team spirit.

It was important that they should all understand the squad system, and that they had to accept that there was fierce competition for places. Nobody had a divine right to be in the team. I have often been accused of being anti 'the star' player. That is nonsense. There is nothing I like better than to see a beautifully poised and skilful player dictating a game, but no matter how talented and worshipped he may be he has to work for the team when the opposition has the ball. Liverpool are the prime example of a team in which every player is prepared to work for the good of the team rather than his own selfish means. They have had plenty of world-class stars, but they have always happily accepted that the team is more important than the individual. This has been the secret of their success, and I was making it work for Arsenal. I needed players who helped to win matches, not just decorate them.

I also wanted a team that would not easily cave in under pressure. The 'southern softies' jibes could never be aimed at Arsenal during my days in charge at Highbury. We were never a dirty side, but opponents did not relish playing against us because we had players who knew how to mark and how to tackle, and they would never surrender. We developed our championship-winning style behind closed doors at London Colney, and the Press were peeved that I would not allow them in to watch our training sessions. I demanded privacy because I wanted nothing affecting our concentration, and there was no knowing what some of the more imaginative reporters might have found to write about. To me, the training ground is sacrosanct and should never be open house for photographers and reporters. It is where the vital match-winning work is done, and it needs to be in private. How would the reporters like it if I stood looking over their shoulder while they were trying to write? There was a section of the Press that seemed anti-Arsenal and anti-George Graham. I made it work in our favour by building on the 'them v. us' scenario that they had created, and I used to stick every knocking headline on the players' notice board to help motivate them. The 'Boring Boring' headlines used to have the best effect.

Henry Ford had a saying: 'The secret of success is being ready.' I understand exactly what he meant, and I have always been a great believer in getting everything properly organised. I am meticulous with my planning, and we never went into a game without the players having total knowledge of the individual strengths and weaknesses of the opposition. Whenever possible I made personal checks on the opponents, and I also had one of the best 'spies' in the business in Steve Rowley, who worked with our youth side and on match days went out as an opposition assessor. His reports were always superbly written and gave an in-depth assessment of each team that he watched.

Steve was a member of what I rated the best backroom team in the League. Theo Foley had a warm, infectious personality to go with his enthusiastic approach to every job, and it was one of the hardest tasks I ever faced when I needed to tell him that I wanted to promote Stewart Houston as my righthand coach. Terry Murphy was in charge of youth development and he and our chief scout Steve Burtenshaw must take a lot of the credit for the fact that six of our regular first team squad were home-bred players. Pat Rice and Geordie Armstrong helped bring the young players along in the best Arsenal traditions, and in physiotherapist Gary Lewin we had an exceptional master of medical matters. Gary, who did not quite make the grade as a goal-keeper, switched his attention to the world of treating injuries and he is one of the few qualified chartered physios in the League. There were raised eyebrows when I brought Geordie Armstrong in as reserve team coach, leaving Pat Rice in charge of the youth team. What non-footballing people did not realise is that I considered Pat's job extremely important. It is absolutely essential to get the youth team right and the players brought up with the right habits and accus-tomed to the playing system used by the first-team squad. Bob Wilson used to hold a twice-weekly coaching clinic with the goalkeepers, who could not have been in better hands. Bob has Arsenal-red blood in his veins, and just about manages to bury his bias when doing his TV presentation work.

We had a fine groundsman in Steve Braddock, and our kit manager Tony Donnelly carried out his duties with an efficiency that typified Arsenal. This long-serving Highbury loyalist, who sadly got struck by the curse of cancer, told me after our first championship victory: 'When the club announced you were coming back as our manager I thought what a mistake they were making. I remembered you as the laid back player who was full of fun and mischief. There was no way,

I thought, that you were cut out to be a manager. I could not believe the change in you, and you've proved me completely wrong.' The Boy from Bargeddie had grown up.

I have mentioned how the London Colney training ground is just off the M25, and that notorious traffic trap meant players were often delayed. Any player who had to drive to training around the M25 was allowed to be late just once a month, but after that he would have his name put in the 'late book' and would be fined £10 each time. There were also fines for sloppy dress, not wearing shin pads, putting on unnecessary weight, talking to the press out of turn and lack of discipline on and off the pitch. Gary Lewin was The Collector, and he would pass the fine kitty on to Arsenal assistant secretary, David Miles. At the end of each season the money would be paid over to the Great Ormond Street Childrens' Hospital, and there was one occasion when I was quietly able to give a considerable cheque to Gary Lineker for his leukaemia fund-raising after his son, George, had been a patient at Great Ormond Street. So the fines went to a good cause.

My reward for guiding Arsenal to the championship was the Manager of the Year award, plus a healthy new five-year contract that could earn me in excess of £200,000 a year. I had come a long, long way from the £5-a-week Villa days. Peter Hill-Wood said he was determined to keep me after newspapers had run stories of the interest of several overseas clubs. I would have quite fancied the challenge of the Italian or Spanish leagues because I had seen the way Terry Venables had settled with Barcelona, but my heart was still very much with Highbury.

I was greedy. I did not just want a championship. I wanted a dynasty, Liverpool-style.

11 : The Second Championship

August 1990: The dahlias, chrysanthemums, and, of course, the roses, have brought an unbelievable kaleidoscope of colour and scent of summer to the garden. Fill hanging baskets with trailing nasturniums and lobelias for a further cascade of colour. It's going to be a hot season!

ARSENAL's second championship triumph in three years lacked the extraordinary last lap drama of our first title win, but it was every bit as sweet and satisfying. We never really got the credit we deserved, mainly because of some headline-making of the unacceptable kind, but I am sure that when football historians look back on that 1990-91 season they will be amazed at what we achieved.

For a start, we lost only one First Division match throughout the 38-game season and were within shooting distance of the League and FA Cup double until falling to Tottenham at the semi-final hurdle. Only Leeds in their title year of 1968-69 had come close to that League record with two defeats, and I have already given my assessment of that marvellous Don Revie side. They just did not come better, unless you are going to bring Jock Stein's 1960s Celtic into the argument. You can go through all the great post-war English championship winning sides, such as the Busby Babes, the Wolves Wonders, the Push-and-Run Spurs, Bill Nicholson's Super Spurs, the Best-Charlton-Law Man United, the Bell-Lee-Summerbee Man City, the Ball-Kendall-Harvey Everton and any number of Liverpool teams, and you will not find one of them coming as close to an unbeaten season.

We kept an astonishing twenty-four clean sheets, and it was not until our twenty-fourth League match at Chelsea on 2 February 1991, that we suffered our one and only defeat (and that when our outstanding central defender Steve Bould was crocked in the second-half). Our defence did its job so well that we conceded only eighteen First Division goals, just two more than the all-time record set by Liverpool eleven years earlier. At one stage during the first third of the season we went six matches and 602 minutes without conceding a goal. All our intense homework on the playing fields of London Colney paid off. In fact I worked the players so hard with tactical innovations that at times they were calling them 'the killing fields'.

What the impressive statistics of the season do not reveal is the fact that we had to overcome a mountain of resentment and the deduction of two points before recapturing the championship trophy. I am sure that never in history has a championship-winning team received such a hostile press; and I have to admit here that much of the bad publicity was self-inflicted.

The decades-old 'Lucky, Lucky Arsenal' chants had been replaced by 'Boring, Boring Arsenal' as the main vocal weapon of rival supporters, who must have envied our incredible consistency. You ask dedicated followers of a club whether they would like a team that is good to watch or a team of winners and I'll lay odds that most of them will go for the side that gives them victories to shout about. With only one defeat all season, Arsenal fans had plenty to cheer and there were many occasions when we were very easy on the eye despite the sniping from some quarters of the Press.

There were two major incidents that had the big guns of Fleet Street trained on us. First of all came the brawl at Old Trafford on October 20 when it was reported that twenty-one of the twenty-two players on the pitch were involved in a mass punch-up. The media had a field day, reporting it as if it were the Battle of the Somme. Fair enough. They have a job to do, and this was ripe for big headlines and eye-catching photographs. But I was an eye-witness and have since been able to study detailed video replays, and of the twenty-one players said to be involved in the brawl I can state quite categorically that at least ten of them were trying to stop rather than start trouble. It all began to get nasty when Nigel Winterburn had a rush of blood to the head after he felt he had been brutally challenged. Paul Davis, David Rocastle, Anders Limpar and Mickey Thomas were dragged into battle in support of Nigel as half a dozen United players started throwing handbags at six paces. It was an occasion when the 'all-for-one-and-one-for-all' team spirit I had worked so hard to generate boiled over.

The five Arsenal players involved in the brawl were each docked two weeks' wages by the club, and there was a sharp intake of breath when it was announced that the Arsenal board had also fined me

£10,000. 'This is a brave lead by the Arsenal directors that should be followed by other clubs,' ranted the columnists. 'It is about time that managers were made to take responsibility for the behaviour of their players. George Graham will hate being hit in the pocket where it hurts most, but he deserves the punishment. Well done Arsenal.'

There was a whisper that I was considering walking out because of the punishment, and another story surfaced that the club had considered sacking me but settled for the fine. Now for the truth.

It was my idea to fine me, and it was my idea to make it public. The directors were on the rack because they were taking so much flak from Fleet Street. I was called to a meeting in vice-chairman David Dein's office. Also present were Peter Hill-Wood and Ken Friar. They were the 'three wise men' who had interviewed and appointed me four years earlier. We looked blankly at each other, trying to think of a clever way out of the sudden crisis. Finally, I came up with the solution. 'Gentlemen, the only way to shut everybody up is to show that you have decided on strong action,' I said. 'If we don't announce that we are taking immediate internal disciplinary steps the Football Association could dock us points which just might cost us the championship.'

'So what do you propose, George?' asked the chairman, who hated the fact that he was being dragged into the controversy ('It's not The Arsenal image, old chap.').

'I suggest that we fine each of the five players at the heart of the trouble two weeks' wages,' I said. Then to their amazement I added: 'You must also announce that you are fining me ten thousand pounds. Issue a statement saying that I am responsible for the behaviour of the players, and this will get the press off our backs. It will also, I hope, show the Football Association that we have dealt with the matter internally.'

The press were informed of the 'punishment', but it made little impact at the FA where they had to be seen to be in charge. The fact that the game – and the brawl – had been screened in sixty-four countries added to the seriousness of the incident in their eyes, and both Arsenal and United were charged with bringing the game into disrepute. Both clubs were fined £50,000 each, and we had two points deducted and United one. The committee chairman stressed that our previous record was being taken into account. Our players had been involved in another quick-tempered flare-up at Norwich a year earlier, and four players had been fined £1,000 each for contesting a referee's decision at Villa Park.

Looking back, I would say it was one of the biggest mistakes of my career to take the blame for the trouble on the pitch at Old Trafford. I was crucified, and accused of having no control over the players. I let my love for Arsenal blind me to the fact that I was putting myself up to be shot down. The trouble on the pitch was not my fault. It all grew out of a nasty tackle that sent tempers soaring. No manager can be responsible for how his players react in a situation like that. But I encouraged Arsenal to say that I was to blame, and people suddenly had open house on calling my management into question.

'What's gone wrong with the discipline at Arsenal?' became the question most asked at after-match interviews.

'I will not tolerate any player throwing punches,' I would answer. 'But the incidents have been very isolated. It's just that the publicity given to those few incidents has been so great that it has thrown it all out of proportion. I would say I have the most disciplined squad of players in the League.' And I truly believed it.

Privately, I stressed to the players that they had to remember that they were ambassadors for Arsenal Football Club on and off the field, and that they should bear in mind not only the image of the club but also of the game. I reminded them that they were role models for impressionable youngsters and that they had a responsibility to set a good example. Most of the time they did exactly that, but in the highly charged atmosphere of a fiercely fought match emotions can run high and it is understandable, if undesirable, when things sometimes get over-heated.

Even more hurtful than the punches thrown at us by Manchester United were the six goals they scored against us in a League Cup tie at Highbury five weeks after the 'Battle of Old Trafford' (as the tabloids billed it). They caught us on a night when our minds were not on the job, and after the 6-2 defeat I handed out half a dozen private rollockings to players who had not shown their usual concentration and commitment. But I was able to dip back into Arsenal history to help motivate the team. I convinced them that they had not become a bad team overnight and I recalled how the Arsenal double team of 1970-71 had suffered a mid-season 5-0 crash at Stoke, and that out of the wreckage of that defeat we had become a more determined and disciplined side. And so it proved twenty years on with the 1990-91 team, who were made of similar strong stuff.

I counted myself lucky that I had played for one Arsenal side and now managed another that were each unmatchable when it came to strength of character. Four days after the 6-2 drubbing by United, we handed Liverpool their first defeat of the season. Now that is what you call resilience.

The other major incident that brought the full force of Fleet Street opinion down on us was when our skipper Tony Adams was jailed for a drink-driving offence. It was well known that Tony liked a glass or three to wind down after a match, but this is no crime. I don't encourage it, but the players at Arsenal were grown men who had to be allowed to live their lives the way they saw fit. At every club I have belonged to during all my years in football I have seen some players who like a good drink and others who never touch the stuff. Amazingly enough, footballers are just like other human beings. Tony knew he was totally in the wrong when he was involved in an accident while drunk at the wheel on 6 December 1990, and he accepted his prison sentence like a man.

I was telephoned with the news that Tony had been arrested for driving his car into a garden wall while three times over the limit. My reaction was one of sadness and concern for him. No other player in the League had been under the sort of pressure that he faced virtually every time he ran on to a pitch, particularly away from home. He had once, uncharacteristically, scored an own goal at Old Trafford. One of the more refined newspapers (I'm being sarcastic) devoted virtually the whole of its back page to a picture of Tony depicted as a donkey. From then on, in every match he played he had to put up with rival supporters making 'ee-aw' noises every time he touched the ball. Of all the players I have been associated with, Tony is matched only by Frank McLintock for will-to-win and bloody-mindedness in the face of adversity. In fact he is in the class of one of my all-time favourite players, Dave Mackay, for tenacity and willpower. I can give no higher praise. Bill Shankly used to describe his centre-half Ron Yeats as a colossus. And that was the perfect description for Tony Adams. He was my colossus.

He suffered the disappointment of being dropped from the England team without rancour, and had just earned a recall by manager Graham Taylor. His only sign that the pressure was getting to him came when he responded to taunts from the Queen's Park Rangers fans with a Harvey Smith gesture. The big, powerful man from Essex must have felt the world and his brother were against him when, two days after the drink-drive charge, he became the first player sent off under the new, harsh professional foul rule.

I went to the court hearing at Southend and gave him a character reference that came straight from the heart, stressing that his professionalism and leadership were an example to all other players. 'As a man, as a competitor and as a professional, I have nothing but the highest admiration for him,' I told the court. Despite a previous clean sheet, he was sentenced to nine months in prison, five of them suspended. In my opinion he was being made an example of because of his celebrity status, and as this was close to Christmas he was the ideal high-profile person to give publicity to the seasonal don't-drink-and-drive campaign. I am convinced that had it been Joe Bloggs in the dock, he would not have been sent to prison.

I stated on behalf of Arsenal that the club would stand by him, and we continued to pay his wages. That brought an extra crescendo of criticism, with some writers demanding that Adams should never be allowed to play for England again and claiming that it was disgraceful that we should pay him wages while he was in prison. What on earth did they expect? He still had a mortgage to pay and a wife and children to feed and clothe. I could not believe the hostility in some of the articles; and just to rub it in and kick him while he was down, the Football Association chose to fine him £1,000 for his two-fingered gesture at Queen's Park Rangers while he was serving his time in Chelmsford prison. There are some unfeeling people in this world.

The rest of the Arsenal players had at first been pulling Tony's leg over his crash into the garden wall. 'He was trying to get the wall back ten yards,' was the favourite joke. But all the laughing stopped when the sentence was announced, and from then on we adopted a 'let's win this one for Tony' attitude. Andy Linighan, who I had bought from Norwich for £1.25 million in the summer, did a sound job as stand-in for Adams alongside Steve Bould at the heart of the defence, and I was also able to call on the vast experience of David O'Leary as we set about cutting back Liverpool's commanding lead at the top of the table. We had beaten a strangely defence-minded Liverpool 3-0 at Highbury just four days before the Tony Adams drink-drive incident. It was their first defeat of the season, and we were convinced we could overtake them. The two point deduction had left us eight points adrift of the defending champions, and the bookmakers made them 8-13 on to retain the title. We were second favourites at 5-4, and there were not too many takers.

Apart from Linighan, there were two more new signings in the side from the team that had won the championship in 1989-90. David Seaman had arrived from Queen's Park Rangers for a British record fee for a goalkeeper of £1.3 million, and he gradually won over the Arsenal fans who could not believe I had found somebody I preferred to their hero John Lukic. John was a very good goalkeeper. David Seaman, I knew, could and would become a great one. I might not have pursued my interest in Seaman had John Lukic been prepared to give long-term commitment to Arsenal. But every contract negotiation was like pulling teeth, and John would never agree to commit himself long-term to the club.

That was the main reason I started looking elsewhere, and I knew that in David Seaman I was getting a fantastic replacement. I was disappointed with England manager Graham Taylor when he went public with criticism of David's performance in an international match against the Republic of Ireland. It could have damaged the confidence of a lesser man, but David is certainly not short of self-belief and Bob Wilson's expert coaching was ironing out the few minor faults in his game. The only match in which the candid Yorkshireman had to concede he was at less than his best was in the FA Cup semi-final against Tottenham; and I have to own up as well and admit that I made a tactical error. David Hillier had been doing an excellent midfield marking job for me, but when he was injured I trusted Mickey Thomas with the job of sitting on Paul Gascoigne. Wrong, George! Gazza was allowed too much freedom and took us apart for an hour before going off injured. Tottenham won 3-1 and went on to win the FA Cup. I had been outpointed by my mentor Terry Venables.

My other major signing was Swedish international Anders Limpar, who I bought from Cremonese for £1.1 million after he had struggled to make a real impact in the Italian league. I thought he would be just the player to give us an extra dimension with his ability to break down either of the flanks from a midfield base. The fans fell in love with Anders and his box of tricks, but for a manager he was an infuriating character. One game he would be an explosive match-winner, the next disappear without trace. He turned it on for me more times than not in his first few months, but then his inconsistency started to come to the surface at a time when I could not afford to have anybody in the team not pulling his full weight. One minute he would be indicating that he was injured, and the next wanting to jet off to play international football for Sweden. As we were paying his considerable wages I demanded that he should make getting fit for Arsenal his priority.

Anders and I could not get on the same wave-length. I think I demanded more effort and endeavour than he wanted to give, and he thought his extraordinary skill and vision was enough to help him coast through matches. As I have stated, I wanted match winners not players who merely decorated games. I have to give Anders credit for doing more than anybody to lay the foundation to our championship win with his exceptional form in the first half of the season. If he had produced consistency to go with his class he would have become a superstar of the First Division, but he did not seem prepared to quite give his all. I can hear the Graham-baiters claiming that I was hardly the most consistent of footballers in my playing days. I would accept that criticism, and here is an admission: if I had been a manager watching George Graham week in and week out, I would not have bought him. I was too inconsistent for the sort of team I had built at Highbury. And so, it would prove, was Anders Limpar.

Anders was not the usual stoic Swede. He had buckets of Hungarian blood and a temperament that was more Latin than Scandinavian. There were times when he could pull you up out of your seat with his blinding skill, as for instance when he scored a sensational solo goal in an FA Cup tie at Leeds and also a stunning long-range chip over the head of Liverpool goalkeeper Bruce Grobbelaar. But there was another side to him, and, in my view, Anders started to enjoy his star status too much, forgetting the hard work he had put in to make it all come together.

Anders seemed to me to be getting too close to vice-chairman David Dein and his family. I had warned against this in my job interview, and knew it would lead to difficulties. When I decided that the team would be better off without Anders, the vice-chairman came to me and pleaded for me not to sell him to Everton. Even on the day of the sale he asked me to call off the deal, but I could not let personal feelings get in the way of club business. The team was much more important than any individual, and Anders had to go. I was not top of the Dein family popularity list for that decision.

We had overhauled Liverpool at the top of the table by the time Tony Adams rejoined us after serving two months of his four-month sentence. Seven thousand fans turned up to watch him make his comeback for the reserves against Reading, and he made his return to the first-team after an eight-match absence at Liverpool where a brilliant goal on the break by Paul Merson gave us another memorable Anfield victory. Kenny Dalglish had resigned as Liverpool manager ten days earlier because of the pressures of the job. He had done a fantastic job for the Merseysiders, both as a player and as a manager. Kenny wanted to stop and smell the flowers, and who could blame him. But I knew he would be back. You can't shake off the drug of football that easily.

Even with the two point deduction, we raced away with the championship and had it all wrapped up on the May Bank Holiday Monday when Liverpool went down 2-1 at Nottingham Forest in the afternoon. We had an evening game against Manchester United, and played like the champions we were on the way to a 3-1 victory that included a hat-trick from the ever reliable Alan Smith. Five days later in our final game we crushed Coventry 6-1. This time my 'enigma man' Anders Limpar helped himself to a hat-trick, and Smudger scored his twenty-third First Division goal of the season to clinch the Adidas Golden Boot award for the second time in three years. He also set a record by becoming the First Division's top scorer in two separate championship-winning seasons. Boring, Boring Arsenal!

Paul Davis, who had done a marvellous job as stand-in skipper while Tony Adams was 'away', had a season he could look back on with pride, and Kevin Campbell came through from the junior ranks to show he had been taught all the right Arsenal habits by our excellent coaching staff. I am not sure the Scot in me wants to point out the following fact, but the line-up I favoured most during the season had no fewer than ten English players and Swede Anders Limpar as the one 'outsider': Seaman; Dixon, Bould, Adams, Winterburn; Davis, Thomas, Campbell, Limpar; Smith, Merson.

For me, there was no question about who was the player of the year – and the supporters club agreed with me. It had to be Steve Bould, who gave countless lion-hearted performances in the middle of an unbelievable back line that was close to unbeatable right through the season. I was delighted for Steve because there was a sudden question mark against him the previous season when he got involved in a drunken incident with the walking time-bomb, Paul Merson. Both had made fools of themselves at a dinner to celebrate the first championship triumph, and finished up splashed over the tabloids. I fined them both and suspended Paul from the club for a week. Steve promised me that it was, as far as he was concerned, a one-off moment of madness and proved it by not giving me any more headaches. As for Paul...!

Steve Bould, along with David Seaman, Lee Dixon and Nigel Winterburn, was an ever-present throughout all fifty of the games we played during a season in which we won little praise but a lot of points. At the final count, we won the title by a comfortable margin of seven points – and it would have been nine but for the 'Battle of Old Trafford'.

By now I was a walking record book on the history of Arsenal, and I knew that Herbert Chapman had started the 1930s by winning the League championship twice in three seasons. Something that had eluded even the great Chapman was a European trophy, simply because there was no competition in those days.

The Boy from Bargeddie had his eyes fixed firmly on Europe.

12 : The Cup Double

May 1993: A double is the name for a flower with more than the usual number of petals. Typical examples are double chrysanthemums and dahlias. I have dug the ground and applied eight ounces of bone-meal per square yard and am now ready to plant my young dahlias from my rooted cuttings. I wonder if I will get any more doubles?

WE were literally seeing double in 1992-93 when Arsenal became the first team to win both the FA Cup and Football League Cup in the same season. In each final we conquered Sheffield Wednesday in what became known as the 'carbon copy' campaign. The important thing was that the FA Cup triumph provided us with an instant passport back into Europe after a jarring experience in the European Cup the previous season.

It was Portuguese champions Benfica who produced my biggest disappointment since returning home to Highbury. I was convinced my team was strong enough and skilful enough to make a telling impact in Europe, and I was confident of at least reaching the semi-finals. But we came a cropper in the second round when 'The Lions' of Benfica exposed our lack of experience in European competition, from which English teams had been banned for five years following the Heysel Stadium tragedy.

I had really fancied the challenge of pitting my tactical wits against top Continental coaches, but I was out-manoeuvred before I could get into my stride. In the first leg against Benfica in Lisbon we fell for the three-card trick. Their Swedish coach Sven-Goran Eriksson shrewdly kept his Brazilian ace, Isaias, hidden up his sleeve, making sure he did not play in the matches in which we watched them during the build-up to our tie. They were so dominant in their domestic league that they could afford to play a weakened team, and each time Steve Rowley, Steve Burtenshaw, Stewart Houston and I went to spy on them he would change the formation, not only leaving out Isaias but also his pair of talented Russians Kulkov and Youran.

We were quickly aware of the danger coming from Isaias in the first leg in Benfica's famous Stadium of Light, and I got a message out on to the pitch detailing Paul Davis to sit on him while Paul Merson was briefed to play a deeper role than usual to restrict the Brazilian's movement. The damage had been done by then, Isaias running on to a beautifully weighted through ball to put Benfica in the lead. I made a mental note of the man who had supplied the perfect pass: Stefan Schwarz. We started to get on top once we had controlled the menace of Isaias, and a powerful shot from Kevin Campbell gave us a more than satisfactory 1-1 draw to take into the return leg at Highbury. We were marvellous in Lisbon, but, sadly, mediocre in London. I will always maintain that we were the better side over ninety minutes, but we did not punish them with goals. Benfica survived to extra-time and then, looking fitter and fresher than us, moved up a gear. They showed their superior skill as they went on to win 3-1 on aggregate with two well executed goals in the closing minutes.

This defeat more than any other knocked the heart out of us, and we were still affected by the hang-over when we suffered the deep embarrassment of being bundled out of the FA Cup at Wrexham. It grieves me to admit that this was almost on a par with the infamous 1933 defeat of Herbert Chapman's 'unconquerable' team by Walsall, a result by which all giantkillings are measured. Publicly, I said that one poor result did not mean we had become a bad team overnight. Privately, I told the players that they were letting themselves and the club down by their sudden lack of commitment and passion. I challenged them to take a good hard look at themselves. 'We've had a great run of success but it hasn't just happened by magic,' I told them. 'We've earned that success by hard work that has enabled you to make the most of your ability. Now you must question your application and your attitude. You have stopped doing all the good things that got us to the top. Nobody has a God-given right to succeed. If you're not willing to put in the work that is required then I shall start looking for players who are. Let me see the pride back in your performances, or else ...'

The rocket produced the desired response, and we went through the last seventeen matches of the season undefeated and climbed from eighth in the table to fourth. During that late run we produced some of the most blinding football I had ever seen from an Arsenal team, and that includes my days as a player at Highbury. Limpar and Merson were causing defences all sorts of distress with their inventive work on the flanks, and in the middle we had one of the chief instigators of the sudden lift in our form: Ian Wright, a larger-than-life character who I had snapped up from Crystal Palace for £2.5 million on 23 September 1991. I remember the day well because the deal was negotiated by vice-chairman David Dein while I was a playing guest of *Daily Mail* columnist Jeff Powell, a long-time trusted friend, at the Football Writers' Association's annual golf tournament at Moor Park. We had finished our rounds and were sitting nice and relaxed in the clubhouse when a flushed agency reporter came from the telephone to say: 'You'll never believe this, but Arsenal have just signed Ian Wright for two and a half million quid.'

All eyes were suddenly on me, and the deadline-ticking clock. 'Is this right, George?'

'Yes gentlemen,' I said, a little embarrassed but elated that the deal had been clinched. 'I had to keep dead quiet about it so that other clubs were not alerted. That's why I came along today. I didn't want anybody to guess what we were up to.'

An impromptu Press conference was organised during which I gave chapter-and-verse on the deal, and I was not the most popular person at Moor Park as reporters on their day off and relaxed at the nineteenth hole suddenly found themselves having to write back-page leads. We had been tracking Wright for several seasons, and Crystal Palace reluctantly allowed him to go after their chairman Ron Noades had made some controversial comments in a television documentary about the attitudes of black players. Wright, black and proud of it, took deep offence at the remarks, and he was an Arsenal player eleven days later. Ian lit up the pitch and dressing-room with the electricity of his performances and his personality. Some players you have to wind up before sending them out to play, using psychological ploys to lift and inspire them. With Ian, I had to try to douse the fire that was always burning within him. His bubbling enthusiasm could run away with him, but while getting him to control himself I had to be careful not to rob him of his natural desire to compete.

People are surprised when they meet Ian for the first time off the pitch. They think he is some sort of giant because of the determined and aggressive way he goes about his business, but he is barely 5ft 9in tall and, by today's standards, quite small for a striker. But there is a lot of power packed in his muscular frame, and he has the courage to go in where it hurts if he feels his reward might be a goal.

Wright won instant hero status with the fans by marking his Arsenal debut with a hat-trick at Southampton. He also scored four goals in the dismantling of Everton and in the final match of the season snatched another hat-trick (again against Southampton), his last two goals coming in injury time to lift him above Gary Lineker as the League's top scorer and the 'Golden Boot' winner. He had scored twenty-nine goals in total, twenty-four of them counting for Arsenal after his move from Crystal Palace. And nearly every one of his goals was a gem.

You have to take Ian warts 'n' all, and he has a touchpaper temper to go with his fizzing spirit. He was more victim than villain in an ugly incident at the end of one of his early matches for us at Oldham. Supported by the well-meaning Paul Merson, he got involved in a fracas with a section of the crowd who had been making racist taunts. Ian lost control of his temper when one of the spectators spat at him. I could sympathise with his feelings but not his reactions that brought him a £1,500 fine from the Football Association. Merson was fined £500. Trouble attracted Paul like a magnet.

There is in my view no room for racism in sport. Take the black players out of our game, and it would be much poorer and, in the entertainment sense, less colourful. Right through my time at Highbury I was given tremendous service by black players and in particular Viv Anderson, Mickey Thomas, Paul Davis, David Rocastle, Kevin Campbell and, of course, the irrepressible Wrighty. The Arsenal fans used to call Thomas, Davis and Rocastle 'The Three Degrees' when they were bossing the midfield in my early days as manager. No offence was meant, or taken. Good humour is one way to take the sting and the stench out of racism.

There is not a thimbleful of cowardice in Wright, and he will give as good as he gets if any player goes beyond the boundaries of fair play against him. This means retaliatory tactics often drag him into trouble with referees, who do not see the original foul. In December 1992, a television camera caught him throwing 'paperweight' punches at David Howells in a League match at Tottenham. The Press blew it up out of all proportion and the result was a three-match ban, and I got hit with a £500 fine for letting the referee know what I thought of the way he handled the game. There was no excuse for what either Ian or I did, but anybody who has suffered the inconsistencies and incompetence of some referees will know why Ian loses control of his temper and I lose control of my tongue.

This was not the first time that an Arsenal player had been in trouble because of something missed by the referee but picked up by a television camera. Paul Davis was banned for nine weeks and fined £3,000 in my second season as Arsenal manager after television news cameras had caught him punching Glenn Cockerill on the jaw during the League match against Southampton. I reacted by banning the BBC and ITN news cameras. It was my stand against trial by television. I would never have condoned what Paul did, but it was a matter I wanted to deal with internally instead of having it turned into a TV soap opera. To switch on the TV news and see an incident being shown completely out of context was like having a spy in the camp. Paul should never have thrown the punch, but he was, in my opinion, pilloried and punished out of all proportion.

You could not ask for a more genuine, honest professional than Ian Wright, who was twenty-one before he finally made the breakthrough into League football. This meant he was hungrier than most other players, and explains why he celebrates every goal as if it is a Wembley winner. Even in training if he gets the ball into the net he will run around posing until some appropriate insults from his teammates bring him back down to earth. He is a one-off who has a boyish enthusiasm and love for the game that I wish I could bottle. I would class him among the top half-dozen British strikers I have ever seen. Ian is one player I cannot claim to have improved with my coaching. Everything he does is by instinct. He is a natural like Jimmy Greaves and Denis Law used to be. As with Jimmy and Denis, he can never explain to you after a match how or why he scored a wonder goal. All he knows is that it went into the net, and – like all great strikers – all his concentration and attention is on the next goal. It was often claimed that we had an Ian Wright complex because he scored such a high percentage of our goals. I encouraged the other players to try to match him, but he was out on his own.

His arrival at Highbury meant I was able to give in to Bristol City pressure to sign another of our young black players, Andy Cole, who had made a big impression while on loan with them. I was suddenly overloaded with strikers, and Cole was an untapped prospect whom I did not rate above the likes of Alan Smith, Paul Merson, Kevin Campbell and Ian Wright. I had not worked with him very often at first-team level, but I was concerned about the reports I received about his attitude. There were occasions when it seems he was reluctant to travel to the club from his Nottingham home after Sundays with his family, and my coaches informed me that he did not always give a hundred per cent in training – particularly when it was bitterly cold. He hated the freezing conditions. So did many of our players, but they still turned up for training. I used to have him in my office and give him a good talking to about how important it is to be disciplined and a dedicated professional. I hope I got through to him.

We were paid £500,000 for him by Bristol City, plus a percentage of any fee if they transferred him. When he later signed for Newcastle, Arsenal collected another £400,000. So the club had netted £900,000 for a player who had only once kicked a ball for the first-team. I saw it then as a good deal, and I still see it as excellent business despite all the stick I had to take when he was sold on to Manchester United for £7 million.

Given the same circumstances I have no hesitation in saying that I would do the same again. I hope Cole scores bucketfuls of goals for United, but deep down I have my doubts.

I would be delighted for him to prove me wrong. We shall see.

The turning point of that 1991-92 season came in a League match at Highbury on 15 February. We paralysed Sheffield Wednesday 7-1, six goals coming in a glorious eighteen minute spell in the second-half. Kevin Campbell, entering the game as a substitute for injured Alan Smith, was the inspiration with a cracking goal that lifted the temperature and brought a flood of sensational football that has rarely been equalled at Highbury (or at any British ground for that matter). That victory launched a new attacking attitude that silenced the 'Boring, Boring' chants. We struggled to keep the momentum going in the following birth-of-the-Premiership season, but found our form in the cup competitions when our opponents in both the League Cup and FA Cup finals were the same Sheffield Wednesday.

We made little impact in the League, scoring only forty goals while finishing a far-from-satisfactory tenth. I can say without fear of contradiction that it was the quietest season Highbury had ever known. The North Bank, where our noisiest and most inspiring fans had stood for years, was no more. The famous terraces were being turned into an all-seater stand, and while the work was in progress a huge mural stood at the North Bank end looking on in a silence that did nothing to lift our players. A couple of our players quite properly pointed out that the mural – a painting of hundreds of Arsenal fans – contained only white faces. Some black faces appeared overnight.

All our concentration was trained on the cup competitions. I wish I could report that the two finals were classics. They weren't. But nobody will ever be able to take away from us the fact that we had created history by winning the two cups. Ian Wright was our unquestioned star in that cup-double season, despite his ban. It was his fifteen goals in the competitions that lifted us to the two trophies.

The League Cup final (or the Coca-Cola Cup as it had become known after being variously billed as the Milk Cup, the Littlewoods Cup and the Rumbelows Cup) will always be remembered for the ecstasy and agony of young Stephen Morrow. The Belfast lad was in dreamland when his first ever goal for the club won the League Cup for us. Then it turned into a nightmare. He was celebrating the 2-1 victory over Wednesday when our skipper Tony Adams hoisted him up and then accidentally dropped him. The unfortunate Stephen broke his arm in two places, and while Tony was collecting the cup he was being taken to hospital. It took the edge off our triumph, and Tony was distraught over what had happened. Stephen, a mature young lad, quite rightly accepted that it was just a pure accident. In future it was agreed that we would be less boisterous with our celebrations. There was a happy sequel when Stephen made a lone trip up to the Royal Box at Wembley to collect his League Cup award in an emotional ceremony before the FA Cup Final.

I was upset by the criticism we received following our League Cup final victory. Our tactics in denying space to Wednesday dangermen Chris Waddle and John Sheridan were attacked as being negative, and one experienced football reporter went so far as to say that I had ruined the game as a spectacle. I just could not believe that. My philosophy has always been to work out the opposition strengths, and then nullify them, while imposing our strengths on them. No manager dare approach a game thinking: 'Oh, George Best is playing against us today. That will be great for the spectators. We must give him plenty of room to display his skill.' Sorry, but the professional world of football is just not like that. My thinking would be more like: 'Ouch, George Best is playing against us today. We must stop him making any sort of impact. I shall double park two players on him, one to stop him receiving the ball and the other to mark him as tightly as a second skin and to deny him space in which to make those devastating runs of his.' A manager would not last in his job two minutes if he decided to let the opposition play for the entertainment of the spectators.

Just twenty-seven days after our League Cup victory we were back at Wembley for the FA Cup Final, and again Wednesday were the opponents – the first time that the same two clubs had met in two finals in the same season. I had a touch of *déja-vu* on the way to the Final. As in our double year of 1970-71, we were drawn at Yeovil in the third round; and as in our double year we won 3-0 (with a hat-trick from That Man Wright). There is no doubt that our greatest moment on the way to the Final was a semi-final victory over 'the auld enemy' Tottenham. The hero was 'Captain Marvel' Tony Adams, who galloped upfield to head in a superbly flighted free-kick from Paul Merson in the eightieth minute to clinch our place in the Final. It capped a fantastic week for Tony, who had been outstanding for England in a World Cup qualifying match in Turkey four days earlier. Suddenly people were starting to agree with what I had been saying since he first established himself in the Arsenal team: that Tony Adams was the finest central defender in the game. Alf Ramsey used to rave about the competitive qualities of Jack Charlton in his World Cup winning team. Well I reckon Tony is a class above the old giraffe, who was more than useful. It had taken him six years to become an overnight success. They were no longer calling him donkey, although some enterprising manufacturer did well with a T-shirt that read: DONKEY WINS THE DERBY!

It was extremely satisfying to watch two youngsters off our youth team conveyor belt, Ian Selley and Ray Parlour, playing an important part in our semi-final victory over Tottenham. Their performances spoke volumes for the work of youth team manager Pat Rice and his assistants in bringing up the young players to do things the Arsenal way so that they were able to slot comfortably into the first-team. This semi-final against Tottenham was staged at Wembley, and for many of our supporters it was considered the Final.

The actual Final was an anti-climax. The Wednesday and Arsenal players knew each other too well, and the game petered out into a tame 1-1 draw, David Hirst equalising Ian Wright's first-half goal. Wednesday, who were the form team, played a cautious game out of character with the stylish way their manager Trevor Francis used to grace the football field. All the criticism for the poor entertainment value of the games was aimed at Arsenal. Surely there were two teams out on the pitch. What's that they say about it taking two to tango?

John Jensen was the midfield anchorman in our FA Cup team, making an excellent contribution to my tactical plan for closing off the Sheffield Wednesday supply line to Chris Waddle. I have gone into the facts surrounding Jensen's transfer from Brondy elsewhere in the book. His arrival meant that the Arsenal directors were able to accept a £2 million offer from Leeds manager Howard Wilkinson for David Rocastle, the player he had tried to sign during my first week in the Arsenal chair. It was one of the saddest days in my managerial career when I had to tell David that we were letting him go. I recall that it was a fine August morning in 1992 and 'Rocky' had just arrived for a training work out at London Colney. I met him in the car park and said: 'David, the Board have accepted a bid for you from Leeds. Howard Wilkinson is waiting to speak to you.'

There were tears in Rocky's eyes as he nodded his head. 'Okay, Boss,' he said. 'I don't want to leave Arsenal, you know that. But if I'm no longer wanted here I suppose Leeds is as good a place as any to go to.'

I was so full up with emotion that I could not say what I wanted to say: that he was one of the nicest people I have ever come across in the game, and that he had always been a wonderful advertisement for Arsenal Football Club and for football in general. He had been a class act, and would have still been a key man in the Arsenal midfield but for a recurring knee injury that required surgery. During his lay-off in the 1989-90 season he had put on weight that he struggled to shift. By the time he had got himself fully fit we had a settled team that was putting together a run, and from then on he was in and out of a side to which he had given so much in endeavour and skill. David will always be welcome at Highbury (I wonder if I will be?), and he can look back on his years at Arsenal with great personal pride and satisfaction.

There was a disappointing attendance of only 62, 267 at the FA Cup final replay five days after the first meeting. Neutrals had had enough of Arsenal versus Sheffield Wednesday, thank you very much. But it was a much better game than the first encounter. Ian Wright illuminated the Wembley stage with an exquisitely taken goal in the first-half after neatly combining with Alan Smith, who had settled for a supporting-role back seat since Wright's arrival. Chris Waddle forced a sixty-eighth minute equaliser to take the game into extra-time, and a penalty shoot-out was just a minute away when Arsenal found an unlikely goal-scoring hero in the shape of Andy Linighan. He was nursing a broken nose caused by Mark Bright's disgraceful use of the elbow, but he ignored the pain to bravely head in the winning goal to bring the FA Cup back to Highbury for the first time since 1979 when our youth team coach Pat Rice had proudly held the trophy aloft as Arsenal skipper. It was a magical moment for Andy, who had struggled to win the affection of the Arsenal supporters. He had been an excellent squad member and was popular in the dressing-room. We were all delighted that he had enjoyed his moment of glory. It was particularly memorable for me because I had become the first manager in history to play in and manage teams that had won all three domestic trophies (I was in Chelsea's winning League Cup team in 1965).

Even more important, Andy Linighan's dramatic late goal meant that Arsenal were back in Europe in the Cup Winners' Cup. This time we were determined not to make any mistake.

13 : Wonderful Copenhagen

May 1994: I am spraying a very special plant to ward off greenfly, using a systemic insecticide. It is a rose that will flower this summer and will be the envy of all who see it. It is called an Allgold rose. George's AllGold. And that's what my team will be if we lift the European Cup Winners' Cup in wonderful, wonderful Copenhagen. Allgold Arsenal.

JUST the names of some of the clubs blocking our path to the European Cup Winners' Cup made my mouth water at the prospect of crossing swords with them. Included in the first round draw were the likes of Real Madrid, Ajax, Benfica, Panathinaikos, Ferencvaros, Torino, Paris Saint-Germain, Standard Liége, and the talented holders Parma, who I had watched outclass Antwerp 3-1 in the 1993 final at Wembley. Most experts were agreed that this looked an even tougher competition to win than the European Champions' Cup.

I liked to set out my stall at the start of each season with a target in mind, and it was no secret that what I wanted above all else was the Cup Winners' Cup. Arsenal had only once before captured a European trophy, and that was the Fairs Cup back in 1970 when I was a proud member of the Bertie Mee-managed, Don Howe-coached, Frank McLintock-motivated team. The great Herbert Chapman had never won a European trophy, but that was only because there were no official competitions in those pre-war days when Arsenal were the undisputed kings on the domestic front. But he was a real visionary and had taken Arsenal to such far-flung places as Russia and Brazil in what were trail-blazers for the international club competitions that would be set up in the 1950s.

We made a reasonable challenge for the 1993-94 Premiership, finishing fourth and conceding only twenty-eight goals during a season when we were pegged back by seventeen drawn matches and a worrying impotency in front of goal. The title went to Alex Ferguson's beautifully balanced Manchester United team, which had the added ingredient of Roy Keane's power and Eric Cantona's French flair. I had wanted to sign Keane from Nottingham Forest, but he had a clear preference for Old Trafford and, of course, I was handicapped by the

Arsenal board's wage structure. I was not the slightest bit interested in signing Cantona because I knew he would not fit into the Arsenal jigsaw. He was made for Manchester United, and became a sensational success with them after an indifferent period with Leeds. I had to apologise to my friend Alex Ferguson after I had been misquoted as saying Cantona was a cry-baby. He disappeared from view in several vital Leeds United matches, yet blossomed at Old Trafford because he had players around him who suited his style and moods. Cantona is an artist of a player who can be wonderfully fluent on the ball and can score spectacular goals, but I still harbour some doubts about his temperament and his commitment when the going gets tough.

It was the European Cup Winners' Cup that took my undivided attention in the 1993–94 season. I saw it as a challenge to my tactical perception, and I spent hours studying videos and scouting reports and making secret trips to watch the opposition. I felt like a field-marshal making battle plans, and for me this was the most satisfying part of my job. These are condensed versions of my notes on each team that we met on the way to the final in Copenhagen:

First round: Opponents Odense, of Denmark.

FIRST LEG NOTES: Odense are well organised, particularly in midfield and have a high work rate. I will preach the three P's to the players: Patience, possession and be positive. Must cut out the supply to Alphonse Tchami, a striker from Cameroon who has pace and power. Jess Thorup looks comfortable on the ball and likes to run at the heart of the defence. Deny him space. Goalkeeper Lars Hogh handles the ball well, but his positioning on crosses is suspect. Try firing the ball high to his far post at every opportunity. We should not under-estimate Odense, who are one of only three full-time professional teams in Denmark. They finished second in their league last season, are currently top of the Danish table and this is their sixth European campaign. With Tony Adams suspended, I will play Linighan and Keown in the middle of the back line, with Eddie McGoldrick taking over from injured Lee Dixon at right-back. Counting on John Jensen (who will feel at home) and young Ian Selley to do a containing job in midfield. Weather forecast is for gale-force winds and driving rain. It is going to be a hard slog and we must be prepared to match their work rate.

MATCH NOTES (First leg, Odense, 15 September, 1993): Disastrous first twenty minutes. Doing the opposite to what is required. Diving in on a treacherous surface and leaving ourselves open. Odense awarded a penalty in the third minute after clumsy challenge by Linighan. Thorup hits a post from the penalty spot. Lucky Arsenal! Linighan having nightmare start. His poor back pass should have been put away by Nielsen, but he shot wide. Odense score in the eighteenth minute. We were asleep when they took a short corner, and Skaarup's cross goes into the net off Keown's knee. We are playing like novices. Need to tighten up at the back, and close down in midfield. At last, Winterburn puts goalkeeper Hogh under pressure with a shot from twenty-five yards. He fails to hold it and Wright scores after Merson's first effort was blocked. We go in at half-time 1-1 and I once again underline the three P's ... patience, possession and be positive. I add another 'P': Pride. 'You will be disgusted with yourselves if you lose this to a team not fit to tie your bootlaces.' Stressed that we are giving them too much time and space in midfield, and that we need to work harder. We are much tighter and more competitive in the second-half. Campbell puts Merson through in the sixty-ninth minute, and he scores from fifteen yards after beating two defenders. This is better. We have a 2-1 lead to take into the second leg, but overall I am disatisfied with our performance.

SECOND LEG NOTES: Warn of an opening burst from Odense. They are certain to come looking for an early goal. Must not allow them that confidence booster. They will be going flat out to repeat that opening twenty minutes in Denmark when we failed to show the right commitment and competitive spirit. Forget our goal advantage from the first leg. We need to convince ourselves that we are starting the match at 0-0. Complacency could be our biggest enemy against a team that will be adopting a 'we have nothing to lose, and everything to gain' attitude. Adams and Dixon return to the back line, thank goodness. I will stress again the importance of denying the Danes space. We have the better technique, but in the first leg they more than matched our work rate. I want a hundred per cent effort from everybody. Need the direct route to goal. Could get ourselves in trouble if we try pushing the ball around in what is going to be a crowded and very competitive midfield.

MATCH NOTES (Second leg, Highbury, 29 September 1993): Our fourth game in eleven days and several of our players look jaded. Paul Davis is giving us a monopoly in midfield with that cultured left foot of his, but we are not making anything happen in the penalty area. It's 0-0 at half-time and we are playing without rhythm or confidence. Tell the players they must up the work rate, and I am looking for the midfield players to come through on positive runs to support Wright and Campbell. We go 1-0 up on the night and 3-1 up on aggregate when Campbell heads in a Davis free-kick in the 52nd minute. But we are still loose, and making elementary errors. Six minutes to go and Nielsen has equalised for the Danes. We struggle through 3-2 on aggregate. Very poor performance. If we can't do better than this we have no chance of reaching the later rounds. Must tell the players to improve their application.

Second round: Opponents Standard Liége, of Belgium

FIRST LEG NOTES: Playing cat-and-mouse with Liége coach Arie Haan, one the great old Dutch masters and an old adversary of mine. I played against him twice in the 1970s. What a left foot! He has been to see us twice and I have made sure he has not watched the team Standard will face in the first leg. They're a talented, well-organised team who use the Brazilian Andre Cruz as a sweeper behind two markers. They flood the midfield with lots of movement, play the offside and have front men who can operate from wide positions. Martin Keown is one of my hidden aces. Haan has not clapped eyes on him. I will detail Martin to do a close marking job on their dangerous striker Marc Wilmots, who scored three of the eight Standard goals against Cardiff in the first round. We are going to need lots of patience, because they will pack their defence and look for goals on the break. We need to be watchful while putting them under as much pressure as possible.

MATCH NOTES (First leg, Highbury, 20 October): Tight first-half hour as expected. Standard are packing their defence. They have Romanian Mircea Rednic sweeping in place of injured Cruz, but their in-depth defensive system is exactly as envisaged. We must be patient. Six minutes before half-time a Keown lob from the right. Ian Wright beats the off-side trap to head it in. Perfect timing. It will do wonders for Ian's confidence. First goal for a month. Half-time tell the players to be more positive. Standard chins went down the minute the goal went in. Must apply the pressure from the first whistle. Encourage Paul Davis to go forward more. The Belgians panic every time he is on the ball. We pulverise them second-half. Score two, could have had six. Merson scores with a Koeman-style swerving free-kick from twenty-five yards five minutes into the second-half. Wright makes it 3-0 after a brilliant Merson pass in the 63rd minute. Take Wright off because he is feeling a hamstring. He was booked in the first-half and must be careful. We had seventeen shots to their two, and fourteen corners to two. Sums up our supremacy. A good night's work.

SECOND LEG NOTES: Seriously consider leaving out Ian Wright because I don't want to risk him getting a second booking and missing the quarter-final. I will make a final decision just before the kick-off. I would shoot myself if I left him out and then we lost to Standard. And I would also get crucified by the press and the fans if I get this wrong. Arie Haan has been replaced as coach of the Belgians by Rene van der Ycken. He's a shrewd cookie, and is reminding his players how he was in the Bruges team beaten 3-0 at Ipswich in the UEFA Cup before winning the second-leg 4-0. They will have Cruz back for this leg, so they will be tighter at the back because he is a class sweeper. We have not scored in our last four Premiership matches, so we need goals against Liége to lift our confidence. I shall be looking for speed down the flanks and want us to hunt an early goal while being careful not to let them score early to lift their morale. Now what do I do about Wrighty?

MATCH NOTES (Second leg, Liege, 3 November 1993): I decide to gamble on leaving Ian Wright out. He is choked because he wants to play every minute, but I cannot take the risk of him collecting a second booking that would put him out of the quarter-finals. We silence the critics who have been calling us 'Arsenil' with one of the greatest attacking displays I have ever seen on an away ground. The Liége defenders throw in the towel after Alan Smith scores in the second minute, and if I had been their manager I would have been kicking a lot of backsides. I thought Cruz would tighten a few screws at the back of their defence, but he hardly makes a tackle all night. This is the unacceptable face of South American football. Their players are often too quick to throw in the towel. My note-taking could not keep up with the action. It looked as if we would score with every attack. Finish up winning 7-0. Goalscorers: Smith, Selley, Adams, Campbell in the first-half; in the second-half, Merson, Campbell and McGoldrick (the best of the lot; a fierce shot that provided him with a memorable first goal for the club). It is our twenty-fourth cup tie without defeat. A mind-blowing performance; one of the best since I took over as manager.

Quarter-final: Opponents Torino

FIRST LEG NOTES: Flew to Italy to watch Torino beat Inter-Milan 2-0. They are an exceptional side, and will provide a much more difficult hurdle than Standard Liége. I have no doubts that the Italian Serie A is the strongest league in the world. In Andrea Silenzi they have a world-class striker, and we must stop the ball getting through to him. They play with one up (Silenzi) and two floating midfielders in Uruguayan internationals Enzo Francescoli and Benito Carbone, who can tear you apart if you allow them the space to roam. Francescoli is a support striker, even though he plays from a deep position. He can get into the box at the speed of light, so keep your eye out for him. Torino have three at the back with two markers, and they defend in depth with a sweeper, Luca Fusi, who is disciplined and a real hard man. We must restrict the movement of Francescoli and Carbone in midfield, and Lee Dixon must be on the alert for the left-wing runs of Robert Jarni. I want to smother them with blanket-defensive tactics in midfield. That means important marking jobs for John Jensen and David Hillier, and Paul Davis will need to be less

168

adventurous than usual. I will also want Paul Merson operating in a deep role. I have managed to hide from the Italians that Wright will be out with a hamstring problem (although he is still keen to play). This will throw a big responsibility on Smith and Campbell. For away matches, I play just the lone striker up front, with Merson and Campbell playing wide on the flanks in a 4-5-1 formation. If we are in possession we can quickly switch to a more adventurous 4-3-3. It is going to be a very tight game, and this time I will preach the three C's – composure, control and concentration. I will be more than happy to go back to Highbury with a goalless draw. It's going to be like a game of chess, with physical contact!

MATCH NOTES (First leg, Turin, 3 March 1994): This is football for the connoisseur, a battle of wits and we are winning it. The Torino players cannot understand why they are not flowing as usual. We are murdering them in midfield, where Hillier and Jensen are doing exactly what I asked of them. The two Uruguayans are not being allowed a second to settle on the ball. My tigers are seeing to that. Paul Merson is running a marathon down the left, tackling back and also giving the Italian defence something to think about with his direct running on the ball. It's 0-0 at half-time and I tell the lads to just keep playing the way they did in the first-half, doing the simple things well and giving total commitment. Torino are completely frustrated in the second-half and can make no impact on our back four, with Tony Adams giving a magnificent lead as captain. He and the resolute Steve Bould have made the giant 6ft 4in Silencia look very ordinary. They have now adopted defensive tactics, and are settling for a goalless draw. We have outwitted them, and might easily have won. What a tactical triumph! Now for Highbury, where, make no mistake, it will be just as tight.

SECOND LEG NOTES: Stress that the mountain has still to be conquered. We only got halfway in Turin. They are masters of hitting you on the break with swift counter attacks, and we must put in the same wholehearted effort to stifle them in midfield. Silenzi and Francescoli are the dangermen. Deny them any space in which to work. Frustrate them. Daniele Fortunato will be sweeping at the back in place of Luca

Fusi. He is a more adventurous player, and we must watch out for him coming through to support the attack. I will keep the Italians guessing about my line-up until the last minute. They will be wondering whether Ian Wright will be playing. He will play alongside Alan Smith, but I will not announce the team until just before the kick-off. This is what European football is all about: keeping the opposition in the dark. No general tells his counterpart where and how he will be deploying his troops. That is how it is with a football manager, and why so many of us keep our team plans close to our chest until the last possible moment.

MATCH REPORT (Second leg, Highbury, 15 March): Beware the Ides of March! I prefer the Ideas of March and we have the perfect gameplan to overcome the challenge of Torino. They are expecting us to come at them, but we hold back and it becomes a midfield stalemate. There is a worry when David Hillier has to come off after sixteen minutes, but young Ian Selley does a grand job as his replacement. We are always in control and after a goalless first-half I stress the importance to remain patient. 'Let's make the most of any set-piece situation, because they are suspect to high balls and I want you, Tony and Steve, to come up at every opportunity to add to our strength in the air. Remember all those free-kicks we have rehearsed at London Colney. Now make them work for us.' I could not have scripted it better. In the sixty-sixth minute Paul Davis uses that magical left foot of his to float a free-kick across the face of the Torino goal just as he has done countless times in training, and there is our Captain Marvel Tony Adams rising to head the ball into the net for yet another of his big occasion goals. Proof that we had drawn the sting from the Torino attack is that David Seaman had only one save to make. He has now kept twenty-eight clean sheets in forty-four matches. Over two games I don't think we allowed Torino more than three shots at our goal. Incredible stuff. Now on to the semi-final.

Semi-final: Opponents Paris St Germain

FIRST LEG NOTES: Artur Jorge, the Paris St Germain coach, is the Rommel to my Montgomery as we prepare for the first-leg of the semi-final. I am giving him no clues to my team, and have put out a smokescreen that Ian Wright will not be playing (although I know that he will be). Jorge is the wily old fox who plotted FC Porto's European Champions' Cup triumph in 1987. His PSG side are unbeaten since 15 August, a run of thirty-five games, and they put out mighty Real Madrid in the quarter-finals. Everybody is looking for me to go into the game with the sort of defensive formation that worked for us in Turin. Everybody will be proved wrong. I have decided to attack them from a springboard of a disciplined but not packed defence. Alan Smith will take the front striker's role, with Wright and Merson tucked in just behind him in what Terry Venables has labelled 'the Christmas Tree' formation. I watched PSG beat Metz 1-0 on Friday, and have studied them closely on video. They are easily the best team we have met to date. Unusually for a French team, they have steel to go with their style. Their Brazilian Ricardo is their rock in defence, and they like to pack the midfield from where they launch their most telling attacks. They have incredible strength in depth, and have been leaving Rai, Brazil's World Cup captain, out of their European ties to accommodate Valdo, another Brazilian, and Liberian striker George Weah as the permitted overseas players. World-class David Ginola, French Footballer of the Year, is a potential match-winner with his penetrating pace and two-footed skill, and he is going to have to be watched very closely by Lee Dixon. This is going to be difficult... and exciting! The support of our travelling army of supporters is going to be important to us. Must make a point of menitioning them in my next programme article. They are like a twelfth man to us. You always hear about the passion of the Merseyside, Geordie and Old Trafford fans. Arsenal supporters can match them.

MATCH NOTES (First leg, Parc des Princes, Paris, 29 March 1994): Ian Wright becomes my secret weapon, and rocks PSG with a goal made in London Colney. Paul Davis arrows in one of his precision free-kicks in the 35th minute, and Wrighty scores with a glancing header. One up to Montgomery! The Parisian defenders are guilty of ball-watching. We lead 1-0 at half-time and I am delighted. I warn the players to prepare themselves for an all-out assault by PSG at the start of the second-half, and sure enough they force two quick corners.

Winterburn clears the ball off the line from the first, and then in the 49th minute our marking is atrocious as Ginola heads in a Valdo corner. It is the slackest marking I have seen from our unbeatable back four all season, and the galling thing is that we have been beaten by one of our own near-post specialities. If you get your set-piece play right, there is no counter to it. We quickly regain our composure and concentration, and might have won the game when Alan Smith was through in the 74th minute, but he fluffed his shot. The only really negative note of a memorable night is that Tony Adams and Merson are booked. This means we go into the second leg in two weeks' time with eight players on one yellow card. Should any of them receive another caution, they will miss out on a possible appearance in the final. That is going to put extra pressure on us.

SECOND LEG NOTES: This will be our hardest and most important match of the season. We are tantalisingly close to the final, but Paris St Germain are going to come to Highbury looking for a win of which they are quite capable. In playmaker Valdo and David Ginola they have two class-act players who can dismantle any defence if given half a chance. We watched on video how they had overcome Real Madrid in Spain in the quarter-final, and we know just what to expect. Their counter attacks are quick and incisive, and they have at least five players with the technique to control the ball under pressure. So we must not allow them the time or space to hit back at us. If one of our attacks break down, everybody must be on red alert to mark their nearest opponent. We need to be extra careful not to lose possession and get caught on the break. Once again it is the three Ps: patience, possession and be positive. The only time I will be happy for them to have possession is in their own penalty area! Push them back when they have the ball. We must play the pressing game to perfection. I will delay naming the team until the last minute, because I do not want Artur Jorge to know that Paul Merson is out with a virus. Kevin Campbell will take his place. PSG had their first defeat in thirty-eight matches last week, so their confidence will be down. We must not help them lift their morale by conceding an early goal. If there's to be an early goal I would rather it came from us! Eight of you are on single bookings. You must not let this affect the way you play at all. I want each of you giving a hundred per cent. Anything less, and we could get taken apart by a team that only needs the slightest encouragement to produce football from another planet. Just don't do anything silly to get into the ref's notebook.

MATCH NOTES (Second leg, Highbury, 12 April 1994): What a cracking start. The game is barely five minutes old when Lee Dixon takes a throw-in down the right and accepts the return pass from Alan Smith (another move planned at London Colney). Lee's centre is met by Kevin Campbell who steers the sweetest of headers into the net at the near post. Now all the pressure is on PSG, and we frustrate them by closing down in midfield where they usually expect to dominate. Disaster just four minutes before half-time. Ian Wright gets himself booked for a silly rather than dirty foul on Alain Roche. It is a completely unnecessary challenge, and Ian knows straight away that he has blown his chances of playing in the final. The referee shows him the yellow card, and Ian, who can never hide his emotions, is in tears. He must pull himself together for the sake of the team, otherwise I will have to take him off. What annoys me is that in an earlier incident Laurent Fournier was not cautioned for what I judged a disgraceful tackle on Nigel Winterburn, for which I believe he should have been sent off. Inconsistency yet again! At half-time I tell Ian to calm down. He is inconsolable, but like a true pro accepts he must give it his all in the second-half for the sake of the team. We have only one moment of real crisis in a second-half during which we deny PSG the space they need to come back at us. Ian Selley, who has done a magnificent job for the team as a midfield marker, makes a rare mistake and lets Ginola through. You would put money on Ginola to score as he aims from twelve yards, but he shoots wide. Winterburn is on the receiving end of another vicious tackle, this time from substitute Gravelaine. Nigel is carried off with a sprained ankle, but again there is no card from the referee. We win 1-0, 2-1 on aggregate against one of the finest club teams I have ever seen. They have marvellous skills, but lack real punch. Or should I say we did not give them the chance to show what they could do in the penalty area. It's going to be a fantastic night in Copenhagen next month.

The Final: Opponents Parma, of Italy

PRE-MATCH NOTES: Must be careful not to show the players that I have any doubts about our ability to overcome Parma in the final. I would strongly fancy our chances if we could field a full-strength team, but the squad has been decimated by suspension and injuries. Ian Wright is out, of course. So too are my specialist markers John Jensen, Martin Keown and David Hillier. I am going to have to inspire Ian Selley and Stephen Morrow to play the games of their lives. But am I sending boys to do men's work? I have watched Parma play so many times live and on video that I know them as well as I know my own team. They are sheer class, a beautifully orchestrated team with exceptional individuals of the calibre of Sweden's Thomas Brolin, Colombia's Faustino Asprilla and the gifted Italian Gianfranco Zola. We must be particularly careful of Asprilla's lightning pace and his talent as a free-kick specialist. Parma coach Nevio Scala thinks along the same lines as Terry Venables, in that he brings in players to suit his system. They do not play with orthodox strikers, preferring instead to run from deep, and they will be looking to exploit any weaknesses in our midfield. I will delay announcing that Hillier will not be fit to play, so that they do not realise until the last moment that we have the inexperienced Selley and Morrow doing the midfield marking jobs. We must go out to contain and then strike on the break. Another secret I am hiding is that goalkeeper David Seaman will be playing with a cracked rib. It would be too much of a psychological advantage to Parma to leave him out. This is the Big One.

MATCH NOTES (Copenhagen, 4 May 1994): It sounds more like Highbury than Copenhagen. We have won the support battle before a ball is kicked. Our fans are unbelievable. Once again all our hard work at London Colney pays rich dividends, with our fourth set-piece goal in a row in the Cup Winners' Cup. Parma have started in magnificent style, and we are lucky when Brolin lets us off the hook. Then the turning point. In the twentieth minute Lee Dixon aims a throw-in to Alan Smith deep in the Parma half. As rehearsed on the playing fields of London Colney, Alan plays the ball back to Lee who fires a precision cross into the heart of the Parma defence. Their skipper Lorenzo

Minotti makes a hash of an attempted scissors-kick clearance, and Alan pounces on the loose ball and cracks it on the volley off a post from twenty yards. Smudger has scored many brilliant goals for us, but none as valuable as this one. All my doubts now disappear. I know that with the cushion of a goal lead we can now go on to win because our defence is unbreakable. Now we have breathing space, and the pressure is on the cup holders to try to break us down. Ian Selley and Stephen Morrow are doing a marvellous job in midfield, tackling like Trojans and covering acres of ground to shut down the space available to Parma's multi-talented players. They are proving what I always preach: that commitment and spirit allied to skill is an unbeatable combination. But skill on its own is not enough. At half-time I tell them not to defend quite so deep, but to push up so that we cramp the midfield and deny the Italians time and space to get their passing movements under way. As usual, our back line is magnificent and gives nothing away in the second-half. We have a team of heroes, but special mentions for Steve Bould and Tony Adams for their determination under a second-half siege, and also for Paul Davis, whose passing and vision in midfield matched anything we saw from the Italians, who surprised me with the way they surrendered. It is one of the great moments of my life when our inspiring skipper Tony Adams collects the Cup Winners' Cup.

This victory over Parma is a performance that, for me, matches even that of our first Championship victory at Anfield. I know in my heart that we were not the most skilful team in the tournament. And we were one of the least experienced in terms of European competition. But we were the best prepared, and, even if I say it myself, the best organised. Many of the big guns of Europe were in the draw at the start, and it was Arsenal who were there to collect the trophy at the end of an unforgettable campaign. It underlined what can be achieved by the right application and commitment, and a good dose of what I can best describe as British bulldog spirit (that's my Churchill connection coming out). When I am old and sitting in the football veterans' home alongside my old mate Terry Venables, I shall warm myself with memories of that wonderful night in Copenhagen, the city for fairytales. It was what Peter Hill-Wood would no doubt describe as one of our 'happy' times.

So another season had ended with a trophy in the Highbury cabi-
net.That was six trophies in eight years. Whatever next...? If you had
told me that it was going to be the sack I would have questioned your
sanity. But it was my sanity that was going to be put to the test.

14 : Anatomy of a Sacking

August 1994: My garden is a riot of colour, and the striking flowers of *Lilium auratum* are releasing their heavy scent that is almost overpowering. For the gardener, this is the sweet smell of success and a reward for all the hard planting work in the autumn and spring. But what's this? There is also a scent of scandal in the air.

IT is quite emotive to talk about a stabbing in the back, but that is how I view my sacking by Arsenal. I was made all sorts of promises that I would be allowed to leave the club with my head held high and with a compensation package that would have mirrored all that I had achieved for the club over the previous eight and a half years. As it turned out, I was ejected like a common criminal and without a penny piece. This, by a club for which director Danny Fiszman – a financial wizard – worked out that I had generated £35 million during my glory years.

When I realised my gifts from Rune Hauge were causing concern on several fronts my business manager John Hazell kept for me copious diary-style notes. Little did we know that our diary would become an anatomy of a sacking. These are condensed versions of just some of the entries that give an insight into how my world was turned upside down ...

18 August, 1994: Met John Hazell at the Post House Hotel, Brentwood, in Essex to tell him about my two cash gifts from Hauge. Desperately need advice. Rune Hauge is being investigated by Norwegian tax authorities and they have found a slip of paper with my name on it, and a reference to a sum of money. Do I need to declare the cash to the Inland Revenue, who are taking a close interest in Arsenal affairs? John asks how much it is in total. I tell him £425,000. John, who has been guiding me through the minefield of finance for many years, is of the opinion that as the two payments were unsolicited gifts they may not be liable to tax, but we would need to seek professional advice.

26 August, 1994: Attended a meeting with John in the Charterhouse office of Gerald Lane, a director of the accountants and tax specialists RM Walkden & Co. Mr Lane has no doubt that there is a tax liability, and his strong advice is that the tax authorities must be informed as soon as possible. He has also advised that the Trust I set up for Nicole and Daniel should be wound up because it offers no advantages for income tax and capital gains tax purposes. I was told to also bring the gifts to the attention of Arsenal.

19 September, 1994: A noon meeting at Highbury with Peter Hill-Wood and Ken Friar in my office. John Hazell takes notes. The chairman seems surprisingly relaxed and unconcerned when I tell him about the payments. He does not even ask me the amounts. The chairman advises that I am wise to declare everything and to avoid problems with the Inland Revenue. I apologised to him for my actions, adding that few people would have found it possible to refuse the offer of unsolicited gifts. The chairman nodded his head like a wise old owl. Both the chairman and Ken Friar agreed that the matter would be kept private between the four of us, apart from having to tell Kitsons, the club accountants.

22 September, 1994: Peter Hill-Wood summons me to a meeting at Highbury. Ken Friar and John are also there. The chairman is now agitated compared with his calm manner at our first meeting. He tells us that having had time to consider all the points he could no longer keep the matter between the four of us. 'You have been naughty and I must inform the rest of the Board,' he says. 'I cannot guarantee how they will react.' He asks me the sums involved, and his eyebrows rise when I tell him. The chairman seems not so much concerned about me but the tax man. He said that the club had signed a 'complete disclosure' document that would give Arsenal a clean bill of health with the tax man, but now there would be complications because of my payments on top of those that had been declared by chief scout Steve Burtenshaw. The chairman said, 'I have already signed a statement to the effect that there are no more skeletons in the cupboard. Now this ...' I argued that this was a completely different matter, and nothing to do with the club. It would be between me and the tax man because they were unsolicited gifts made to me and had nothing what-soever to do with club business.

4 October, 1994: I was handed an official letter today by Ken Friar instructing me to attend the Board meeting at Highbury this Thursday. I do not like the tone of the letter. Ken and I have been pals for years. It reads as if he is prosecutor: 'The directors, understandably, have serious concerns about the matter and would wish to have from you, first-hand, a full account of what happened and any other explanations. The Board would decide then what action, if any, needed to be taken.'

6 October, 1994: Sir Robert Bellinger, former Lord Mayor of London, does much of the talking at the Board meeting. He said that the sum involved was substantial, and he questioned whether the payments were unsolicited gifts. I know it is hard for anybody to believe, but I did not ask for the money. When I pointed out that few people would have been able to refuse, Sir Robert said that he had been offered gifts in the past but had said 'no'. Bully for Sir Robert. I told him that his financial situation was probably different to mine. Sir Robert, who I sensed had been elected spokesman, suggested that the money belonged to the club rather than me, but I reacted strongly against that idea because it was my brains that Hauge had been picking. There was no conclusion drawn by the Board at this meeting, but I could already pick out those who were for me and those who were against.

7 October, 1994: Vice-chairman David Dein called in on me at my office, and we talked for two hours. He said that I had lost the trust of the Board, and I responded by saying that I was disappointed that they could not take my word. They knew me well enough to know that I am a basically honest bloke. I had made a mistake, and had admitted it. If I could put right the wrong I would. David got all confidential and said, 'Look, I know the money is out of your transfer deals and that you've got to stick to your story...' I was ready to explode. 'Sorry, David, but you've got it wrong. I'm telling you the truth. The payments were made as unsolicited gifts.' He then insulted me by saying

179

that the Board are now wondering if I have made any money out of my trips abroad. David really knows how to hit below the belt. 'There could be a worry about your involvement in future transfers,' he said. 'No problem,' I replied. 'You look after them.' (He has always given me the impression that this is his ambition, so let him get on with it.) He then started fishing: 'Would you like to go and work abroad?' 'No,' I told him. 'I've got a job here at Arsenal, and I want to win a third Championship. I have no intention of resigning.' He then gave me the friendly bit. 'I want to mend bridges,' he said. 'We don't want this getting into the newspapers.' He explained that the club were concerned because the Inland Revenue had stopped all dialogue with Arsenal. They were worried as the chairman had signed a statement saying that everything about the club business has been disclosed. 'He signed it in good faith,' I said, 'and as far as my business goes that is between me and the tax man. It is not club business.'

22 October, 1994: My tax adviser Gerald Lane received a worrying letter from the Inland Revenue today. They are considering preparing a report so that the Board of Inland Revenue can decide whether in their opinion I have commited any criminal offence. I am positive that I have not broken any laws, but must seek legal advice.

4 November, 1994: Danny Fiszman, the most influential of all the Arsenal directors and a near neighbour living just a few roads and several million pounds away, invited me to his palatial home to talk things over. David Dein was also there. Danny told me that the Board are considering sacking me. They have taken legal advice and feel they can dismiss me, leaving me with no recourse for wrongful dismissal. I told him that I would fight the Board all the way because I still do not believe that I have done anything wrong. Stupid, yes. Unlawful, no. I said that the Board wanted my head on a plate, but they were not going to get it. Danny suggested there were two alternatives for me to consider: 1) The sack, and a subsequent court case which would be bad for everybody concerned; 2) I could write a letter of resignation that would be implemented at the end of the season, and in return get a suitable compensation package. I suggested a third alternative that brought wry smiles to their faces: 'Let's forget all about it!'

7 November, 1994: Danny Fiszman talked to me again this evening, just one to one. He said the Board wanted to make a decision either way at their meeting in ten days' time ... to either sack me or to come to an agreement on a resignation. By doing nothing, they could be seen by the Inland Revenue to be condoning what I had done. Two of the directors, he said, were of the opinion that I should be sacked without any further discussion. He claimed that he and David Dein were fighting for a dignified way to settle the problem. I said that I would only consider the resignation route if I was guaranteed that my contract would be honoured (it had until June 1997 to run, and was worth considerably more than £1 million).

8 November, 1994: John Hazell had a meeting with Rune Hauge today at the Royal Lancaster Hotel. Rune confirmed everything that I said about the money being unsolicited gifts, and that he had wanted to thank me for opening up the British transfer market to him. Rune said that he would be prepared to come to London to speak up for me if he was ever needed.

9 November, 1994: One of my solicitors, Rob Eldridge, of Berwin Leighton, has produced a five page report analysing the entire employment situation. His confidential summary includes the view that the sum of £425,000 might be seen as being too large a figure to represent a gift.

10 November, 1994: John Hazell and I meet Danny Fiszman and David Dein again at Danny's place to discuss a compensation package. John opens up by making an impassioned speech of support for me. It was highly charged stuff, and Danny and David both hastily assured us that they had been working hard on my behalf talking certain directors out of option one, the sack and no compensation. But they were now able to talk about option two, the compensation package. 'The club,' Danny said, 'wants a happy ending. After all that you have done for Arsenal, we want to see you go out a hero, not a villain.' He pointed out that the club felt that the 'gift' money by rights belonged to Arsenal. They asked what compensation I was seeking. John, who is a respected financial consultant, had spent the previous

181

48 hours working out what my guaranteed earnings, pension rights and calculated bonuses would be up to June 1997, and he came up with a figure of £1.7 million gross, which would be a net payment of just over £1 million. They were thinking more in terms of £500,000, taking into account that I was in possession of the gift money. After a lot of haggling and juggling, John and I came down to a figure of £850,000 gross, £500,000 net. Danny and David agreed to put the case to the Board.

14 November, 1994: Anthony Arlidge QC, one of the country's leading barristers, today advised me that I should hand the gift payments over to Arsenal. This opinion was forcibly seconded by Charles Falconer QC, a specialist in Employment Law. This would in their view clear me of any serious problem with the Inland Revenue. It was explained to me that legally the money belonged to Arsenal because it had been given to me while I was in their employment and as a result of work that I carried out as an employee of Arsenal. I shook my head in disbelief, but as the best legal brains in Britain are telling me I suppose I had better listen.

16 November, 1994 (5.00pm): John Hazell and I met Danny Fiszman and David Dein at David's swish home in Totteridge. There had been an unofficial Board meeting at Highbury yesterday, and they have been authorised to tell me that the Board were prepared to offer the following package that is not negotiable: 1) I would write a letter of resignation, giving notice that I would leave the club on 31 May 1995; 2) I would receive a lump-sum payment of £250,000, plus a testimonial match (which it was estimated would produce a minimum of £250,000) and a bonus of £250,000 if Arsenal qualify for Europe. This package acknowledged that Arsenal would not press me to pay to them the gift money. John Hazell made the point that if this leaked out to the press, I could hardly expect a well-supported testimonial match. It was agreed that a pre-announcement of my decision to resign 'with honour' would be made to the media. It seems some directors are concerned that I would be unable to motivate the players in these circumstances, but I insisted I had no worries on that score. David Dein said that while they could not dictate to me, they would be very unhappy if I joined one of their major competitors in my next job. He was thinking in particular of Tottenham. It was also agreed that if at the season's end both the Board and I wanted to change our minds and continue working together, the 'retirement' plan would be kicked into touch. 'This offer,' said diamond merchant Danny Fiszman, 'is set in stone.'

16 November, 1994 (8.00pm): With John Hazell, visited the chambers of Anthony Arlidge QC. Also present were Charles Falconer QC, and my legal advisers Tony Bunker and Rob Eldridge. Mr Arlidge repeated his advice that it was his considered opinion that I should hand the money to Arsenal or risk prosecution by the Inland Revenue. Charles Falconer, the leading expert in these matters, suggested that I should draft two letters, one offering to hand the money to Arsenal; two, a letter of resignation. Letter number one, written in my own hand, reads:

> Dear Mr Chairman, You will remember that on 19 September I told you and Ken Friar about payments of money I had received from a football agent called Mr Hauge. It was suggested at the next Board meeting that the money might in fact belong to Arsenal FC. I have now taken advice from Charles Falconer QC that, despite the fact that they were unsolicited payments, the monies should be regarded as belonging to Arsenal FC. None of the money has been spent. It has been invested. Instructions have been issued to realize these investments and I will pay the monies together with any profit to Arsenal FC as soon as possible.
> Yours sincerely, George Graham.

Letter number two reads:

> Dear Mr Chairman, I would like to inform you that I have decided to leave my job as manager of Arsenal FC after the end of the current season. I have greatly enjoyed my time as manager of the club and do not want my departure to jeopardise its future. I will do everything I can to co-operate with my

successor if he is appointed before I leave. Whilst I intend to remain active in football management I will never forget the opportunity that the club has given me. Yours sincerely, George Graham.

16 November, 1994 (11.15pm): Back to Totteridge for further meeting with Fiszman and Dein. Reported the opinion of Counsel, and that I would be handing in my letter of resignation at tomorrow's Board meeting. They were also delighted with the news that I would be handing over the money.They once again promised that they would see to it that I would leave with dignity and with a suitable package that would reflect the success I had brought to the club.

17 November, 1994: Handed my resignation letter to chairman Peter Hill-Wood today. I was too choked up to say anything, and left the Boardroom with tears in my eyes. This is not how I envisaged ending my days at Arsenal.

25 November, 1994: Paul Merson tells the *Daily Mirror* that he has drink, gambling and drug problems. For months I have been warning him against drinking and gambling, but I had no idea he was also taking cocaine. This is not the time to discipline him. The boy needs help, and I pledge full support to him. Paul's problems put my troubles in perspective.

30 November, 1994: Fifty years old! At least I've got something to celebrate – a 2-0 victory over Sheffield Wednesday in the fourth round of the Coca-Cola Cup at Highbury. Cancel a planned birthday bash and settle for small family dinner with Daniel, Nicole and her husband Carl. We dine at Harvey Nicols (absolutely fabulous), and then go on to Tramp's for a drink. Stories are beginning to leak out in the Press about my resignation, but the club and I decided on a policy of 'no comment'.

1 December, 1994: Pay over a cheque to Arsenal for £465,500, inclusive of £40,000 on account of interest (They will eventually have £482,205 sitting in their account.) Call me a stubborn Scot, but I still feel the money is rightfully mine. Rune Hauge had wanted to thank me as an individual, not Arsenal the club. I never had any intention of breaking Inland Revenue rules, and I genuinely believed that you did not have to declare unsolicited gifts. Now I have put right the wrong. I wish I had never accepted the money in the first place. If only ...

3 December, 1994: I was having a quiet evening meal at the Mezzaluna restaurant in Hampstead with friends when we were interrupted by a reporter from the *Mail on Sunday*. She showed me a copy of the front page of their first edition. The lead story was that Arsenal are investigating payments made to me. I am just surprised that it has taken so long to leak out. I thank the reporter for her interest but tell her that I have nothing to say.

4 December, 1994: The *Mail on Sunday* front page exclusive prompts David Dein to contact Premier League chief executive Rick Parry. He tells him that I have already paid the money to Arsenal.

8 December, 1994: Ken Friar receives a letter from Premier League solicitors Denton Hall confirming that an Inquiry team has been set up to look into the 'alleged irregularities in the transfers of Mr John Jensen and Mr Pal Lydersen to Arsenal FC'. The Inquiry team will consist of Rick Parry, Steve Coppell and Robert Reid QC.

11 December, 1994: More *Mail on Sunday* revelations. They have found out about the £285,000 payment and have tied it in with the John Jensen transfer. Wrong! This will give more fuel to the Inquiry team.

15 December, 1994: I was questioned today by the Premier League Inquiry team at the Chancery Lane offices of Denton Hall. I willingly told them that I had accepted two payments from Rune Hauge, and I stressed that they were unsolicited gifts which were not connected in any way to the Jensen and Lydersen transfers. I know that Hauge will confirm this when he is interviewed.

18 December, 1994: According to the letter from Denton Hall, the

Inquiry is supposed to be conducted in strict confidence. Yet I open my Sunday papers today to find 'Graham guilty' and 'Graham to be banned' stories all over the back pages. So much for confidentiality. It's diabolical, and I complain bitterly to my lawyers. It is as if I am being hit from all sides.

23 December, 1994: I am being ripped apart by the media, and have taken legal advice about the possibility of suing for libel. Counsel advises against it 'at this moment in time', but stresses to keep all cuttings for future reference that would help me make out a case of 'persecution' at a later date. Counsel quotes Henry Ford to me: 'When dealing with the media, never complain, never explain.' So it continues to be open house on George Graham. It is three years to the day since I accepted the first gift from Hauge. Merry Christmas.

13 January, 1995: Paul Merson is in tears at a press conference as he reveals how he is determined to fight his personal problems. We are all behind him. I concentrate on footballing matters, and clinch the transfers of John Hartson from Luton and Chris Kiwomya from Ipswich. I would like to bid for the major stars, but the Arsenal board's wage structure will not allow it. We urgently need a pick-up in the League because we are down in thirteenth place. That's virtually unheard of in my time as manager at Highbury.

2 February, 1995: Gave David Dein a lift home from the ground today. He has recently come back from the United States where he watched the Superbowl with Rick Parry. Parry has apparently told Dein that he is desperate to keep the matter exclusively under the umbrella of the Premier League, and that he did not want the Football Association to get involved. Dein said that Arsenal were now not only under pressure from the press but also from the government because MP Kate Hoey has been asking searching questions in the House. I report the conversation to John Hazell, who says: 'George, they will not be happy until they have your head on a platter.'

9 February, 1995: I never thought I would admit it, but I have now had enough at Arsenal. Our performance last night against AC Milan in the second leg of the European Super Cup was just about the worst in my time at Highbury. There is no doubt that I have 'lost' some of the players. I just cannot motivate them like I used to. I'm tired, a few of them are past their peak and the payments affair is hardly helping matters. The majority of the press are slaughtering me without being in full possession of the facts, directors are being off-hand and distant, and there is an unhealthy atmosphere. I convey my thoughts to John Hazell, and tell him that I don't want to wait until the end of the season before resigning.

10 February, 1995: John Hazell reported on a meeting he had yesterday at Danny Fiszman's Farringdon Road office. They went through the financial package which has been changed in view of the fact that I have paid the gift money to the club. It was decided that there would be a termination of contract by mutual consent, and it was provisionally agreed to announce my departure at a Press conference on 15 February, this of course subject to a satisfactory financial arrangement. John had negotiated a deal that would bring me a £750,000 settlement of my contract, plus another £250,000 in lieu of a testimonial match that was shelved because of all the recent publicity. While this will sound a fortune to many people, it was a cut-price deal as far as I was concerned. I would have earned a minimum £1.7 million by staying to the end of my contract, and I no longer had the gift money. In my opinion this would be a cheap get-out for Arsenal after all the money I had generated for them during the past eight and a half years. I have just been given the go-ahead to buy Dutch international winger Glen Helder from Vitesse Arnhem for approaching £2 million, so reports of my imminent dismissal are exaggerated.

15 February, 1995: Danny Fiszman contacted John to tell him that there was a major problem. The IK Start officials had allegedly given damaging evidence about the Pal Lydersen deal. Danny said that I should contact the chairman urgently. I rang the chairman's home (as Danny had arranged) and talked to his son, Charlie. He said that his father was not there, but that he would tell him that I had rung. My call was not returned. David Dein had told me that he understood that the IK Start officials were suggesting that I had manufactured the figures for the Lydersen deal. Untrue!

18 February, 1995: Attended the Premier League Inquiry meeting, but did not give evidence because we had lost confidence in the ability of the Inquiry to be impartial. All concentration now seems to be on the IK Start/Lydersen deal. Apparently the three IK Start officials could not give any details about Lydersen's £110,000 signing-on fee, but they were able to recall how long the dinner had lasted after our negotiations.

20 February, 1995: The newspapers are full of informed gossip about the findings of the Premier League Inquiry. 'Graham guilty of taking bungs,' is the tabloid theme. This Inquiry committee seems to have more leaks than a Welshman's garden.

21 February, 1995: The boot goes in, and I go out without a penny compensation. I am now counting on the Football Association tribunal to clear my name (I can hear Tommy Docherty: 'Don't hold your breath, George.').

15: Drugs, Drought and Despair

February, 1995: A good time of the year to apply worm-killing preparation to my lawn. While worms in the cultivated parts of the garden can aerate the soil and be beneficial, they should be eradicated from the lawn because they produce slippery casts that can spoil the appearance of well-manicured turf. Get rid of the worms!

IT seemed so unreal as I sat in my Hampstead lounge on the evening of 10 May 1995, watching Arsenal lose to a freak last-kick goal in the European Cup Winners' Cup Final. A year earlier in Copenhagen it had been one of the greatest nights of my life when we won the trophy. Now here I was sitting in front of my television set watching the team I had built being beaten in the cruellest way possible. I was mortified for the players, with whom I will always have a bond; and I was desperately sorry for Stewart Houston, my old pal who had taken over from me in a caretaker capacity when I had been kicked out of the manager's job eleven weeks earlier.

I sensed that Stewart had no chance of being made manager on a permanent basis. He was too much in my mould, and I doubt that even a victory in the Cup Winners' Cup Final would have got him the job. But his chances disappeared completely with Nayim's incredible last minute goal for Real Zaragoza. Arsenal had shown all the character which I had embedded in them to claw their way back into the match with a John Hartson equaliser after trailing 1-0 with fifteen minutes to go. Then, with just seconds to go to a penalty shoot-out, ex-Tottenham midfielder Nayim lobbed the ball from way out on the touchline, and David Seaman – the semi-final hero – scrambled back but was unable to stop the ball dipping over his outstretched fingers and into the net. It was as dramatic a goal as that scored by Michael Thomas to clinch our first Championship triumph at Anfield, and I sank into my sofa in helpless despair as Arsenal finally relinquished the trophy we had worked so hard to win.

My last season at Highbury, all six months of it, had been one long nightmare. I had lost some of my rapport with a few of the players and was struggling to motivate them. Everybody, including the players, the directors and the fans, had been spoiled by all our success. I remember Stan Cullis saying when he was sacked by Wolves after a barren season following years of winning trophies: 'I have given them a yardstick by which they can measure me, and it has become a stick with which they can beat me.' That was how it was for me. In the previous May we had won the Cup Winners' Cup, our sixth trophy in eight seasons. The 1994-95 season was barely three months old before our critics were bandying around that over-used word 'crisis' because, by our sky-high standards, we had made a poor start to the Premiership campaign and there was a worrying drought of goals.

But then we were overtaken by a real crisis; a personal crisis for Paul Merson, who admitted in an exclusive series in the *Daily Mirror* that he was addicted to gambling, alcohol and cocaine. The story broke at the same time as I was trying to cope with the sensitive (to say the least) Rune Hauge gift issue. Suddenly my predicament seemed minuscule alongside that of Paul's. I had seen it all coming to a boiling point for months, but even I was astonished by the depth of his problems. Long before these revelations, some members of the Board had wanted me to get rid of Paul because 'he's not quite the Arsenal image, old boy.' I pointed out that if we were going to take that sort of high moral ground we would not be left with much of a team.

I wanted to persevere with Paul because I knew that, clear of his problems, he could be a real asset to the club. Walter Smith, Rangers manager, was very keen to take him to Ibrox, but I would not give him any encouragement (the thought now of the two Pauls – Merson and Gascoigne – loose in Glasgow together on a Saturday night is mind blowing!).

Once again, I was crucified over the situation. 'Why has Graham not kept a closer eye on him?' was the chief criticism. Anybody who knows anything about alcoholism or any addiction will know that there is nothing or nobody as crafty as the addict. No one at Arsenal knew the extent of Paul's problems. Time and again I had tried to help this likeable lad, quietly giving him lectures and advice and occasional disciplinary fines to try to get him to straighten himself out. He was basically a nice person, and worth trying to help. It had reached the point where I had twice had secret meetings with his wife, Lorraine, and we were working out how we could get him some professional advice when the story broke. I found out about it the day before it appeared in the newspaper when Paul, accompanied by Arsenal players' agent Jerome Andersen, called in to Ken Friar's office to tell him of the problem. Ken, who at heart is a really caring man, has since gone to extreme lengths to help Paul get himself on the recovery road.

When trying to advise Paul, I had always centred my comments on his drinking and gambling habits. I had no idea whatsoever he was also into drugs, and I like to think that part of the story was exaggerated, as were the tales about him turning up drunk at training and with hang-overs on match days. The only time I knew he might perhaps have been the worse for wear was when Stewart Houston had to send him home from a training session. If I had thought Paul was ever 'drunk on duty' I would have given him the rollocking of his life. As for the use of drugs, I would not have tolerated that under any circumstances.

I am from the old-fashioned school that detests all drugs, and I have not got a clue how to get hold of them or how to use them. But I recognise that the young generation is heavily into a drug culture, and that recreational drugs are in wide use. Chris Armstrong was the most highly publicised case of a footballer being found positive in one of the random drugs tests that the football authorites have wisely introduced, and many of us in the game fear that the problem of recreational drug-taking is widespread. I was astonished when a random test in December 1994 caught our midfield player David Hillier in the net. It showed that he had been smoking cannabis, but I had to accept his explanation that it had been a spiked cigarette slipped to him by a mischief maker. David did not seem the type of boy to get caught up in the drugs scene, but you just never know these days.

I was even more amazed when Paul Merson confessed that he was hooked on cocaine. I was just hoping he had made that statement to try to bump up his serialisation fee.

My advice to Paul once he went public with his problems (he sold his story to help pay gambling debts) was three-fold: one, get expert help; two, ditch those hangers-on who are dragging you into trouble; three, fight to hold your marriage together because, in Lorraine, you've got a wife who loves you.

The entire Arsenal club – Ken Friar in particular – got behind Paul in his battle to beat his addictions, but in the end it was down to him to do it on his own. He went into a rehabilitation centre in Southampton for six weeks, and then joined Alcoholics and Gamblers Anonymous and started to overcome his demons a day at a time. It has given me enormous pleasure to watch Paul getting his act together. He gradually became a new man, with a shining light in his eyes and the confidence to start helping others facing his sort of problems.

At his lowest moments, Paul told me that he had even considered taking his own life because of the crushing pressures brought on by his three addictions. His recovery is nothing short of miraculous, and the Football Association now use him as a spokesman for their Fit for Football campaign. Keep it up, Paul.

The first match Paul watched after his rehabilitation treatment was our FA Cup third round replay against Millwall at Highbury. We were a suitable case for treatment that night as we crashed to a humiliating 2-0 defeat. It was wrongly reported that I had an up-and-a-downer in the dressing-room afterwards with several of the players. We did not argue, but all agreed that our application and attitude was wrong.

I knew deep down that I was approaching the end of the road with Arsenal, and the feeling was nothing to do with the cash controversy. The team was not functioning properly, despite the arrival of a beautifully composed midfield player in Stefan Schwarz. He unfortunately came into a struggling side. A year or so earlier he would have been a sensation when all the other players were on song.

But I felt I had temporarily lost the motivating powers needed to inspire the players as in my peak years at Highbury. The team needed an injection of new blood, and the directors released £5.9 million for me to buy John Hartson from Luton, Chris Kiwomya from Ipswich and the Dutch international winger Glen Helder. So much for the lack of confidence from the Board! I would have preferred to have signed Marc Overmars from Ajax, but they tied him to a long-term contract just when I thought I was on the point of capturing him. So I switched my interest to Helder.

If I had been allowed the time I am confident I could have moulded the new players into the Arsenal team that could have maintained the standards of my previous sides, but I was shown the door before

Helder's signature had hardly had time to dry on the contract.

One of the accusations constantly levelled at me was that I was lax in my disciplining of the players (while other critics said I was too much of an iron-fisted manager and likened me to Gadaffi and Saddam Hussein!). It was always being shoved down my throat that Herbert Chapman would never have stood for the drinking, nightclubbing and (in Paul Merson's case) drug taking that occasionally had my players splashed across the newspapers. All I can repeat in my defence is that I could not spend twenty-four hours a day with the players. Although I had control over them during working hours, I had to put them on trust and treat them as adults when they were out of my sight. London is a giant city with temptations on nearly every corner, and once they have gone off into the night after a match you can only hope that they will be professional and responsible (as most of them were). Herbert Chapman did not manage in an era when players were earning thousands of pounds a week, had fast cars, and were the target for headline hungry newspapers.

I like to think I was hard but fair with the Arsenal players. What I asked from them in return for my loyalty and support was total effort and pride in their performance. We had some great years together, and I hope that one day when they look back they will appreciate that I gave them standards that could set them up for life.

One of my most memorable moments came a few days after I had been sacked. I paid a secret visit to London Colney for one last goodbye to the players who had done so much to make my eight-and-a-half years so rewarding. I thanked them for all their support and said that I knew I had been a demanding manager. 'But one day,' I told them, 'you'll look at your medals and you will realise all the hard work was worth it.'

Then, for the last time, I drove away from London Colney – the place where I had plotted all our victories. And yes, there were tears in my eyes.

Now I could only kick my heels until the Football Assocation hearing where I was convinced I was going to have my greatest victory. Wrong, George!

16 : A Worldwide Ban

August 1995: We are deep into a long, dry summer and I am busy with the hose pipe bringing life and sparkle to my thirsty garden. There is talk of a possible hose pipe ban. That would be a disaster for my plants. They need water like I need football. We are feeling very parched.

TRUE to his word, Rune Hauge turned up to give evidence at the Football Association hearing that followed a frustrating five months after the Premier League Inquiry findings and my brutal sacking by Arsenal. Hauge, whose English some would say is better than mine, repeated what I had been saying from day one: that the money he gave me had been an unsolicited gift as a gesture of thanks on behalf of his company, InterClub, for helping him become established in the British transfer market.

You could have heard a boot-lace drop in what was a courtroom atmosphere when FA barrister Brian Leveson QC tried hard to get him to admit that he had made payments to other British managers. Under fierce cross-examination, Hauge would only go so far as to say that it was 'usual' to pay managers. I was pleased when, despite the continual probing of Mr Leveson, he refused to name names.

I would not want any one in the game to go through the nightmare I had suffered since this whole issue had blown up like a grenade going off in my hand. I am not the sort of vindictive person to start pointing the finger at anybody else in football.

It sickens me to think I have been made a scapegoat, but that does not mean I want to drag others down with me. They will understand what I mean when I pose the question: Where is the rule in any football book (or in my Arsenal contract) that says: 'You must not receive gifts'?

Yes, it is probably morally wrong. But if we start analysing morals in the game, I would think that come Judgment Day some club chairmen and directors will be perspiring in the queue along with managers.

I am not allowed to give chapter and verse on the FA hearing because evidence was given in confidence, but I can paint a picture of what it was like in the temporary 'courtroom' that was set up in a conference suite of the Watford Hilton National Hotel.

If I had not been the man 'on trial', I would have been thoroughly absorbed in it as a spectacle. The cut and thrust of the courtroom has always held an appeal for me, and representing me I had a fencing master. Anthony Arlidge QC is a Rumpole-style character with a wit as quick as a professional comedian and a brain as sharp as a razor-blade. His adversary making out the case for the FA was Brian Leveson QC, much more serious and sombre but just as smart and perceptive (He was the barrister briefed to prosecute Rosemary West, and I had to smile at the suggestion from one of our team that maybe the FA thought I had buried some money in the garden; somebody else said no stone would be left unturned – laughter was keeping me one step the right side of sanity.) Michael Brindle QC was also there as legal adviser to the tribunal, but he only played a back-seat role. It was an education to listen to these word masters at work, and I might even have enjoyed it except that I was having to pay through the nose for the privilege of listening. I was paying the piper, but I was not calling the tune.

The men in charge of the case and my destiny were the three panel 'judges': Geoff Thompson, chairman of the FA disciplinary committee and also chairman of the panel; Gordon McKeag, the Football League President; and Lincoln City chairman John Reames. They were all reasonable men, and I looked forward to an honest judgement based on all the facts.

Over the course of eighteen hours of evidence spread across three days, I feel I got a fair hearing. If it had been a boxing match between Anthony Arlidge and Brian Leveson, the referee would have scored a clear points win for my man. He was particularly tough on the two IK Start representatives who made the trip from Norway, leaving a third one behind. It had been their evidence to the Premier League Inquiry (along with that of the missing third man) that had persuaded the Arsenal board to fire me, but Arlidge made them extremely uncomfortable under penetrating cross-examination. They contradicted each other on important points to such an extent that I was confident it would be confirmed that I was 'not guilty'.

Ken Friar and Peter Hill-Wood, from whom I was now distanced since my two-and-a-half-minute dismissal, barely nodded to me. For more than eight years we had worked as a tremendously successful team. Now they could not look me in the eye. Both were given some quite harrowing moments under cross-examination, and they contradicted each other on a vital point of transfer procedure.

Howard Wilkinson, Leeds manager and a founder member of the League Managers' Association, appeared as a character witness for me, and all in all I thought our case was powerful enough and revealing enough to have cleared me.

The Prosecution Case against me was summarised in three alternative ways:

(1) most seriously, that Mr Graham had effectively conspired (with Mr Rune Hauge, a football agent) to make a personal profit from the Lydersen and Jensen deals;
(2) that the payments arose out of or in connection with the transfers, and he knew that was so when he received them;
(3) that the payments were connected to the transfers but Mr Graham did not realise this.

The panel took three hours considering their verdict, and then found me not guilty on the most serious charge. They said they were not satisfied that I had asked for the money or that I had negotiated the transfers to obtain any personal gain. I had not, they felt, set up the transfers to make money for myself. That was the good news. The bad news is that they were satisfied that when I received the money I must have known it was connected with transfers. The receipt of the payments, they decided, constituted misconduct.

Twenty-four hours later the panel announced the punishment: a one year ban, plus a share of the FA's legal costs (which felt to me like a £50,000 fine).

I could not believe it. The main case against me had not been proven, yet they still decided to hang me over what were relatively minor charges. I could only lean on the famous Lee Harvey Oswald quote: 'I'm the patsy.'

Anthony Arlidge had done such an outstanding job representing me, including a powerful plea for leniency, that I thought at worse I might get a hefty fine. But the one year ban was like double punishment. Not only was it 12 months out of football (on top of the five months since my dismissal by Arsenal), but I had also been virtually prohibited from earning a proper living for seventeen months. Then there was the sting in the tail: the legal costs. How on earth did they expect I was going to pay them if I was unable to earn my daily bread in the game of football that had been my life for thirty-five years?

The costs kept piling up. Not only had I repaid the gift plus the interest, I had lost a contract worth £1.7 million and had huge legal fees to pay for my own lawyers and Counsel.

Like most people, I have a mortgage. Like everybody, I have to eat, drink and clothe myself. Like any driver, I have to pay to put petrol in the car. But suddenly my main means of making a living had been denied me.

It would have been easy for me to have taken the Manchester City job while I was waiting for the FA panel to get their act together, but I did not wish to embarrass City chairman Francis Lee, who had chatted to me about the vacancy at Maine Road before giving the job to my old Arsenal team-mate Alan Ball.

I also lost out on three possible jobs abroad. In March I had secret talks at a Piccadilly hotel with Bilbao general manager Señor Fernando Ochoa, who was keen for me to make a commitment to take over the Basque club regardless of the FA hearing. I told him that it would not be fair for me accept his offer with the threat of suspension hanging over me. I then had an approach asking if I was interested in joining Sporting Lisbon, but this was more tentative. I also had a meeting in London with a representative of the Turkish club Fernebahce. I told him I would be making no plans until after the hearing. All three jobs went out of the window once FIFA confirmed that the FA's ban was worldwide.

I have not profited from my folly in accepting the gifts. The money has been handed on to Arsenal and is now sitting in their bank account. In fact, out of the whole episode I consider that I am the only one whose financial health has been seriously damaged. Arsenal have profited greatly from my predicament. I wonder if anybody at Highbury feels at all embarrassed when they think of the £1.7 million in earnings they will not have to pay me, and of the £482,205 in their bank gaining interest? That was money given to me and which I was going to put in Trust for my children. I have conceded that I was greedy in accepting it, but I had noble plans for the money.

The most rewarding thing about the whole mess has been the wonderful support I received from Arsenal players, good friends and marvellous supporters. I got a load of calls from my old players wishing me luck and encouraging me to keep my head up, and the response from Highbury fans has been just unbelievable. I have lost count of the number of people who have stopped me in the street to give me their support, and I received hundreds of letters from the Highbury faithful giving me strength during my rockbottom days. It was theraputic for me to reply to each and every one of them by hand to tell them how grateful I was for their thoughts and good wishes.

My relationship with the Arsenal fans had always been strong without being soppy. I never tried to milk their support or to play to them, but I know we had a deep respect for each other and I like to think I gave them plenty to feel proud about during the eight-and-a-half years that I was privileged to be Arsenal manager. *Their* manager.

On the evening of 3 April 1995, the condemned man was given a memorable supper. Susan, a very special lady who had been a source of strength to me during these difficult times, talked me into taking her out for a meal at our favourite Mezzaluna restaurant. When we arrived, we found it shut to the public. Nicola, the owner, opened the door and as he ushered us in a piper in full Scottish regalia led the way. Inside were more than one hundred of my closest friends gathered for a surprise party organised by Nicola, Susan, my daughter, Nicole, and John Hazell. They included my Arsenal buddies Stewart Houston, Steve Burtenshaw, Pat Rice, Fred Street, Geordie Armstrong, Gary Lewin, Theo Foley, Bob Wilson, Frank McLintock, and Doc Crane, the club doctor.

Nicola had got his chef to make a huge cake in the shape of a football pitch on which were mounted miniature players and the words in red icing on a white background, 'George's Gunners'. It was my pal Terry Venables who said: 'This, George, is an unsolicited gift.'

I had a song request for Terry. 'Chestnuts Roasting on an Open Fire'.

I gave deep consideration to lodging an appeal against the verdict. It was in my view scandalous that I had been banned for effectively seventeen months after the panel of 'judges' had found me not guilty on the main charge of conspiring to make a profit from the Lydersen and Jensen deals. What on earth would the punishment have been had they found me guilty? A public hanging, no doubt.

There were three main reasons why I finally decided against an appeal. The first was purely financial. I do not have a bottomless pocket, and I have been cleaned out since my dismissal in February 1995. I just simply could not afford the costs of an appeal. A football club like Tottenham can afford to take on the Football Association in court and expose that the FA do not live by the laws of the land, but it is beyond the means of most individuals to take a legal battle to court. My second reason was that I felt in my heart that I would not get a fair hearing because in my opinion the FA had to be seen to be hanging somebody out to dry. My third reason was the much more basic one of simply wanting to get on with the rest of my life. I have lived with the burden of the gift controversy for too long. Now I just want to kick it into history, and to start living again and to start preparing for my return to the game of football that I love above all else.

John Hazell and I have been doing our sums, and we calculate that my year in exile plus the five months I spent waiting for the FA hearing will have cost me far in excess of £2 million (taking into account lost earnings, anticipated bonuses and extra-curricular income, plus crippling legal costs).

Arsenal, meantime, are having a great time spending the millions that I helped earn for them. Their transfer transactions since I was kicked out of Highbury make the deals I used to conduct seem like petty-cash affairs by comparison.

I did not know whether to laugh or cry when, with my bloodstains still on the boardroom carpet, Arsenal bought Dennis Bergkamp and David Platt for around £12.5 million. I am sure that if, say a year earlier, I had gone to managing director Ken Friar and told him I wanted to spend that amount of money on two players he would have thought I had gone round the bend. 'There is no way we can afford that,' he would have said, and I am sure that it would not have even been considered by the directors.

It was Arsenal policy – not George Graham policy – to operate a tight, even-handed wage structure. Arsenal will no doubt dispute that, but I will not give ground on the fact that it was the club that laid down the wages policy, not me. No player was allowed to earn heavily in excess of a team-mate. Time and again I had my hands tied by the board's wage restrictions when trying to bring the best players to Highbury. Roy Keane, Paul Parker, Chris Sutton, Tony Cottee, Jan Wouters, Didier Deschamps and David Ginola are just some of the quality players I missed out on because I could not compete with the wages being offered by other clubs. More than once I made the point to the directors that Manchester United, in particular, were getting the players that I wanted simply because they were paying the sort of wages that today's star footballers expect. I was convinced that Chris Sutton was going to join us from Norwich, but I understand that once he found he could probably earn twice as much at Blackburn we had no chance of signing him.

'If we give in to one player, we will have a queue of players at the door,' Ken Friar used to say.

Several times I told members of the board that we needed to change our wages policy if we were to compete with our rival clubs for top players, but my pleas fell on deaf ears. I managed to keep Arsenal in the chase for the major trophies despite the wages handicap imposed by the directors. Yet no sooner had I been dismissed than the wage policy was turned upside down. The likes of Bergkamp and Platt were, on their arrival, no doubt earning three and four times what some of their Arsenal team-mates were picking up each week.

I heard on the grapevine that the queues quickly started forming at the boardroom door, and that several of the players were given substantial pay rises to keep the peace.

As an Arsenal shareholder, I am looking forward to seeing the balance sheet at the end of the 1995-96 season. The wages section will make interesting reading. I used to take all the flak for being tight while I was merely carrying out the board policy. Now I wonder just how successful I might have been had they allowed me the freedom to meet the astronomical wage demands of today's top players. Might I have done even better than winning six trophies?

And here's another question that I keep kicking about in my head: *Who really holds the power at Arsenal Football Club?* Inspector Graham investigates ...

17 : Arsenal Stadium Mystery

October 1995: It is autumn in my garden, and the intensity of colours in the autumn foliage is beautiful beyond belief. Soon the brown, orange and gold leaves will start falling as nature strips down for winter. My time is taken up with removing summer bedding plants ready for the planting of my spring bedding. Nature's cycle goes on.

THERE was a murder film made at Highbury back in 1939 called *The Arsenal Stadium Mystery*. It was a whodunnit and features Arsenal players of the time delivering lines that are unintentionally hilarious. Now there is a new Arsenal Stadium Mystery, and it's not so funny. The big mystery is: *Who holds the real power at the club?*

As an Arsenal shareholder with thirty-two shares to my name I am keen to know the answer to that question. So, too, perhaps is the Archbishop of Canterbury, who I understand has just one share. Back in my playing days there was no doubt about who held the power at Arsenal. The Bracewell-Smith and Hill-Wood families were in firm control,with Denis Hill-Wood a powerful chairman. His son, Peter Hill-Wood, is now in the chair, but with drastically reduced influence.

There has been a quiet but sensational shift of power at Highbury. David Dein, who was a season ticket holder, was first to break the 'old boy' network at Arsenal when he started buying shares in the 1980s. He joined the Board in September 1983, and four months later he became vice-chairman by which time he had become one of the largest shareholders. Dein was so hungry for shares that it was reported he once travelled all the way to Scotland just to purchase two. He at one stage got his stake up to forty-two per cent of the club, but he has since reduced his holding while bringing in Danny Fiszman as a major shareholder.

Fiszman is a near-neighbour of mine in Hampstead, and is a diamond merchant who is seriously wealthy. He is a dynamic financial genius who I believe would make the best chairman of Arsenal if and when Hill-Wood steps down. Fiszman, the new power behind the throne, holds 15,200 of the gilt-edged 'ordinary' Arsenal shares. He has a recorded common interest in another 7,126 of the 16,736 shares held by Dein. Hill-Wood now has just 448.

When I was a player, we used to call Arsenal the Upstairs, Downstairs club. We were like servants below stairs, and never allowed up to the wood-panelled boardroom where City brokers and Old Etonian types ruled. It was 'them' and 'us'. The Toffs and the Toilers. But Dein and Fiszman, two powerful businessmen with earth-moving energy and imaginative commercial schemes, have smashed the old image, and those of us looking on from the outside wonder how long it will be before they convince the club to go public.

Just before the kick-off to what proved to be my final season the Arsenal board met to consider a top-secret report prepared by City brokers Smith New Court. The report discussed the one subject which I know Denis Hill-Wood used to consider taboo: *should the club float on the Stock Exchange?*

Although the controversial 1991 bond scheme to convert Highbury into an all-seater stadium (and which alienated so many of the supporters and made a hole in the Royal Bank of Scotland) was seen as an alternative to flotation, there were, I know, some on the board who felt that Arsenal should copy Manchester United and go public. As I understood it, David Dein was the main driving force behind the idea for a flotation. His chief opposition, I believe, came from the Carr brothers, Richard and Clive, who between them own 26 per cent of the shares and represent the old money on the board. They inherited much of their holding from their grandfather, Sir Guy Bracewell-Smith, former Lord Mayor of London, who was an influential Highbury director when I was a player. The Bracewell-Smiths have held even more power at Arsenal than the Hill-Woods, even though Peter Hill-Wood has followed his father and grandfather as chairman.

It was around 1929 that Samuel Hill-Wood started the Hill-Wood dynasty when he took over as chairman from Sir Henry Norris, who had been kicked out of the game in a scandal about under-the-counter payments to players (and to the club chauffeur!). These days they would have been called bungs. Samuel's son, Denis, took over from Bracewell-Smith as chairman in 1961, and he became one of the most respected men in the game. He was chairman during my playing days, and had a passionate love for the club. Surprisingly, his son, Peter, has never shown the same passion, and I got the impression that he was reluctantly carrying on the family tradition as chairman. The club could not have had more success, yet Peter never gave an indication that he was enjoying it as I would have expected. It was as if the job was more of a burden than a joy. He is an affable and courteous man, but can obviously be ruthless when he thinks it necessary. I followed Terry Neill and Don Howe as the third manager to depart while he was chairman. His sons, Julian and, in particular, Charlie, seemed more interested in the team than he was, and I suppose that one day they will carry on the Hill-Wood tradition and join the board ... but how many shares will they have left to play with?

He owned fourteen per cent of the club when I took over as manager in 1986. By 1991, with the share capital raised to 56,000, his holding had dropped to 0.8 per cent. Surprisingly in my view, the bulk of his shares had moved across to Dein.

The one thing Peter Hill-Wood shared in common with his father was the determination not to let Arsenal go public. He, along with the Carrs and the rest of the Board apart from Dein and Fiszman, would, I am sure, have breathed a sigh of relief when the report from the City brokers advised against it.

Flotation would mean that directors with large holdings could make a financial killing by selling some of their shares while retaining control. It is a scheme that has worked extremely well for Manchester United chairman and chief executive Martin Edwards. It will be interesting to see if Dein and Fiszman make a new bid to get the club floated on the Stock Exchange.

I was always disappointed and surprised at what seemed the lack of real interest shown in the team at away matches by the majority of the Arsenal directors, including Peter Hill-Wood. More often than not, by the time I got to the boardroom after a match the few Arsenal directors who had bothered to make the trip had left. This to me seemed very discourteous. Richard Carr, a retired solicitor who, with his brother, has a big stake in the Park Lane Hotel, was the one director apart from Dein and Ken Friar who continually showed close interest in the team. He even liked to watch the reserves and youth teams to see who was coming through, but he never interfered or got busy on the business or social sides of the club. I was very disappointed when it came down the gossip grapevine that Richard was apparently one of the two directors who wanted me out at Arsenal regardless of the Inquiry findings. He always seemed the one most impressed by my systems and tactics. Obviously, we did not have the rapport that I thought we had. Cheers, Richard.

Dein, whose parents were fruit importers and who made his money in sugar commodities, is a human dynamo who wants to get involved in everything at the club. I am sure that if I had let him he would have selected the team. I remember him once asking if he could join me on scouting trips, and was clearly hurt when I told him that I preferred to go alone. He is a likeable, walking jack-in-the-box of ideas, always coming up with commercial plans that have raised a lot of money for the club. But he seems to be insensitive to the fact that he is often treading on the toes of others when poking around into every area at the club, and he also seems to forget that the main reason he finds it so easy to raise money on the commercial side is because of the success of the team and the explosion of interest in spin-offs of the game. He often got too close to the players for my liking, and – as I had warned right from day one of my appointment as manager – it caused embarrassment when the time came for me to make a decision in the interests of the club. David and his family were keen supporters of Anders Limpar, and it was tough enough having to put up with the fans saying I was wrong to sell him without the Dein family on my back as well.

When the team started to run out of steam in my last year, Dein came to me and asked: 'What needs to be done to get back on top?'

'I've got to start rebuilding,' I replied, truthfully. 'The team needs a complete overhaul.'

'How many new players do you need?'

'I would reckon at least five, maybe six.'

'What would that cost? Give me a ballpark figure.'

'It would be in the region of twenty million pounds.'

He did not bat an eyelid. 'If you put that to the Board,' he said, 'I'll back you.'

I did not bother because I was convinced that the Board would just laugh at me.

Since my dismissal, Dein must be in his element because I understand he is now in charge of transfers. He clinched the deals for

Bergkamp and Platt, but I reckon Arsenal paid at least £3 million too much for them. There is no way that the Board would have sanctioned me spending more than £12 million on two players. I just wonder how Ken Friar, an Arsenal man through and through who holds 200 shares, is reacting to the new set up when he is no longer able to run a tight budget. He is not far off retirement age and will have given Arsenal getting on for fifty years meritous service as first a protégé of the outstanding Highbury administrator Bob Wall and then his successor. Should Ken retire, my money is on David Dein to take over the complete running of the club and to become the Arsenal supremo. In fact I don't think David will be happy until he is in the chairman's seat. Or even the FA chairman's seat of power. My forecast is that in the near future Peter Hill-Wood will step down as club chairman. The man best suited to take over from him is, in my opinion, not David Dein, but Danny Fiszman. It remains to be seen whether he has the desire for the job. That is something that David Dein does not lack.

I never found out from the other directors how they felt about the shift of power at Highbury. The Carr brothers, former Lord Mayor of London Sir Robert Bellinger and Sir Roger Gibbs, all of them wealthy businessmen, kept their cards close to their chest. Do they know or are they are as puzzled as I am as to why Peter Hill-Wood appears to have almost encouraged David Dein to move in and grab such a big piece of the action?

Yes, it's an Arsenal Stadium Mystery. *Who holds the real power at Arsenal?*

I shared a lot in common with Herbert Chapman, legendary manager of the Arsenal whose bust I used to nod to every time I walked through the Marble Halls. We were both single-minded, and brought a tableful of trophies to Highbury. It has been lost in the mists of time that the great Chapman was also once exiled from football. He was suspended *sine die* after his club of the time, Leeds City, were kicked out of the League in 1919 for making illegal payments to players. Chapman was allowed back in after a year and captured two League championships with Huddersfield, who were on their way to a hat-trick of titles when he quit to join Arsenal in 1925. The advertisement for the job in the *Athletics News* stressed: 'Anyone who considers paying exorbitant transfer fees should not bother to apply.' Chapman ignored his brief, and bought what became known as 'Arsenal's Bank of England' team. Charles Buchan, David Jack – the first five-figure footballer – and Alex James were among his buys as he built one of the great teams in English football history. In January 1934 Arsenal were on top of the First Division and on the way to the second of their three consecutive championships when Herbert caught a cold while watching Arsenal's third team playing. Three days later he died, and I have a report in my library collection of Arsenal books that describes how in the next game against Sheffield Wednesday 'players and spectators wept as the match was played'.

I know that Herbert would have approved of the Ten Football Commandments that we preached to young Arsenal players under the guidance of youth team manager and old Highbury hero Pat Rice:

* Desire must come from within, not as a result of being driven by coaches or parents.
* The only thing that counts is your dedication to the game. You run on your own fuel, it comes from within you.
* Whenever two teams of players of equal ability play, the one with the greater courage will win.
* You cannot get much done in life if you only work on the days when you feel good.
* A team wins with the elimination of mistakes and with people who want to win and can't stand losing. There is no letter 'I' in the word teamwork.
* If anybody uses 'tired' as an excuse for losing then I will find someone to play that position who isn't tired.
* Physical pain can't stop you if your mental outlook is strong enough.
* A man wrapped up in himself makes a very small bundle.
* The critic is one who knows the price of everything and the value of nothing.
* A man who has committed a mistake and does not correct it, is committing another mistake.

That last commandment is particularly poignant for me. I made my mistake, and tried hard to correct it. And now I am paying the price for it, just as Herbert Chapman paid the price when he was exiled from the game. Herbert would not recognise Highbury if he came back today. Even Bertie Mee, manager of the Double team in 1970-71, would get lost. The changes, many of them triggered by the Lord Justice Taylor report following the Hillsborough disaster, have turned the stadium from a mausoleum into one of the finest grounds in Europe. The capacity has been reduced from 57,000 to 39,000 all seated, and the facilities are now in keeping with a club of Arsenal's great pedigree.

Call me conceited, but I like to think I deserve a lot of the credit for helping to shape the club for the second millennium. My friends used to rib me that one day there would be a George Graham Stand, and that they would have to erect a statue of me to stand alongside the bust of Herbert Chapman. When the directors who kicked me out are sitting watching Arsenal play I hope they are haunted by the fact it was the feats of the team that I built that helped bring them their super new stadium. They will never be able to exorcise the ghost of George Graham from Highbury.

I won't get a bust in the Marble Halls, but they will never be able to hide the fact that my team – players with whom I had a special, unbreakable bond – won six trophies in eight seasons. Even Herbert Chapman did not match that.

The Boy from Bargeddie is very proud of his Highbury record. In the words of the Gershwin song, *They can't take that away from me; no, they can't take that away from me.*

18 : The Exile's Files

ANYTIME: It is often necessary to move plants from one place to another to provide them with more growing space, or to check their root growth. Shrubs and trees raised in nurseries, for instance, are transplanted annually to keep their roots compact, so that they will establish quickly and easily after lifting. A well-planned transfer can transform a garden.

DURING my eight and a half years in charge at Arsenal I was involved in forty-seven transfers, twenty-five players coming in and twenty-two going out. As I sit in enforced exile, I can take a considered look at each deal and give an honest assessment of the players and whether I spent the money wisely, and also whether I sold well. Following are my verdicts on twenty of the deals, plus an in-and-out transfer market balance sheet ...

June 9 1986, **Martin Keown** to Aston Villa. *Fee: £200,000*
My first deal, and one which was forced on me. Martin was ambitious for first-team football and also for better than first-team wages. I refused to pay him more than the likes of Tony Adams and David Rocastle, and so he was off to Aston Villa. I regretted having to make the deal, but I am sure not as much as Martin, who would have won more medals and earned more money had he stayed with us. The fee was a joke, set by a transfer tribunal. In 1993, it would cost ten times more to bring him back to Highbury where he had first been taught all the right habits. Martin developed into one of the best markers in the business and was known in the dressing-room as 'Rash' because he was all over the opposition.

Sept 11 1986, **Perry Groves**, from Colchester. *Fee: £65,000*
There was a lot of behind-the-hand sniggering when I made Perry my first investment. But what a buy. He joined us from Fourth Division Colchester as a squad member, and gave excellent service as a utility forward with electric pace. I had taken note of him when I was manager at Millwall, and I knew he had good potential. Perry could play on either wing or straight down the middle. He didn't have the great-

est technique, but when he was really bombing defenders would panic because he took some stopping. I was later able to sell him on to Southampton for £750,000 after he had played 155 League games for us and scored twenty-one goals. A real bargain if ever there was one. Perry had a bouncing-ball personality, and nothing could keep him down for long. He accepted the squad system, and knew that he was never going to be guaranteed a first-team place. His attitude was a lesson to so-called star players who thought they had a God-given right to be first on the team-sheet. Arsenal were served well by the Groves Family. Vic Groves, a relative of Perry's, had been a Highbury idol back in the fifties. One of the last things I did before leaving Arsenal was to get the Board to agree to send the first-team to Colchester for a testimonial match for Perry, who had sadly been forced into early retirement by an Achilles injury.

Jan 7 1987, **Stewart Robson** to West Ham. *Fee: £700,000*
An enigmatic player, who I admit I never got through to; and neither did any of my coaches. He had enormous potential but never realised it, mainly because of atrocious luck with injuries. A lesson I learned from the old Liverpool maestro Bill Shankly was, 'Before commiting yoursel' tae a transfer, it is as important tae check on a player's injury record as his playing record.' You need a player who is going to play for you week in and week out, and sadly for Stewart he was continually in the treatment room. I had problems negotiating with Stewart and his father, and did not take kindly to being told that, as in his previous contract, it should be stipulated that he would play in only one position, that of central midfield. I tried to make the breakthrough with him by appointing him captain on a couple of trips, but he was too introverted for that important role. He scored sixteen goals in 151 League appearance before I sold him to West Ham. I got a lot of stick from the Arsenal supporters over the deal, but they did not have the headache of trying to handle him. He was a deep, intense boy and I would liked to have helped him make the most of his great natural ability, but I just could not prise him open. A coach must be able to communicate with a player, but Stewart and I were never on the same wavelength.

Mar 26 1987, **Alan Smith** from Leicester. *Fee: £850,000*
One of the most dedicated and exemplary professionals I ever had the
pleasure of working with. Nothing ever phased Alan, and the only
time I knew him get really upset was when in his final season he collected his one and only booking. He and Gary Lineker used to play in
harness together at Leicester, and were both gentlemen of the first
order. It must have been something they put in their tea at Leicester.
Alan was a master at finishing and positioning, and could bring other
players into the game with neat touch-offs. There were few better target players than Smudger at his peak. He did not really get the credit
from the fans that he deserved because he played without fuss or frills, .
and always put the needs of the team first. I think if he had had a little devil in his play, he could have become one of the finest of all
England strikers. It was Steve Burtenshaw, our chief scout, who kept
on at me to take a good look at him, and I had to agree that he was
perfect for the striking job I had in mind. He was overshadowed by the
arrival of Ian Wright, but got on with his business without a moan or
a groan and accepted his role as second fiddle. It was sad that he was
forced to retire with a knee problem just a couple of months after my
departure. Arsenal owe him a debt of gratitude because he was top
scorer in both our Championship seasons, and also netted the vital
goal that won us the Cup Winners' Cup. Well done Smudger. You have
been a credit to our game.

May 26 1987, **Nigel Winterburn** from Wimbledon. *Fee: £350,000*
Nigel was a player I had in mind from the moment I took over at
Arsenal because I had been impressed by his performances for
Wimbledon against Millwall. The change from Wimbledon to Arsenal
was, I know, a shock to his system. It was well known that Wimbledon
were the 'Crazy Gang' of football with a relaxed, fun-and-laugh
approach to the game. He found that at Arsenal we were the exact
opposite, and we treated football with deadly seriousness. If I had to
judge Nigel on his training input I could not give him too good a
report, but what a competitor when it really matters! He is a self motivator, and would get himself stoked up for a game without need of any
words from me. He is quiet and calculating, and overcame a tough
first six months – when he was understudy to Kenny Sansom – to

establish himself as a key player in what I considered the finest back line in football. I would say that over a period of four or five seasons, Nigel was our most consistent performer. He has started his own coaching clinic for youngsters, and it will be interesting to see if he takes on board some of the things he learned under me at London Colney. He will produce a conveyor belt of exceptional left-backs if he can teach them to tackle as firmly as he can and also to pass with his style of educated left foot. But also work on the right, Nige!

July 9 1987, **Viv Anderson** to Manchester United. *Fee: £250,000*
Another player that I did not want to let go, but I had my hands tied by the Arsenal board's wage structure. Even though he was thirty-one, Viv was ludicrously valued by the transfer tribunal. He was without doubt one of England's finest post-war right-backs, but he was allowed to get out of contract and there was nothing I could do to persuade him to stay once he knew that United were ready to meet his wage demands with which I could not compete. I would not only miss his skill at right-back but also his infectious good humour that was an important ingredient for our dressing-room spirit. The only time he used to lose it was when he considered I was working him too hard in training. I wonder how hard he works his players now that he is in management as number two to Bryan Robson at Middlesbrough?

Aug 26 1987, **Kevin Richardson** from Watford. *Fee: £220,000*
I bought Kevin from Watford because I knew he had been educated in the Arsenal-style system during his seven years at Everton. He was a steal, and did a marvellous job for me as a midfield buccaneer. Kevin, with his willingness to run all day and his desire to win, was a perfect balance for the more skilful David Rocastle. A tough Geordie, he is a self-opinionated character who I often had to cut down because he had so much to say for himself. But I respected him for his commitment, and when he ran on to the pitch I knew I would be getting all-out effort every time. Kevin once told me that he was disappointed that I never relaxed and socialised with the players, as Howard Kendall had apparently done when he was at Goodison. That was just not my style. It works for other managers, but I never believed in getting too close to my players away from football. Do you know of any boss who goes

out on the town with his staff at the end of a day's work in the office? It is vital that you keep some distance otherwise you will quickly lose their respect. I made around £500,000 profit when selling Kevin to Real Sociadad in September, 1990. That's good business by any standards.

Jan 7 1988, **Charlie Nicholas** to Aberdeen. *Fee: £750,000*
Ah, Charlie, Charlie, Charlie. What a character. What a player, and what a headache! Charlie is one of the warmest and friendliest and most likeable of all the people who have played under me. If I was picking a social team, he would be number one on the list. By the time I inherited him at Highbury, he had become more famous for what he did in nightclubs than at the football club that paid his wages. I had to try to get him producing his old style and form, but failed. He promised in fits and starts to regain the magic that had made him an idol at Celtic (the first League Cup final, for instance, when his two goals won us the match), but I could not afford to have a player in the team who was going to turn it on only occasionally. That would not have been fair on the other players. I was getting through to Charlie that he had to be more consistent when he was sidelined by a nasty injury, and while he was out of action the team began to put together a winning run. I realised I could do without Charlie, who might have been better off missing out on the distractions and bright lights of London and choosing the Old Trafford or Anfield stage for his skills. He had the choice of Manchester United, Liverpool or Arsenal when he moved from Celtic. Had I been advising him at the time I would have told him to avoid London because there were too many temptations waiting to trap a boy who loved a good time off the pitch. Many of the Arsenal fans hated me for selling him to Aberdeen, but I am sure that even they knew in their hearts that the time had come for a fond farewell to the aptly nicknamed Bonny Prince Charlie. The story got around that I disliked star players. Distrusted would be a better description. There is no greater fan than me of the player who can make a ball talk and who can dismantle a defence with one glorious pass or sudden change of pace, but I want him sharing the workload with his team-mates when we do not have the ball. I love a star player. I hate a prima donna. I loved Charlie Nicholas, but I thought he was a

fool to himself. Cheers, Charlie.

Jan 29 1988, **Lee Dixon** from Stoke City. *Fee: £350,000*
Lee is an example to every professional in the country in how to make
the most of your ability. There are more skilful right-backs, better
tacklers, more accurate passers and certainly those with better first-
time control of the ball. But when it comes to concentration, commitment and maximising what you've got going for you, then Lee takes
some beating. He has distinguished himself with both Arsenal and
England after a chequered early career during which he was rarely
given the big-time chance he deserved. Lee had to learn his trade with
Burnley, Chester and Bury before we discovered him at Stoke. I found
out about his consistency by regularly reading the local newspaper
reports (that I had sent to me from all over the country). Lee was
taught good footballing habits very early in life by his father, Roy,
who had been the goalkeeping understudy to the legendary Bert
Trautmann at Manchester City. He is a natural sportsman, who is
expert at cricket, golf, water-skiing and deep-sea diving. The only
trouble he ever gave me was when he went off on a deep-sea diving
expedition with David Seaman while we were on a tour of Australia.
They did not ask permission, and gave us all sorts of anxiety before
they reappeared. I would rate Lee and Nigel Winterburn the best pair
of attacking full-backs in the Premiership. Lee could be having a
nightmare but he would never hide and always continued to try his
best. I recommended him to Bobby Robson and Graham Taylor for the
England team because I knew they would get a player who would give
them every ounce of effort. A great role-model for any youngster not
blessed with natural skill. You can still make it to the top. Ask Lee
Dixon.

Mar 25 1988, **Brian Marwood** from Sheffield Wed. Fee: *£450,000*
Brian reminded me of Geordie Armstrong, who was one of the unsung
heroes of our double team of 1970-71 (and later the Arsenal reserve
team trainer). He could play on either flank, gave us width and was an
excellent crosser of a ball. I tracked him for a year before finally land-
ing him from Sheffield Wednesday. He did not have the flair of an
Anders Limpar or the speed of a Perry Groves, but he had good all-

round ability. Brian would have been in the first title-winning team but for unluckily collecting an injury after playing a key role all season. I wish I could have had him under my wing when he was younger because I am convinced I could have made him an even better player. Brian was also an active member of the Professional Footballers' Association and became their powerful chairman. I could not hide from him the fact that I thought he was giving too much time to union matters to the detriment of his football. Brian, who joined Sheffield United for £350,000 in 1990, now works in commercial management for the PFA. He can look back with pride on what he achieved with Arsenal, even if he did not always agree with the manager!

June 13 1988, **Steve Bould** from Stoke. *Fee: £390,000*
The most under-rated player in the Premiership. He is immensely strong and single-minded, and has a good footballing brain to support his physical output. Just watch him in set-piece situations. He is nearly always a thought and a deed ahead of his opponent. At their peak, he and Tony Adams formed the best central defensive partnership in Europe. Yes, Europe. He had the character to overcome a bad injury, and caught the eye of our chief scout Steve Burtenshaw when he went to Stoke to watch Lee Dixon play. He joined Arsenal as a squad member and quickly established himself alongside Adams, and they became the twin rocks of our defence. Steve likes a lager or three, but only once gave me problems when he got out of control one night while in the company of the one and only Paul Merson. A fine did the trick, and he never let me down again. The sort of man's man you want alongside you in the trenches.

Dec 28 1988, **Kenny Sansom** to Newcastle. *Fee: £600,000*
I had played with Kenny when he was a kid at Crystal Palace and thought then that he was the most naturally gifted left-back I had ever seen. I had no reason to change this assessment by the time I inherited him at Highbury. Kenny was captain when I arrived, and on my first day said, 'Well, what's it going to be ... George, or Boss?' He knew that friendship was going to take a back-seat when I replied, 'From now on it will be Boss.' I meant to start as I would carry on. As well

as being a superb player, Kenny was excellent in the dressing-room where his perky personality always kept things alive. His impersonations were professional class and he could keep his team-mates in stitches. Unfortunately he got himself weighed down with personal problems caused by a well-publicised gambling habit, and it suited him to make a move to new pastures. I was lucky to have Nigel Winterburn ready to fill his place. At his best, Kenny was a rival to even 'The Master' Ray Wilson as England's greatest left-back. I borrow from dear old Joe Mercer his quote about Stan Bowles: 'The only thing he couldn't pass was a betting shop.' Kenny is a coach now, and has a wealth of experience to pass on to players lucky to have such a talented player teaching them the basics. It was a privilege to have watched him play.

Mar 21 1990, **Niall Quinn** to Manchester City. *Fee: £800,000*
Niall did a tremendous job for me in my early days as manager, carrying the responsibilities of front-striker on his wide shoulders. He was barely twenty and reminded me of a thoroughbred foal that had not quite found its feet. At 6ft 4in and yet to fill out properly, he was all gangling arms and legs and could look clumsy on the ball. But he stuck to his job despite taking some unnecessary stick from a section of the crowd, and there were also some members of the board who were continually urging me to drop him. A likeable, uncomplicated lad, he accused me of putting his career on hold for a year when he had to make way for Alan Smith. I understood his feelings, but needed a strong squad of which he was an important member. Nobody was more delighted than me when things started to go right for him following his move to Manchester City. I am sure he would give credit to Arsenal for providing him with a strong foundation to his career.

May 18 1990, **David Seaman** from QPR. *Fee: £1.3 million*
The Gentle Giant of Highbury has proved himself not only a rival to Bob Wilson, Pat Jennings and Jack Kelsey as the greatest of all Arsenal goalkeepers but, in my opinion, is now at least on a par with Peter Schmeichel as one of the best in the world. I have explained earlier why I had to find a replacement for John Lukic, who would not make a long-term commitment to the club. The fans loved Lukic, but

they quickly learned first to respect Seaman and then to accept that he was the better goalkeeper. What he has over most other goalkeepers is an intimidating physical presence. He is built like a brick outhouse, and yet is as agile as a gymnast and has a racing driver's reflexes. David is a proud Yorkshireman, who has a lovely, even temperament. What I like about him is that he is still ready to listen and learn when working with the knowledgable Arsenal goalkeeping coach Bob Wilson, who knows a thing or three about how to be a success between the Highbury posts.

July 4 1990, **Andy Linighan** from Norwich. *Fee: £1.2 million*
I bought Andy from Norwich because I wanted competition at the centre of the defence. Steve Bould responded by producing the best form of his life, and so there was no regular place for Andy. He did an outstanding job for me filling in as a specialist marker, but he was not always appreciated by the fans. I was thrilled for him when he scored the goal that won us the FA Cup because it was a contribution that was visible to those critics who did not appreciate the all-round work that he did for the team. He showed tremendous bravery in that FA Cup final replay after having his nose broken by Mark Bright's reckless use of the elbow. His performance at Wembey at last won him the warmth and acceptance of the Arsenal fans. Andy is a quiet, pleasant man, who was popular with the other players and a good squad member.

July 12 1990, **Anders Limpar** from Cremonese. *Fee: £1.1million*
If Anders could have maintained the brilliance of his start with Arsenal he would have proved himself the greatest of all my buys, but he lost the magic touch once he forgot that even the most talented players need to show full commitment all of the time. I have never known anybody able to match Anders for the things he was able to do with the ball in training. I was proud of my skills honed in the roads of Bargeddie, but Anders left me for dead. What a pity for him, for Arsenal and for the fans that he could not always transcend this to the pitch on match days. I was not the only one who had doubts about his commitment. For all his ability, he was never sure of his place in the Swedish team during the 1994 World Cup finals. Anders could have

been up there in the George Best, Jairzinho bracket if only his application had matched his ability. Other players at Arsenal began to lose confidence in him, and I knew that meant he had to go. I made £600,000 profit when selling him to Everton.

Sep 24 1991, **Ian Wright** from Crystal Palace *Fee: £2.5 million*
When the Arsenal history books are written at the end of this century, they will struggle to find a better striker in the club's 100 years. He was my Mission Impossible man. I have seen him score goals from impossible angles, in impossible situations and against impossible odds. It is not just a goal when Ian scores – it's an occasion. Nobody salutes a goal quite like Wrighty, and while I tried to curb his at times over-the-top enthusiasm I could never deny him his celebrations that have helped lift him into the land of legend with Arsenal fans. He wears his emotions like a badge, and is sometimes as quick to tears as he is to laughter. There were moments when he used to get so high on excitement in the dressing-room before a match and at half-time that I would have to try to bring him down with harsher words than I really meant. Ian Wright is a one off, and a player in a million.

Dec 16 1991, **Michael Thomas** to Liverpool. *Fee: £1.5 million*
How sad that the player who gave me my most memorable moment in football also gave me some of my biggest headaches. Michael's goal in the last minute of the season that won the League championship for us at Anfield has clinched a lasting place for him in the football history books. And quite rightly, too. But I am afraid that for a while the goal and the glory seemed to go to his head. He was so feted and applauded for his historic strike that he appeared to think he had arrived as a superstar, forgetting all the hard work that had helped win him a place in the team. Suddenly he was relying just on his exceptional skill to try to make an impact, but without the work rate he was only half the player. He has given me some pretty heavy stick in the press over my training methods and playing systems. I will just point to my six trophies in eight years and rest my case. Michael was a great fan of Continental and Brazilian football, and he was a little disappointed when it was Liverpool rather than one of the major Continental clubs that came in for him after we had failed to agree

contract terms. What a pity he could not continue the way he had been taught as a youngster in the outstanding Arsenal youth squad. Young footballers just starting out can learn a lesson from Michael: If you are born with a gift for playing football, never ever take it for granted. But thanks to that goal at Anfield, Michael will never be forgotten by either the Arsenal fans or by me. At his best, he is an exceptional player.

July 14 1992, **John Jensen** from Brondby. *Fee: £1.57 million*
Forgetting the controversy surrounding the John Jensen deal, I want to go on record with my assessment of his contribution to Arsenal. It became a standing joke that he was unable to find the net (just one memorable goal against QPR), but his failure to score was far out-weighed by the job he did for us as a marker operating just in front of the back line of defence. Once he had settled to the faster pace of English football, he came into his own, particularly in our European matches when he shut out some of the finest players in the world with a commitment that was always commendable. John was com-fortable on the ball and could pass accurately, but for the supporters he was never ever able to live up to expectations raised by his spec-tacular goal for Denmark in the European championships final against Germany. It gave a false picture of his style of play. He is a very agreeable man, and dedicated to playing the game to the best of his ability. There are few better midfield anchormen in the Premiership.

Aug 4 1992, **David Rocastle** to Leeds. *Fee: £2 million*
If there was one player I would liked to have kept at Arsenal it was David. He epitomised the Arsenal team spirit, and would always accept defeat and victory with the same dignity. He was in tears when I revealed to him the board had accepted a bid from Leeds United. When he was at his peak and before knee problems started to take the edge off his game, David was as good as any midfield player in the land. He had great pace and vision, and gave us an extra dimension in midfield when working in unison with his gifted partners Michael Thomas and Paul Davis. David was never quite the same power after leaving Arsenal, the club that I know will always be closest to his

heart. He was a credit to the club and to football with his behaviour on and off the pitch.

Here is a full list of my major in-and-out transfers from when I took over as Arsenal manager on 14 May 1986, with approximate fees:

DATE	PLAYER	FROM OR TO	FEE
June 1986	Martin Keown	to Aston Villa	£200,000
June 1986	Tony Woodcock	to FC Köln	£125,000
Sept 1986	Perry Groves	from Colchester	£65,000
Jan 1987	Stewart Robson	to West Ham	£700,000
Mar 1987	Alan Smith	from Leicester	£850,000
May 1987	Nigel Winterburn	from Wimbledon	£350,000
July 1987	Viv Anderson	to Manchester United	£250,000
Aug 1987	Kevin Richardson	from Watford	£220,000
Jan 1988	Charlie Nicholas	to Aberdeen	£750,000
Jan 1988	Lee Dixon	from Stoke	£350,000
Mar 1988	Brian Marwood	from Sheff Wed.	£450,000
June 1988	Steve Bould	from Stoke City	£390,000
Aug 1988	Steve Williams	to Luton Town	£300,000
Dec 1988	Kenny Sansom	to Newcastle	£600,000
Sept 1989	Siggy Jonsson	from Sheff Wed.	£400,000
Jan 1990	Colin Pates	from Charlton	£250,000
Mar 1990	Niall Quinn	to Man City	£800,000
May 1990	David Seaman	from QPR	£1.3 million
June 1990	John Lukic	to Leeds	£1 million
July 1990	Andy Linighan	from Norwich	£1.25 million
July 1990	Anders Limpar	from Cremonese	£1.1 million
July 1990	Martin Hayes	to Celtic	£700,000
Sep 1990	Brian Marwood	to Sheff United	£350,000
Sep 1990	Kevin Richardson	to Real Sociadad	£450,000
Sep 1991	Pal Lydersen	from IK Start	£500,000
Sept 1991	Ian Wright	from Crystal Palace	£2.5 million
Oct 1991	Jimmy Carter	from Liverpool	£500,000
Dec 1991	Michael Thomas	to Liverpool	£1.5 million

July 1992	John Jensen	from Brondby	£1.5 million
July 1992	Andy Cole	to Bristol City	£900,000*
Aug 1992	Perry Groves	to Southampton	£750,000
Aug 1992	David Rocastle	to Leeds United	£2 million
Feb 1993	Martin Keown	from Everton	£2 million
June 1993	Eddie McGoldrick	from Crystal Palace	£800,000
Mar 1994	Anders Limpar	to Everton	£1.7 million
May 1994	Stefan Schwarz	from Benfica	£1.8 million
Jan 1995	John Hartson	from Luton	£2.4 million
Feb 1995	Chris Kiwomya	from Ipswich	£1.25 million
Feb 1995	Glenn Helder	from Feyenoord	£2.3 million

*Andy Cole's fee includes a percentage of his transfer on to Newcastle United
Transfers not shown in the table: Rhys Wilmot, Gus Caesar, Andrew Marriott, Colin Pates. Neil Heaney and Alan Miller (sold for a total of £1,085,000). Craig McKernon (£150,000) and Lee Harper (£60,000) are two buys not listed.

The total income from transfers while I was in charge at Arsenal was an estimated £13,076,085, while I paid out a total of £22,095,210. That's a debit balance of £9,019,125.

The club was around one million in the red when I arrived on 14 May 1986. When I was unceremoniously kicked out on 21 February 1995 they were extremely comfortable at the bank. The stadium had been completely refurbished, and sponsors were queueing up to be associated with the club.

Club director Danny Fiszman, a financial genius, worked it out that in my eight-and-a-half years at Arsenal I generated more than £35 million for the club through the success of the team.

I had hardly been out of the door five minutes when much of the money had been spent, and the wage structure that had restricted me throughout my time as manager had been kicked out. Things would never again be the same at Highbury, the stadium that I helped to build.

19 : A Team for All Seasons

ANYTIME: There is beauty in all changes of season, winter giving way to the promise of spring ... then summer with its burst of colour, and the slow stripping of autumn before the cycle is completed with the return of the invigorating snap of winter. I love all the changes, and enjoy most of all making my selection of plants for each of the four seasons.

IT was Norman Giller, an old friend from way back and the man who has helped me put my jigsaw of thoughts together for this book, who cruelly tortured me with the challenge to select an Arsenal team from all the players I played with and managed during my fifteen years as a Highbury servant.

I invite you to join in the selecting game, just so that you can appreciate how difficult it can be picking a team. It is not choosing who to select that is so hard as deciding which players should be left out. After much arguing and discussion, I got my shortlist down to the following thirty players, fourteen from my playing-days era and sixteen from my managerial reign:

1960s-70s
Goalkeeper: Bob Wilson
Full-backs: Pat Rice, Bob McNab, Sammy Nelson
Central defenders: Frank McLintock, Peter Simpson
Defensive midfield: Peter Storey, Eddie Kelly
Attacking midfield: Alan Ball, Liam Brady
Winger: George Armstrong
Strikers: John Radford, Ray Kennedy, Charlie George
1980s-90s
Goalkeeper: David Seaman
Full-backs: Lee Dixon, Viv Anderson, Nigel Winterburn, Kenny Sansom
Central defenders: Tony Adams, Steve Bould, David O'Leary
Defensive midfield: John Jensen,
Attacking midfield: Paul Davis, Mickey Thomas, David Rocastle
Winger: Anders Limpar
Strikers: Alan Smith, Ian Wright, Paul Merson

Yes, I know. What about Charlie Nicholas, Graham Rix, Martin Keown, Stefan Schwarz and so many more not on the shortlist? Sorry, but the rules are thirty players only in what is almost a Fantasy League team. This is my selection of an Arsenal Team for All Seasons (picked for a 4-4-2 formation):

In goal, **David Seaman** ... winning by a fingertip from Bob Wilson, the man who has taught him so much as an outstanding coach. Bob was not a natural goalkeeper. He made himself great by studying and really working at his game. David has all the attributes for an exceptional goalkeeper – fast reflexes, good positional sense, gymnastic agility, a safe pair of hands, courage and a powerful physique. I would put him number one in Europe.

At right-back. **Viv Anderson** just gets the nod ahead of Pat Rice and Lee Dixon. There was little to choose between the three of them, but Viv's attacking play just gives him the edge. Pat was probably the most consistent of the three of them, and Lee the most enthusiastic and determined.

At left-back, it has to be **Kenny Sansom**, who at his peak was as good a full-back as I have ever seen. He had excellent ball control and could dig with his tackling when necessary. Bob McNab was the better defensive player, and Nigel Winterburn the best all-rounder of the three. But for flair, it has to be Kenny who I watched developing from his young days at Crystal Palace.

In the centre of the defence I have paired the two captains, **Frank McLintock** and **Tony Adams**. With Tony's authority in the air and Frank's marvellous positional sense I think they would be the perfect foil for each other. It is a toss up which of them would make the most inspiring captain. Both led by example, and had the ability to lift the performances of the players around them.

For my midfield anchorman I go for old ice eyes, **Peter Storey**. He had a tackle like a clap of thunder, and was – along with Chopper Harris – the finest ball winner that I played with at club level. John

Jensen was a better deliverer of the ball than Peter, but was not quite in his class when it came to tackling.

The playmaking would be the responsibility of **Liam Brady**, just getting the vote over Alan Ball whose peak years were at Everton. Liam would use his famous left 'Claw' to dismantle defences. I confess to cheating a little by including Liam in the squad because I only played with him for Arsenal reserves. He was just a teenager then, but it was already clear that he was a star in the making. He made his breakthrough into the first-team the season after I left for Manchester United and he quickly established himself as one of the most influential Arsenal midfield players of all time.

Making runs from deep positions I would have the smooth as silk **David Rocastle**, just getting my vote ahead of Paul Davis and Mickey Thomas. **Geordie Armstrong**, two wingers in one, would operate on either wing and give my team necessary width. He just edged out Anders Limpar from my final selection, even though he was one of the most naturally gifted players I ever managed.

I would share the twin striking duties between **John Radford** and **Ian Wright**, who together would be a handful for the tightest defence. Alan Smith and Charlie George would be another interesting combination, but I think big Raddy and the inventive Wright would make a perfect partnership. I tried hard to find a place for Paul Merson, who when he is really motoring can take any defence apart. It was also devastating having to leave out Ray Kennedy, who was equally effective as a striker for Arsenal and as a midfield attacker for Liverpool.

On the sub's bench I would have **Alan Ball**, who would walk into most other teams.

So that is my Arsenal Team for All Seasons. I would be proud to manage it.

Epilogue: The Wilderness Months

I have been forcibly unemployed now for nine months, and doesn't it show here in my garden. When not locked in discussions with lawyers or trying to lower my handicap on the golf course, I spend every spare moment here preparing for the changes of the seasons. It is the first opportunity since climbing aboard the football management roundabout to give the garden my full attention. Winston Churchill, the man whose birthday I share, built a wall during his Wilderness Years. All my energy is going into my garden. Winter arrives later here at Hampstead than it used to up in Bargeddie where I reckon gardening chores have to be done a month earlier. My plan now is to collect all the fallen leaves for compost, and then dig beds ready for the planting out of hardy perennials that I have raised from seed. I look on it as digging for victory, a personal victory over the trials and torment of the last year which I would not wish on my worst enemy.

You never really find out about yourself until you have to face a crisis. I am proud to say that I have come through my experience a stronger man, and feel that I have won a battle of confidence. It would have been easy to have caved in and fallen into the trap of feeling bitter and twisted and sorry for myself. I could, for instance, have tried to find the answer to my problems in the bottle, which is a solution I know several managers have attempted before me. I have a display cabinet containing more than 200 malt whisky bottles in a collection that I started back in my playing days. The good news is that they remain unopened. In my lowest moments I have remembered those words Joe Mercer used to say to me when I was a young player just starting out in the foothills of the soccer mountain: 'Head up, son. Walk tall. You have plenty to be proud about.'

I know in my heart that few people could have resisted the temptation that came my way, but I did my best to make amends and (as my bank manager will testify) I did not profit from my mistake. Even writing this book has been described in one newspaper as 'the wages of sin'. Well I have to do something to earn my daily bread, and I have seen this book as a way of putting my side of things. Watch out for a hotter novel to follow!

I have been seeing the football world from another angle, with regular media work and particularly with the excellent BBC Radio 5 Live team. The experience is doing me the world of good, and I am finding out the problems that football reporters and commentators can face. I am prepared to admit that I was not the greatest PR manager in the history of the game. I was often too blinkered, and interested only in the team and what was happening on the pitch and at the training ground. Something I have learned about myself during my exile is that I need to be a little more relaxed and forthcoming with the media. But I will still not tolerate the sort of gutter journalism that ridicules players (Donkey Adams) and managers (Turnip Taylor). It is now much clearer to me that the managers and media must work in closer harmony, but there must be common sense and dignity on both sides.

While sitting out on the touchline, I have had my problems brought into perspective by the dark shadow of tragedy. Cancer has struck several close friends, including our loyal old kit man Tony Donnelly and a personal pal, Bob Silver. So why should I feel sorry for myself?

Do I have any regrets? Just three major ones... that I ever accepted the cash gifts from the well-meaning Rune Hauge; that I allowed the Board at Highbury to dictate a too-tight wages policy; and that Arsenal – the club to which I had given the best years of my life – did not stand by me when I faced a crisis.

But there is no time for bitterness or recrimination. What happened at Arsenal is history, nearly all of which I will look back on with pride at what I achieved. I gave fifteen years of my life to Arsenal, and the club – the players, the supporters and the backroom staff – will always have a special place in my affections. But I would not cross the road to greet the directors. What I am missing nearly as much as the football during my months in exile are the little things, like the afternoon cuppa brought by the always cheerful Irish tealady, Maureen, the diary organisation of my secretary Sheila, and the perfectionism of groundsmen Steve (at Highbury) and Ken (at London Colney), who always grew what Bill Shankly would have described as 'professional' grass. Then there was the odd-job man, Paddy, who I could always rely on for an honest opinion.

'What did you think of the performance last night, Paddy?'

'A load of old rubbish, Mr Graham,' he would say. 'Rubbish, so it was.'

I will always have Arsenal red blood running through my veins. They may have taken my job away, but they can never take away all that I achieved at Highbury. The record books will show that George Graham was there.

But now Highbury is history. I must look forward to the future, and I am determined that it will be a future in football. The game has been my life, and I am as much in love with it as when I first learned to kick a ball in the Bargeddie road games. I was rarely without a ball at my feet from the age of about five, and it was my living from the day I joined Aston Villa at fifteen.

Life is a rollercoaster ride, and sometimes you are up and sometimes down. I hit my personal rockbottom on 21 February 1995, when Arsenal showed me the door. Things cannot get worse than that, and I am now in a positive frame of mind and looking forward to climbing back on to that crazy football roundabout.

The moment my exile is over I shall be applying for the best jobs. My CV is here in this book: promotion with Millwall, and six trophies in eight seasons with Arsenal. I wonder if Peter Hill-Wood will give me a reference after all the 'happy times' I gave him?

I am a great believer in fate, and have never sat down and plotted my course. I tend to let things happen. It was, for instance, fate that took me to Chelsea from Aston Villa when I had made up my mind on Southampton. It was fate that took me to Arsenal as a player, and then on to Manchester United, Portsmouth and Crystal Palace. And it was fate when Terry Venables sat me down to talk about a coaching job when I was making plans to go into the pub business. The Millwall job came out of the blue and gave me the chance to find my feet as a manager, and the call to join Arsenal only came after they had made a mess of signing my mate Terry.

A flash forward here to the year 2025. The scene, the old footballers' veterans home somewhere on the South Coast. Over there in the far corner, Tommy Doc is chatting up the physiotherapist. Sir Bobby Charlton is dribbling in the opposite corner, and there's the Doog rushing around in his bathchair pretending it is an Inspector Morse-style Jaguar. George Best is chasing the nurse, and Jimmy Hill is on the sofa interviewing himself. Look, there's Bob Wilson dropping his plate (sorry, Bob) and over there is Alex Ferguson getting French and kung-fu lessons from Eric Cantona. Ron Atkinson is on the sunbed, and Graham Taylor is refusing to eat his orange. Tommy Smith and Ron Harris are kicking the table, and Frank McLintock is wearing matron's jacket and has torn it down the back. Rodney Marsh passes the salt with his right foot and Denis Law heads it wide of a diving Catty Bonetti. Kenny Dalglish is laughing away to himself, and Saint and Greavsie are asking if anybody has any questions. Steve Coppell is holding a one-man committee meeting, and Jack Charlton is playing with his shillelagh.

In the middle of the room, a white-haired old boy is trying to get them all to stand in a Christmas tree formation. It's Terry Venables. I go over to him in my wheelchair, and I say: 'Tel, you and I must have been blankety-blank mad.'

'What's that, George?' he says, cupping a hand to his ear.

'I said we must have been blankety-blank mad,' I shout.

'You don't have to shout, George,' he says. 'I'm not deaf. What d'you mean, mad?'

'Well,' I say, 'giving all that money to the lawyers. We must have been blankety-blank mad.'

'You're right,' says Terry, and then he starts singing 'Chestnuts Roasting on the Open Fire'. Tommy Doc shouts, 'Venables, go to your room.'

I head for the garden and sanity.

Back in the here and now, I am watching as much football as possible because I do not want to be out of touch when I return to the game. I am also keeping an eye on the European leagues, and have just started Spanish and Italian lessons. Well you never know.

I count my many blessings. A son and daughter who love me,

brothers and sisters who have never given me less than a hundred per cent support, Susan, a beautiful lady in my life, friends both in and out of football who keep in constant touch, and good health. What more can a man want? Well a job back in football, for a start. I know that I have the organisational skill to do for another major club just what I did for Arsenal. I will need a board prepared to give me full backing, and players who are ready to give me their total commitment to go with their skill. Herbert Chapman, the man with whom I am always being bracketed, won championships with two clubs. I would like the chance to emulate him.

But for now, it's back to gardening for the Boy from Bargeddie. Thanks for the visit. Next time you see me, everything will be coming up roses.

George Graham: A Chronology

1944: Born at Bargeddie, Lanark, Scotland, on 30 November (Shares same birthday as Winston Churchill and Gary Winston Lineker).

1961: Joins Aston Villa groundstaff as a fifteen-year-old apprentice professional after winning Scotland schoolboy cap.

1963: Scores the winning goal in his youth international debut for Scotland against Switzerland.

1963: Manager Joe Mercer selects him in April for the first of eight First Division matches for Aston Villa. He scores in his debut against Liverpool.

1964: Signs for Tommy Docherty at Chelsea. Fee: £6,000. Plays the first of 72 First Division games for Chelsea. Scores 46 goals in 102 games, and is leading Chelsea marksman for two successive seasons.

1965: Wins first of two Scotland Under-23 caps against Wales. Plays in Chelsea's winning team against Leicester City in the League Cup final. Chelsea beaten 2-0 by Liverpool in the FA Cup semi-final.

1966: Chelsea beaten 2-0 by Sheffield Wednesday in the FA Cup semi-final at Villa Park. Chelsea lose to Barcelona in the Fairs Cup semi-final. September 30: Signs for Bertie Mee at Arsenal. Fee: £50,000, plus Arsenal striker Tommy Baldwin. Plays the first of 227 First Division games for Arsenal (eight as substitute; scores 59 League goals).

1967: Top scorer for Arsenal in the First Division with 11 goals in 33 games.

1968: Arsenal lose 1-0 in the League Cup final against Leeds.

1969: Substitute for the Arsenal team beaten 3-1 by Swindon in the League Cup final at Wembley on 16 March.

1970: In the Arsenal team that captures the UEFA Fairs Cup, beating Anderlecht in the two-leg final. Lose 3-1 in Brussels and win the return leg 3-0 at Highbury.

1971: Arsenal League and FA Cup Double year. Voted Man of the Match after the extra-time FA Cup Final victory over Liverpool. Scotland manager Tommy Docherty selects George for his full international debut against Portugal.

1972: Collects FA Cup runners-up medal in the centenary final against Leeds. December 27: Signs for Tommy Docherty at Manchester United for £120,000. "He is in the class of Gunter Netzer," says The Doc. He makes George his captain and United beat off the threat of relegation.

1973: Wins the last of his 12 Scotland caps as substitute against Brazil. Plays 43rd and final League game for United, who are relegated.

1974: Joins Portsmouth in a swap deal for veteran Welsh international centre-forward Ron Davies. Plays 61 League games, scores five goals.

1976: Signs for Terry Venables at Crystal Palace (13 November). Plays 44 League games for Palace (one as substitute, scores two goals). Palace win promotion to the Second Division.

1977: Has two metal screws inserted in a broken ankle following an injury received while playing on loan to California Surf in the North American League.

1978: Breaks leg playing in a friendly match with Crystal Palace in Memphis. Retires, and is invited by Terry Venables to coach the Palace youth players.

1980: Appointed Crystal Palace youth team manager. Terry Venables moves to QPR and appoints George youth team manager at Loftus Road.

1982: Appointed manager of Third Division Millwall on 6 December by chairman Alan Thorne..

1983: Millwall win Football League Trophy.

1985: Steers Millwall to promotion to the Second Division.

1986: Returns to Arsenal as manager on 14 May.

1987: Arsenal win the Littlewoods Cup, beating Liverpool 2-1.

1988: Runners-up to Luton in the Littlewoods Cup final.

1989: Arsenal win the League championship for the first time since 1971; dramatic last-minute winner by Michael Thomas at Anfield in the final game of the season clinches the title.

1991: Guides Arsenal to the second League title under his management despite the handicap of having two points docked following a brawl at Old Trafford.

1993: Arsenal achieve League Cup and FA Cup double over Sheffield Wednesday, which means that George has won all three domestic trophies as player and manager. It is the first time that a club has won these two trophies in the same season.

1994: Arsenal beat Parma to capture the European Cup Winners' Cup.

1995: Arsenal beaten 2-0 on aggregate by AC Milan in the European Super Cup. Dismissed by Arsenal on 21 February.

OVERALL ARSENAL MANAGERIAL RECORD

	P	W	D	L	F	A
League	350	162	106	82	522	310
FA Cup	35	18	9	8	54	38
League Cup	52	34	10	8	96	36
European Cup	4	1	1	2	8	6
ECWC	13	9	4	0	27	7
Total:	454	224	130	100	707	397